T.S. Eliot

THE COCKTAIL PARTY

T.S. Eliot

THE COCKTAIL PARTY

[Edited with Introduction, Author's Information, Complete Text, Summary and Analysis and Study Questions]

Misha Kandhari
M.A., M. Phil. English,
Delhi University

ANMOL PUBLICATIONS PVT. LTD.
NEW DELHI - 110 002 (INDIA)

ANMOL PUBLICATIONS PVT. LTD.

H.O.: 4374/4B, Ansari Road, Darya Ganj,
New Delhi-110 002 (India)
Ph.: 23278000, 23261597

B.O.: No. 1015, Ist Main Road, BSK IIIrd Stage
IIIrd Phase, IIIrd Block
Bangalore - 560 085 (India)
Visit us at: www.anmolpublications.com

The Cocktail Party

First Published, 2009

PRINTED IN INDIA

Printed at Balaji Offset Press, Delhi.

Contents

Preface

T.S. Eliot (1888-1965), American-English poet, playwright, and critic, a leader of the modernist movement in literature. Eliot was awarded the Nobel Prize for literature in 1948. His most famous work is THE WASTE LAND, written when he was 34. On one level this highly complex poem describes cultural and spiritual crisis.

Eliot attended Smith Academy in St. Louis and Milton Academy in Massachusetts. In 1906 he went to Harvard, where he contributed poetry to Harvard Advocate. After receiving his B.A. in 1909, Eliot spent a year in France, attending Henri Bergson's lectures at the Sorbonne and studying poetry with the novelist and poet Henri Alain-Fournier

The Cocktail Party concerns a married couple, Edward and Lavinia Chamberlayne, who are separated after five years of marriage. The first and last acts of the play feature cocktail parties held at their home where their marital problems are aggravated by the pressure of having to keep up social appearances.

Author

Chapter 1

Introduction

Eliot is one of the greatest literary critics of England from the point of view of the bulk and quality of his critical writings. His five hundred and odd essays occasionally published as reviews and articles had a far-reaching influence on literary criticism in the country. His criticism was revolutionary which inverted the critical tradition of the whole English speaking work. John Hayward says:

"I cannot think of a critic who has been more widely read and discussed in his own life-time; and not only in English, but in almost every language, except Russian."

As a critic Eliot has his faults. At times he assumes a hanging-judge attitude and his statements savor of a verdict. Often his criticism is marred by personal and religious prejudices blocking an honest and impartial estimate. Moreover, he does not judge all by the same standards. There is didacticism in his later essays and with the passing of time his critical faculties were increasingly exercised on social problems. Critics have also found fault with his style as too full of doubts, reservations and qualifications.

Still, such faults do not detract Eliot's greatness as a critic. His criticism has revolutionized the great writers of the past three centuries. His recognition of the greatness of the Metaphysical poets of the 17th century resulted in the Metaphysical revival of the 20th century. The credit for the renewal of interest in the Jacobean dramatists goes to Eliot. He has restored Dryden and other Augustan poets to their due place. His essay on Dante aroused curiosity for the latter middle ages. The novelty of his statements, hidden in sharp phrases, startles and arrests attention. According to Eliot, the end of criticism is to bring readjustment between the old and the new. He says:

"From time to time it is desirable, that some critic shall appear to review the past of our literature and set the poets and the poems in a new order."

Such critics are rare, for they must possess, besides ability for judgment, powerful liberty of mind to identify and interpret its own values and category of admiration for their generation. John Hayward says:

"Matthew Arnold was such a critic as were Coleridge and Johnson and Dryden before him; and such, in our own day, is Eliot himself."

Eliot's criticism offers both reassessment and reaction to earlier writers. He called himself "a classicist in literature". His vital contribution is the reaction against romanticism and humanism which brought a classical revival in art and criticism. He rejected the romantic view of the individual's perfectibility, stressed the doctrine of the original sin and exposed the futility of the romantic faith in the "Inner Voice". Instead of following his 'inner voice', a critic must follow objective standards and must conform to tradition. A sense of tradition, respect for order and authority is central to Eliot's classicism. He sought to correct the excesses of "the abstract and intellectual" school of criticism represented by Arnold. He sought to raise criticism to the level of science. In his objectivity and logical attitude, Eliot most closely resembles Aristotle. A. G. George says:

"Eliot's theory of the impersonality of poetry is the greatest theory on the nature of the process after Wordsworth's romantic conception of poetry."

Poetry was an expression of the emotions and personality for romantics. Wordsworth said that poetry was an overflow of powerful emotions and its origin is in "Emotions recollected in tranquility". Eliot rejects this view and says that poetry is not an expression of emotion and personality but an escape from them. The poet is only a catalytic agent that fuses varied emotions into new wholes. He distinguishes between the emotions of the poet and the artistic emotion and points out that the function of criticism is to turn attention from the poet to his poetry.

Eliot's views on the nature of poetic process are equally revolutionary. According to him, poetry is not inspiration, it is organization. The poet's mind is like a vessel in which are stored numerous feelings, emotions and experiences. The poetic process fuses these distinct experiences and emotions into new wholes. In "The Metaphysical Poets", he writes:

"When a poet's mind is perfectly equipped for its work, it is constantly amalgamating disparate experiences; the ordinary man's experience is chaotic, irregular, fragmentary".

Perfect poetry results when instead of 'dissociation of sensibility' there is 'unification of sensibility'. The emotional and the rational, the creative and the critical, faculties must work in harmony to produce great work of art. Critics stressed that the aim of poetry is to give pleasure or to teach morally. However, for Eliot the greatness of a poem is tested by the order and unity it imposes on the chaotic and disparate experiences of the poet. Wimsatt and Brooks are right in saying:

"Hardly since the 17th century had critical writing in English so resolutely transposed poetic theory from the axis of pleasure versus pain to that of unity versus multiplicity."

Eliot devised numerous critical concepts that gained wide currency and has a broad influence on criticism. 'Objective co-relative', 'Dissociation of sensibility', 'Unification of sensibility' are few of Eliot clichés hotly debated by critics. His dynamic theory of tradition, of impersonality of poetry, his assertion on 'a highly developed sense of fact' tended to impart to literary criticism catholicity and rationalism.

To conclude, Eliot's influence as a critic has been wide, constant, fruitful and inspiring. He has corrected and educated the taste of his readers and brought about a rethinking regarding the function of poetry and the nature of the poet process. He gave a new direction and new tools of criticism. It is in the re-consideration and revival of English poetry of the past. George Watson writes:

"Eliot made English criticism look different, but not in a simple sense. He offered it a new range of rhetorical possibilities, confirmed it in its increasing contempt for historical processes and yet reshaped its notion of period by a handful of brilliant institutions."

His comments on the nature of Poetic Drama and the relation between poetry and drama have done much to bring about a revival of Poetic Drama in the modern age. Even if he had written no poetry, he would have made his mark as a distinguished and subtle critic.

Chapter 2

Introduction: Eliot

In 1163, a quarrel began between the British King Henry II and the Archbishop of Canterbury, Thomas Becket. The men had been good friends, but each felt that his interests should be of primary concern to the nation and that the other should acquiesce to his demands. Becket fled to France in 1164 in order to rally support from the Catholic French for his cause and also sought an audience with the Pope. After being officially (although not personally) reconciled with the King, Becket returned to England in 1170, only to be murdered as he prayed in Canterbury Cathedral by four of Henry's Knights. Three years later, he was canonized and pilgrims—Henry among them—have made their way to his tomb ever since.

The allure of such a story for a dramatist is obvious: there is a great conflict between human and divine power, a strong central character and a number of complicated spiritual issues to be found in his death. In 1935, T. S. Eliot answered this "calling" to compose a play for that year's Canterbury Festival; the result was a work that revitalized verse drama—a form that had not been widely employed for almost three hundred years. Critics praised Eliot's use of verse and ability to invest a past historical event with modern issues and themes, such as the ways in which lay persons react to the intrusion of the supernatural in their daily lives. In part because it is a religious drama which appeared long after such plays were popular, Murder in the Cathedral is still performed, studied and regarded as one of Eliot's major works, a testament to his skill as a poet and dramatist.

Chapter 3

Biography of T.S. Eliot

Thomas Stearns Eliot (1888-1965)

American-English poet, playwright and critic, a leader of the modernist movement in literature. Eliot was awarded the Nobel Prize for literature in 1948. His most famous work is THE WASTE LAND, written when he was 34. On one level this highly complex poem describes cultural and spiritual crisis.

"The point of view which I am struggling to attack is perhaps related to the metaphysical theory of the substantial unity of the soul: for my meaning is, that the poet has, not a 'personality' to express, but a particular medium, which is only a medium and not a personality, in which impressions and experiences combine in peculiar and unexpected ways." Thomas Stearns Eliot was born in St. Louis, Missouri, the seventh and youngest child of a distinguished family of New England origin. Eliot's forebears included the Reverend William Greenleaf Eliot, founder of Washington University in St. Louis. Isaac Stearns on his mother's side was one of the original settlers of Massachusetts Bay Colony. Henry, Eliot's father, was a prosperous industrialist and his mother Charlotte was a poet. She wrote among others a biography of William Greenleaf Eliot.

Eliot attended Smith Academy in St. Louis and Milton Academy in Massachusetts. In 1906 he went to Harvard, where he contributed poetry to Harvard Advocate. After receiving his B.A. in 1909, Eliot spent a year in France, attending Henri Bergson's lectures at the Sorbonne and studying poetry with the novelist and poet Henri Alain-Fournier. He then returned to Harvard, where he worked on a dissertation on the English idealist philosopher F.H. Bradley. Eliot also studied Sanskrit and Buddhism.

In 1915 Eliot made England his permanent home. With Ezra Pound, his countryman and an advocate on literary modernism, he started to reform poetic diction. Pound was largely responsible for getting Eliot's early poems into print, such as THE LOVE SONG OF J. ALFRED PRUFROCK in the Chicago magazine Poetry in 1915. The title character is tormented by the uncertainty of his identity and the difficulty of articulating his feelings. Prufrock is a perfect gentleman and tragic in his conventionality. He has heard "the mermaids singing" but is paralyzed by self-consciousness-"I do not think that they will sing to me." Denis Donoghue has pointed out in Words Alone that in his early poems Eliot didn't start with a theme but with a fragment of rhythm, or motif. Prufrock has not the qualities of a person, he is a fragmented voice with a name. "Eliot's language here and in the early poems generally refers to things and simultaneously works free from the reference. He seems always to be saying: "That is not what I meant at all./That is not it, at all." When he gives a voice a name—Prufrock, Gerontion—he makes no commitment beyond the naming."

Pound also introduced Eliot to Harriet Weaver, who published Eliot's first volume of verse, PRUFROCK AND OTHER OBSERVATIONS. Eliot taught for a year at Highgate Junior School in London and then worked as a clerk at Lloyds Bank, where he wrote acticles for the monthly in-house magazine Lloyds Bank Economic Review on foreign currency movements. A physical condition prevented his entering in 1918 the US Navy. Eliot's second book, ARA VOS PREC (published in the U.S. as POEMS), which appeared in 1919, was hand-printed by Virginia and Leonard Woolf at the Hogath Press.

In an early essay, 'Tradition and the Individual Talent', Eliot propounded the doctrine, that poetry should be impersonal and free itself from Romantic practices. "The progress of an artist is a continual self-sacrifice, a continual extinction of personality." Eliot saw that in this depersonalization the art approaches science. With his collection of essays, the sacred wood and later published the use of poetry and the use of criticism and the classics and the man of letters, Eliot established his reputation as a literary critic.

In 1922 Eliot founded the Criterion, a quarterly review that he edited until he halted its publication at the beginning of World War II. With the help of Pound, who had raised money from friends and patrons, Eliot left the bank. In 1925 he joined the publishing house of Faber and Gwyer (later Faber and Faber), becoming eventually one of the firm's directors. Between the years 1917 and 1919, Eliot was an assistant editor of the journal the Egoist. From 1919 onward he was a regular contributor to the Times Literary Supplement.

In the 60 years from 1905 to his death, Eliot published some 600 articles and reviews. Eliot's principal purpose in his literary-critical essays was "the elucidation of works of art and the correction of taste." He wanted to revive the appreciation of the 17th-century "Metaphysical poets, " referring to such writers as Donne, Crashaw, Vaughan, Lord Herbert and Cowley. He admitted that it is extremely difficult to define metaphysical poetry and decide what poets practiced it, but praised the complex mixture of intellect and passion that characterized their work. In the essay 'Religion and literature' Eliot stated that "literary criticism should be completed by criticism from a definite ethical and theological standpoint."

Eliot's first marriage from 1915 with the ballet-dancer Vivienne Haigh-Wood turned out to be unhappy. She was temperamental, full of life, restless. Her arrival at menstruation brought extreme mood swings, pains and cramps; her condition was diagnosed as hysteria. From 1930 until her death in 1947 she was confined in mental institutions. Later Eliot married his secretary, Valerie Fletcher. Carole Seymour-Jones has argued in Painted Shadow: A Life of Vivienne Eliot that Eliot's sexual orientation was fundamentally gay. Eliot avoided sharing bed with Vivienne, who started an affair with Bertrand Russell. Virginia Woolf once said: "He was one of those poets avoided sharing bed with Vivienne, who started an affair with Bertrand Russell. Virginia Woolf once said: "He was one of those poets who live by scratching, and his wife was his itch."

After a physical and mental breakdown in 1921, Eliot went to Lausanne for treatment. There he completed The Waste Land (1922), a poetic exploration of soul's - or civilization's - struggle for regeneration. Following Pound's suggestion, Eliot reduced The Waste Land to about half its original length, but Pound was not responsible for the form of the poem, its transitions, or lack of them. The first version, with Pound's revisions, was published in 1971.

Eliot's long poem, which caught the mood of confusion and feelings of nostalgia for a "paradise lost" after World War I, was not unanimously hailed as a masterpiece. Conrad Aiken noted that "What we feel is that Mr. Eliot has not wholly annealed the allusive material, has left it unabsorbed", but Aiken also argued that the poem succeeds "by virtue of its incoherence, not of its plan; by virtue of its ambiguities, not of its explanations." (New Republic, February 7, 1923) To critics who said that Eliot had expressed the "disillusionment of a generation" the poet himself answered that "I may have expressed for them their own illusion of being disillusioned, but that did not form part of my intention."

Divided into five sections, The Waste Land is a series of fragmentary dramatic monologues, a dense chorus of voices and culture historical quotations, that fade one into another. In the centre is the immortal prophet Tiresias. The waste land is contrasted with sources of regeneration, such as fertility rituals and Christian and Eastern religious practices. Moreover, Eliot didn't hesitate to combine slang with scholarly language. Material for the work Eliot drew from several sources, among them the Grail story, the legend of the Fisher King, Sir James George Frazer's Golden Bough, and Dante's Commedia, but when Dante finally is reunited with Beatrice in 'Heaven', The Waste Land ends ambiguously with a few words of Sanskrit. In a way the work, bristling with symbols, quotations and references, fulfilled Eliot's "impersonal theory of poetry": "The poet's mind is in fact a receptacle for seizing and storing up numberless feelings, phrases, images, which remain there until all the particles which can unite to from a new compound are present together." In 1927 Eliot became a British citizen and member of the Church of England. His way towards his own particular brand of High Anglicanism may be charted in his poetry, starting from 'The Hollow Men' (1925) to visions in FOUR QUARTETS (135-42), which Eliot himself regarded as his masterpiece. It consisted of four poems, 'Burnt Norton', 'East Coker', The Dry Salvages', and 'Little Gidding,' into which he integrated his experiences in World War II as a watchman checking for fires during bombing raids. These quartets represent the four seasons and four elements. Helen Gardner has described the whole work as an "austere and rigorously philosophic poem on time and time's losses and gains." (The Composition of Four Quarters, 1978)

Eliot's other works include poetic dramas, in which his dramatic verse became gradually indistinguishable from prose. MURDER IN THE CATHEDRAL (1935) was written for a church performance and treated the martyrdom of St. Thomas à Beckett. After the publication of the play, Eliot was appointed to the committee in charge of a new English translation of the Bible. In THE FAMILY REUNION (1939) Eliot took a theme of contemporary life, and tried to find a rhythm close to contemporary speech. THE COCKTAIL PARTY (1950) was partly based on Alcestis of Euripides.

"What we have to do is to bring poetry into the world in which the audience lives and to which it returns when it leaves the theatre; not to transport the audience into some imaginary world totally unlike their own, an unreal world in which poetry can be spoken. What I should hope might achieved, by a generation of dramatists having the benefit of our experience, is that the audience should find, at the moment of awareness that it is hearing poetry, that it is saying to itself: "I could talk in poetry too!" Then we should not be transported into an artificial world; on the contrary, out own sordid, dreary, daily world would be suddenly illuminated and transfigured." (from Poetry and Drama, 1951)

Eliot was an incurable joker and among his many pranks

was to seat visiting authors in chairs with whoopee cushions and offer them exploding cigars. To the poet's pleasure, the American comedian Groucho Marx was his great fan. In 1964 he wrote to Groucho: "The picture of you in the newspaper saying that, amongst other reasons, you have come to London to see me has greatly enchanted my credit line in the neighborhood, and particularly with the greengrocer across the street." OLD POSSUM'S BOOK OF PRACTICAL CATS (1939), Eliot's classical book of verse for children, has achieved a considerable world success in a musical adaptation. His most influential exercise in social criticism was NOTES TOWARDS THE DEFINITION OF CULTURE (1948).

Eliot died in London on January 4, 1965. His ashes were taken to St Michael's Church in East Coker, his ancestral village. Eliot's fame has been shadowed by accusations of racism, misogynism, fascism, emotional coldness, and anti-Semitism. However, Eliot avoided being labelled as a Communist. Hints of Eliot's anti-Semitism, especially the poem 'Burbank With a Baedeker: Bleistein With a Cigar,' has been considered a questionable outgrowth of his theology, or due to a class prejudice, but never the centre of his thought. The possibility that Eliot perhaps was parodying antisemitism also offer an alternative way of reading this controversial piece. (see Patricia Sloane's work T.S. Eliot's Bleistein Poems, 2000)

For Thine is
Life is
For Thine is the
This is the way the world ends
This is the way the world ends
This is the way the world ends
Not with a bang but a whimper
(from The Hollow Men

Chapter 4

T.S. Eliot: Poet and Critic as Historical Theorist

Most people suppose that some people, because they enjoy the luxury of Christian sentiments and the excitement of Christian ritual, swallow or pretend to swallow incredible dogma. For some the process is exactly opposite. Rational assent may arrive late, intellectual conviction may come slowly, but they come inevitably without violence to honesty and nature. To put the sentiments in order is a later, and immensely difficult task: intellectual freedom is earlier and easier than complete spiritual freedom.

Thomas Stearns Eliot

Many writers, philosophers, and artists contribute theories to the field of history without intending to do so. Because most writers and philosophers write about the past at some point or another, and because artists do not create in a vacuum, but in the context of cultural tradition, they often develop ideas about why and how past events occurred as they did and postulate what might take place in the future. For example, historian Karl Lowith's *Meaning in History* examines the historical theories of Comte, Condorcet, Voltaire, Bossuet, Joachim, and Augustine, thinkers who probably never thought of themselves as historians in the formal sense.

Thomas Stearns Eliot, best known for writing "The Waste Land," which literature scholars still study and acknowledge as *the* poem of the twentieth century, also wrote literary criticism and cultural philosophies. In confronting the world and its past, present, and future in art and philosophy, Eliot developed an approach to history as complex and mature as any professional historian's. Like Vico and Toynbee, Eliot viewed history in terms of the development of cultures. Grounding himself in the absolute authority of Anglo-Catholic Christianity, Eliot posited religion as the source of all cultures, describing how these cultures develop through the dynamic interactions of unity and diversity, tradition and novelty, and individual perspective and cultural context.

Unlike the Enlightenment historians and their heirs, he did not see progress as an escalating improvement in culture, but as the regeneration of cultural tradition. Like many thinkers of his time, Eliot believed Western culture was a fragmentary mess. He cited the decay of religion — the source of culture — and tradition — the permanence of culture — as the cause of cultural collapse. Though he believed this decay had proceeded too far to be easily reversed, he enjoined thinkers to adopt his theories and draw hope from the understanding they provided. And though Eliot was staunchly conservative in outlook and disposition, his focus on individual perspective made him one of the fathers of post-modem thought.

Born to a well-established Anglo-American family in 1888, Eliot confronted both the early twentieth century's frightening alienation and the collapse of the Western bourgeois synthesis. Western thought had replaced the Christian religion with a combination of capital, progress, and the reification of natural science and positive philosophy. The disaster of world war had proved to Eliot and thinkers like him that the stomping progress of technology and material wealth without a broader meaning or system of values was bankrupt and hopeless. Since the Renaissance, philosophers had tried to fill the vacuum left by the abandonment of Christianity, but no system they could devise had the authority of traditional religion. Their faith gone and its substitute revealed as an ineffectual charlatan, the Europeans and Americans stumbled about in a shellshocked daze, desperately scrabbling for a foothold of hope and authority and able to find none. Eliot, who detailed this alienation in poems like "The Love Song of J. Alfred Prufrock" and "The Waste Land," himself participated in this search, exploring the philosophy of Henri Bergson, Eros, aestheticism, humanism, idealism, and even Buddhism for doctrines to explain and repair the fragmentation of culture.

Eliot's disposition and intellectual rigor required something more substantial to solve his inner conflicts; the philosophies were, no matter how urgently presented and grasped, wispy artificial constructs, and Eliot feared that Buddhism, though an admirable religion, could strip him of his identity as a Westerner. Five years after writing "The Waste Land," he found the stability he sought, converting to Anglicanism in 1927. As he had grown up in the Unitarian Church, a faith which watered down Christianity to make it amenable to Enlightenment thought, and which Eliot believed encouraged skepticism rather than belief, this conversion constituted a completely new belief system for Eliot. It would shape everything he wrote, from poetry to drama to criticism, from that point onward. It would also provide the foundations of his cultural and historical theories.

From this religious basis, Eliot formulated the most basic tenet of his cultural theory, that religion and culture are essentially "related." In fact, Eliot argued that "no culture has appeared or developed except together with a religion: according to the point of view of the observer, the culture [appears] to be the product of the religion, or the religion the product of the culture." They might be thought of as different aspects of the same thing; culture was "the incarnation of the religion of a people."

Civilizations which appeared to be secular or humanistic, such as ancient Greece and Rome, were actually religious cultures in decline. Culture could not be preserved, extended, or developed in the absence of religion, nor could religion be preserved and maintained if culture was not. Eliot reached this connection between religion and culture because he lived in a time in which he saw people, including himself, wandering aimlessly in search of meaning, and because he was finally able to find meaning through Anglicanism. There is much evidence, however, that his conversion was not a conversion of passionate belief, but a conversion of will. Eliot had reached the end of his philosophical rope and so turned reluctantly but determinedly to the last available source of authority and meaning. His friend Virginia Woolf said of his conversion that "a corpse would seem to me more credible than he is." E.M. Forster noted that he was "not a mystic. [His work] contains several well-turned compliments to religion and Divine Grace, but no trace of religious emotion He has not got it; what he seeks is not revelation, but stability."

This said more about the context of Eliot's Christianity and its importance to his cultural theory than it does about his belief itself; Eliot was certainly a sincere Christian who openly acknowledged the intellectualism of his conversion (note my opening quote). He believed that, as Christianity did so for him, "any religion, while it lasts, and on its own level, gives an apparent meaning to life, provides the framework for a culture, and protects the mass of humanity from boredom and despair."

Culture, according to Eliot, began in primitive societies as a unified entity, then expanded and specialized, developing a dynamic relationship between its unity and diversity. The aspects of culture, which included religion, politics, science, and art, gradually became distinct from one another; the witch doctor and the king came to have different roles. As they diverged in interests and goals, these societal divisions struggled with one another for dominance, their competition pushing them to flower and prosper. Despite this rivalry, no aspect of culture — urbanity and civility, learning, philosophy, the arts, and so on — could flourish independently of the others. Few definitions of culture included all of the attributes which might be considered, but no one of them alone could confer the wholeness of culture.

Culture, out of necessity, had many other divisions. In one of his most controversial assertions, Eliot insisted that, for a culture to be transferred hereditarily, that culture must preserve its social classes. Culture, to Eliot, was not some exalted holding of the upper classes, but the sum total of the activities of all classes. The upper classes merely preserved the more specialized and conscious domains of culture. Privilege rewarded the efforts of the upper classes, and familial love inspired them to pass this privilege and culture on to their children. Eliot emphasized that he was not interested in the aristocracy as a ruling class so much as the specialized gradation of classes, in which the aristocracy played an important role.

How does the contemporary mind deal with Eliot's seeming endorsement of inequality? Well, to give him the benefit of the doubt, not all people are created equal. Many people have talents and gifts which set them apart from others; others may have deficiencies or handicaps which make them less competent or able than others. Eliot believed that "a democracy in which everybody had an equal responsibility in everything would be oppressive for the conscientious and licentious for the rest." Perhaps this makes sense; the logical conclusion is a merit-based rule, is it not? Well, no, not for Eliot. He toyed with the idea of rule by an elite who rose to prestige and power by their abilities, but rejected it, worried that an elite would not have the social commonality and camaraderie that the classes would; he had not seen an elite system work. An elite system would also serve to disenfranchise the masses from their duties and privileges within society. Eliot did not reserve much sympathy for the unwashed masses, but they are almost as important to his system as the upper classes. The unity of each class would facilitate the passing on of their cultural trusts to their posterity, and it took all of the classes working in tandem for the process to work.

Had Eliot ever experienced the essence of working class life and what it meant to work with his hands for a working class wage? Probably not. He never asserted that members of the upper class are better people than the masses, although his passions and upbringing suggested such chauvinism, but his theories reified the high classes' position in society and allowed for little or no social mobility. He spoke out against the "overeducation" of working people, believing it lowered overall standards of learning and was unnecessary. Only Marxists would argue hotly against Eliot in favour of a classless society, but Eliot should have been able to appreciate a society in which social mobility was possible, if not easy, and in which the best members of society could rise to positions of leadership. Despite the flawed execution of its ideals, the United States of America had always striven for such a society, and many European countries had followed suit by Eliot's time. Nevertheless, the class system was necessary to the unity and diversity in Eliot's cultural theory.

Eliot also looked for this dynamic in geographic regions within culture and in the religion of the culture. He believed that in a healthy culture, several regions surrounded a dominant central region. People in the central region had a nationalistic allegiance to the culture, while people living in the satellite regions balanced their loyalties between their region and the larger culture. The distinct character of the subculture then contributed a wider perspective and special flavour to the generally blander, less passionate central culture.

The friction between these regions bolstered creativity and kept the entire culture fresh. Imbalance-whether in the form of exaggerated regional conflict, which endangered the culture, or cultural uniformity, which threatened other cultures as the central culture sought new satellites-had to be vigorously avoided. Eliot cited the relationship between the regions of Great Britain-England, as a dominant nation, and Scotland and Wales, as satellites-as an example of regional unity and diversity. Also important was unity and diversity within religion, which, religion being the lynchpin of culture, linked the other two aspects of unified diversity. Although the entirety of a culture should have subscribed to the same religious doctrines, sects and cults should have healthily varied by class and region as well as conviction. This way, the believer could follow his or her conscience regarding religious practice as an individual or as a member of a class or region. Sect and cult thus helped both the gradations of class and distinctions of regions have a voice in society.

To Eliot, the prime mover of culture was the preservation

of tradition in a constantly changing world. All of the aspects of culture he enumerated, but especially class, worked to maintain tradition and keep it fresh. Yes, the world changed, and culture expressed itself in new ways as time passed, but in order for these expressions to have structure and context, a body of the best past expressions and ways of life had to endure. Tradition was not a symptom of antiquarian stuffiness, but rather the preservation of something from the past for an appropriately timely use in the present.

This tradition, this canon of continuingly accepted expressions, periodically took in new material, new stimuli which kept it relevant to the present. This evolutionary development was not just a shift in quantity, but also in quality, as the new information changed the culture's perception of the older matter. As Eliot described it: the artist] must be aware that the mind of Europe [Western culture] — the mind of his own country — a mind which he learns in time to be much more important than his own private mind-is a mind which changes, and that this change is a development which abandons nothing en route, which does not superannuate either Shakespeare, or Homer, or the rock drawing of the Magdalenian draughtsmen... the difference between the present and the past is that the conscious present is an awareness of the past in a way and to an extent which the past's awareness of itself cannot show.

In other words, what historians had over the makers of history was hindsight, the ability to understand the context of events and activities as was not possible while they were taking place. Tradition's purpose lay not in futile antiquarianism, but in improving the present, and by extension, the future. If a teaching or tradition had no proper use or relevance to a contemporary culture, the culture threw that teaching out. Studying past cultures gave the present culture a different perspective by which it could become more selfaware through the contrast. At the same time, cultural expression could not simply study the traditional canon, but had to constantly strive to build upon it. If the propagation of culture fell into decay, not only would there be no present culture, but the culture would lose touch with its past and lose all sense of being a culture. A robust culture would apply its generational reflection of mercurially changing standards to the canon. Every new addition to tradition would change the contemporary perspective, giving the society a larger tradition than it had before, a new criterion of appreciation. Each generation had a different interpretation of each work of culture which was appropriate to its time. Eliot's was a progressive theory, not one of hope for steady and inevitable improvement, but one of regenerative utility.

If this view of tradition sounded very relativistic, it also provided a modicum of security, stability, and virtual absolutism. The community as a whole held a common perspective which acted as a grounding, a mortar, for the various individual perspectives within it. This communal prejudice provided a standard of "objectivity" that all within the culture accepted. The preservation of the past and induction of new ideas in tradition served to enlarge this consensus, providing a greater field of objectivity. Eliot felt that language was one of the prime detern-dners and vehicles of expression of a cultural world view; language defined a civilization's perspective. He believed poets made their greatest contribution to their culture by expressing the inexpressible, expanding the language and thus the consciousness of their society.

This communal background stood as the context for the experience of the individual in the world. Personal identity was very important to Eliot's personal concept and to his philosophy, and most of that identity came from the culture in which one had been raised and had learned to think. World view, culture, tradition-the individual learned all through his or her native society, and they composed much of what that person was. Hence Eliot's fear of losing his "Westernness," which kept him from converting to Buddhism. Language, the expression of culture, was another practice Eliot guarded fiercely: One of the reasons for learning at least one foreign language well is that we acquire a kind of supplementary personality; one of the reasons for not acquiring a new language *instead* of our own is that most of us do not want to become a different person. Despite the need to preserve identity, the best way for an individual to recognize and understand identity was to explore other cultures and, especially, to cultivate aesthetic experience. Eliot believed the experience of art not only brought people greater joy, but also greater self-understanding:

It is ultimately the function of art, in imposing a credible order upon ordinary reality, and thereby eliciting perception of an order in reality, to bring us to a condition of serenity, stillness, and reconciliation.

Art appreciation served to organize tastes, beliefs, and experiences into a whole, satisfying the human desire for unity and self-realization. It was "a fusion of what was not oneself with oneself," developing and becoming "more [one]self by becoming more not [one]self." Reflexively, the self-awareness granted by the study of art facilitates the understanding of other aspects of art and culture the individual might encounter.

This concept of the individual in relation to his or her culture and to the rest of the world served as a central point in Eliot's philosophy. Grounded in Anglican belief, Eliot insisted upon the imperfectability of humanity. No one could see with a perfect, holistic, unprejudiced, "God's-eye view." A human being who tried to see with such unstructured sight saw nothing at all. However, though total objectivity was beyond reach, Eliot believed that tremendous empathy, effort, and understanding could make it possible to merge one's horizons with those of an artist or another human being, and thus broaden those horizons.

Eliot also asserted the individual's role in bringing a perspective to a work of art. The standard for interpretation was not the intent of the artist but rather the reading of the observer, who might be viewing the work from a much later perspective. Moreover, that perspective was not just the worldview of the interpreter's culture, as discussed earlier, but a wholly unique, individual bias. This focus on individual perspective, which approached relativism but had groundings in Eliot's beliefs in religion, local cultures, and traditions, made him one of the primary literary innovators toward post-modern thought. Eliot's willingness to allow innovation within what appeared to be a very conservative scheme stemmed from his belief that a healthy culture depended on a balance between the old and the new. If many now interpret him as a stuffy reactionary, he only emphasized tradition so fervently because of the times in which he lived.

The rapid change of the nineteenth and twentieth centuries threatened to whisk away Western tradition in a Heraclitian hurricane. Eliot wanted to sound alarms to stop the rapid decay of tradition; temporary reification of that tradition seemed to him the best way to preserve it. Eliot's cultural theory was no absolute theory of history — though he did have a scheme for what had happened and what should happen — but rather a diagnosis of the modern malaise and a plan of action for how to deal with it.

Eliot's Anglicanism was, of course, the root of all of his theories. His Christianity did not sit well with many of his contemporaries, who uncomfortably dismissed it as a throwback to the Dark Ages. In fact, his colleagues often made him feel like an outsider after his conversion. Indeed, as already indicated, Eliot himself found the path to belief a tremendous struggle, but the Christian scheme which would provide the stability he sought would work no other way. The alternatives, particularly secular humanism, provided no solace; its ethics comprised "a s stem of morals which seem[ed] to be founded on nothing but itself. Religion seemed to him the much more viable alternative:

> The religious habits of the race are still very strong, in all places, at all times, and for all people. There is no humanistic habit: humanism is, I think, merely the state of mind of a few persons in a few places at a few times. To exist at all, it is dependent upon some other attitude, for it is essentially critical — I would even say parasitical. It has been and can still be, of great value; but it will never provide showers of partridges or abundance of manna for the chosen peoples.

What particularly set Eliot apart from Enlightenment, humanistic, progressive thinkers was his fundamental belief that perfection was reserved for God. Humanity could improve itself, but there would always be an unattainable flawlessness that the race could look to as incentive to improve further. The Platonic absolute could be imagined but not won. If Joachim and the Enlightenment thinkers he influenced predicted a perfected earth, Eliot could not be absolutely optimistic:

We have to remember that the Kingdom of Christ on earth will never be realised; we must remember that whatever reform or revolution we carry out, the result will always be a sordid travesty of what human society should be-though the world is never left wholly without glory.

In the twentieth century, Western civilization was far from Eliot's cultural ideal. After his conversion, Eliot believed that the culture was falling apart not just for its abandonment of tradition, but also for its neglect of Christianity. According to his theory, the past two thousand years of European culture rested on the Christian foundation. Unfortunately, modernism and skepticism had eroded the Christian basis, and what Europe and America had left to them was a negative society which could not succeed either economically or spiritually. To Eliot, the options for endurance were to either establish a new Christian society, or enact a positive pagan society — an idea which curdled Eliot's blood.

The new Christian society would not force belief on all those living within it, but would instead operate under rigorous Christian value systems under the custodianship of an elite called the Community of Christians. Eliot noted that, in the situation in which he wrote, modern society was hostile to Christianity, promoting un-Christian aims; therefore, society would have to be re-organized to conform to Christianity. Moreover, in the interests of promoting religion and tradition, a uniform system of education would be executed. A National Church similar to the Church of England would exist in tandem with, but not controlling or under the control of, the state.Eliot's Christian society may appear to be a megalomaniacal projection of his own beliefs on the entire culture. Still, others have proposed utopias, and they, too, drew from their own beliefs and dreams. For Eliot, nothing else would suffice in what increasingly appeared to him to be a morally bankrupt and spiritually desperate society:

The number of people in possession of any criteria for discriminating between good and evil is very small; the number of the half-alive hungry for any form of spiritual experience, or what offers itself as spiritual experience, high or low, good or bad, is considerable.

Significantly, Eliot put forward his proposal for a Christian society shortly after his England, his chosen homeland, abandoning principle in Eliot's eyes, knuckled under to Adolf Hitler in the crisis of September 1938.

In essence, Thomas Stearns Eliot's theory of history was not concerned with wars or great political events and movements, nor was it a typical Enlightenment theory of progress. These it replaced with the monolithic flow of tradition, a tradition passed from generation to generation with an occasional infusion of novelty to keep it appropriate to the times. This dynamic combination posited a conservative tradition which kept itself fresh through the struggles and growth of its new artists and philosophers. It was Eliot's hope that such a firm tradition would save what he feared was otherwise a doomed culture. In short, his theory was that of a conservatively-minded critic and artist who was intently interested in laying out a future course for Western civilization.

Eliot died in 1965. What would he have thought of the student riots at Columbia University and what they said about the future of authority and tradition? What would he have thought about the youth cultures of the United States and Europe in the 1960s? What would he have thought of the spread of feminism, multiculturalism, and relativism? Of the decline of Christian practice and traditional moral values? All have called for an end to Western tradition. Needless to say, Christianity, abandoned in the West with an increasing sense of lethargy, has played little role in cultural preservation in the past half-century. Doubtless Eliot would pronounce his life's work and efforts a failure and say a prayer for the soul of Western culture. Still, despite the intellectual and moral difficulties contemporary life presents, a richer community demographic now contributes to our culture; more races, religions, and genders speak the peace of their fresh Eliot perspectives to change culture as we know it and as Eliot knew it. These groups have found their voices both through religious cult (the non-violent Christian efforts of Martin Luther King, Jr. come to mind), as Eliot might have predicted, and through allegiance to ideals which haven't proved nearly so insubstantial as Eliot thought.

To Eliot, due to Western hegemony, Western civilization meant, by extension, world civilization. Now many other cultures play a much larger role in defining world civilization. If the postmodern world seems morally bankrupt, human beings are becoming increasingly accountable to one another; if society has not embraced Christianity as a panacea for aimlessness, each individual is learning to follow his or her own path rather than marching on a unified path in a group; distinct perspective no longer indicates aimlessness. Even if the currently subordinate state of tradition might disappoint Eliot, a much more open, inclusive, and diverse human family, a unity in diversity he might have appreciated, will contribute to the tradition of tomorrow.

Chapter 5

T.S. Eliot and the End of Bourgeois Poetry

I believe T. S. Eliot has no equal among the bourgeois poets of today, in France or in England. I know the regime of the literary society which has established itself now for more than one generation of bourgeois poets makes it all the more difficult to sustain this claim; the glories of poetry are confined to Chapels and I have not nearly visited all of them. It is quite possible that those which I have not visited may be concealing poets no less remarkable than Eliot. The technical difficulty of paying a visit to all these Chapels is, however, not as great as the difficulty of learning all of the resident languages: a fundamental aspect of these kind of societies is that each has its own exclusive idiom and they are idioms of a kind that cannot be quickly mastered.

Eliot's own growing fame has contributed more than one example of this linguistic difficulty. Thousands of readers have failed when confronted by the obscurity of his poetic grammar and even experienced critics (notably I. A. Richards and Edwin Muir) have been careless enough to analyse his work without learning his language first. This obscurity of contemporary poets cannot be reduced to the simple problem of logic, to these almost mandatory elliptical accumulations, which on first sight make contemporary poetry seem a disquieting and indecipherable shorthand. Even worse is that each poet has his own symbolic language, but does not bother to explain this language to the reader so that it becomes intelligible only to experienced psychoanalysts. The poet does not want to be understood. The reader does not want to understand, either. Poetry has ceased to be a means of communication; the poetical forum has become a market of snobbism on which one learns to trade without considering its intrinsic content. Poetic glories have become mere fortuities, linked to poetically insignificant individuals. On the stock exchange of values, poets possess nothing that yields interest to either the literature scholar or the sensibility of the dying bourgeoisie. Nothing is being said about anything the reader likes or understands. Poetry has devaluated to being merely an aspect of social organization, relevant perhaps to sociologists or economists, but to nobody else.

But do bourgeois poets deserve any better? Is there anything more to them than their disconcerting displays of originality? Poetry has never been as devoid of meaning and of valid social content1 as now. The worlds these poets construct are rigorously 'private' – they are as arbitrary and exclusive as dreams. Nobody needs this. Watching them pass by has become a mere mind-game. Sentiment (with which I mean all that contains a value judgement) can find nothing to react to. All that remains of these poets' efforts is their deformation of the language (in the widest sense of the term), emptying it of all social content, 'demagnetising'2 it.

Standing out from this core of crossed-word and mixed-image brokers are a small number of poets whose work holds at least some interpersonal interest. And among them, an even smaller number actually has anything truly significant to say. The importance of a poet derives from two variables: his poetic power and the human and historical relevance of his topic. The poetic power itself has a neutral value, comparable to a cannon whose destructive power does not depend on the cause it is used for.3 These two elements had a strong tendency to coincide in the grand poets of preceding times: Dante, Milton and Goethe were at once the mightiest voices *and* the most representative spirits of their respective eras. Victor Hugo was the last of the great poets4 who were at the same time popular and a representative of the living forces of their era. But bourgeois poetry, emasculated of the last remnants of its revolutionary power, ceased to be fertile even before Hugo's death. From Tennyson, Longfellow and Sully-Prudhomme onwards poets have become no more than eunuchs detaining the public ear and the only poetic power left were the "poetes maudits", with Rimbaud as their prime representative. These poets were no longer moved by the hopes and ideals of a vigorous class, but by the tragic contradictions of a society dominated by a class in a stage of latent but incurable decomposition. They were no revolutionaries, but symptoms of a state of affairs where revolution should have been the only issue. Their poetry became a button which set off the bourgeoisie's festering decomposition at an explosive speed and with likewise power. Being a 'poete maudit' was not easy, these were "tragic heroes", scapegoats singled out to be sacrificed for the sins of the tribe.

The truest of them perished literally. Their deaths left behind a potent vaccine for posterity, which, after the tragic deaths of Verlaine and Rimbaud, degenerated to a spicy seasoning for the meals of the decomposing middle-class. The contrast between the disgrace of Rimbaud's living conditions and his posthumous glory among today's elite – a glory so tangible that the most expensive bar of the *quartier latin* in Paris bears the name of Rimbaud's most celebrated poem – represents the contrast between a time when the death of bourgeois civilization haunted only the most inspired of Cassandras and a time when that same death has become an object of daily consumption – after all, one might as well make death consumable when one is forced to consume it anyway. Today, the potent chemicals left us by the "poetes maudits" have been reduced to a harmless goo.

For most poets, they have become only more or less dominant ingredients to be added to their bowl of stirred images. Other poets who did imbued the vaccine, have become immune by making the vaccine a springboard, a point of departure from which they can leave a positive value system. But unfortunately, under the current regime of bourgeois civilization, which is itself incapable of producing a value system, they can only produce dummy values, intellectually unacceptable and historically false, borrowed from more fertile eras but profoundly alien to ours. Such is the nature of Claudel's Catholicism.

Asked who was the greatest poet in France andre Gide answered: "Victor Hugo, alas", which is a respectable answer from one the last members of the bourgeois decadence, who finds the robust self-sufficiency of a less corrupt age ridiculous and vulgar; an answer worthy enough of an intelligent critic who knows how to appreciate without liking. One ought to answer the question who is currently our greatest French poet in the manner of Gide: "Paul Claudel, alas". There can be no doubt that Claudel's voice is the ablest among the French authors of today. But this poetic ability serves an ideology, the acceptance of which only demonstrates the extent of the bourgeois poets' moral and intellectual disintegration.

Hugo's democratic vitality was a religion that lived for its time; Claudel's Catholicism is a hole in the sand in which the ostrich-like poet believes to be sheltered from sad, sad reality, a refuge where the shirker of history tries to shelter himself from the approaching future. Morally it is a flight, a cowardice; intellectually an abdication, for only by blinding one's intelligence can such a fantastic and unreal system be accepted. Claudel's poetry is not empty in the way typical decadent bourgeois poetry is; it is worse. He has inflated his poetry with negative matter, invested it with a power that serves an unreal and negative goal – all too typical of the dying bourgeois civilization: Claudel's poetry is not unlike the immense amount of negative energy that was shed in the Great War. What distinguishes Eliot from all these poets is that in him, an exceptional poetic power has allied itself to a truly important social theme, indeed, the only historically valid and sincere theme that remains a bourgeois poet in our time. Where his contemporaries are themselves nothing but manifestations of the death of bourgeois civilization, he alone has been able to create a poetry of death.

Eliot's theme is the only one available for a poet of the decadent bourgeoisie. For a true poet is a true poet also for having an understanding, an 'intuition' if you will, of the historical reality that his understanding has to be more or less self-conscious. One could object that there is another possibility, that the fight against the past by a class dedicated to death could well be the source of inspiration for a poet of bourgeois imperialism. But Lucain's Caton, the typical militant of this condemned class, is a figure devoid of high poetry. Why could fascism not inspire a poet of Eliot's size? Because long before its physical and military defeat bourgeoisie lost everything justifying, even to itself, its struggle against the class that will superannuate it. The bourgeoisie is devoid of values and all the living values are on the side of the working class. If a bourgeois poet, or ideologist, wants to confront the revolution with something positive and convincing (convincing to himself also), he has no other option but to rely on the resurrection of some medieval ghost – such is Claudel's Catholicism – with the consequence that inevitably he will become irrelevant to his contemporaries.

The fight of the bourgeoisie against the revolution is ideologically sterile. Fascism is merely an *atto puro*, an action without rational aim or justification beyond the action itself.5 Fascism is a mere binge, a drinking-bout that blinds all reason and intelligence and reduces mankind to a system of reactions, sterile from conscience. Like Dr. Watson's rats, the system constitutes of behaviour only and of the hypothesis that conscience is superfluous to explain its movements. Fascism cannot have its own poet and for today's bourgeois poet Fascism cannot be a topic: the only one left to him is Death.

Death is a very interpersonal theme, since it is firmly grounded in both history and society. But it is hardly a popular theme. The poet who takes it as the leitmotif of his oeuvre by definition lacks popular elements, in every sense of the word 'popular'. Besides, the 'private' and exclusive style developed by the bourgeois poets of recent decades serves excellently for poker-facing a lost game and insisting on that to which one can but resign oneself.6 Taken from that point of view, Eliot's obscurity becomes very interesting. Eliot is obscure. He is so consciously, aggressively – obscure with a vengeance. One might even call him a champion of obscurity, of the poet's right not to be understood. But his complexity is different from that of most of his contemporaries. The latter go to great lengths to be incomprehensible simply because they have nothing to say worth understanding. For Eliot, obscurity is a weapon with which he defend defends himself; it allows him to speak of secret things the populace was never *meant* to understand. Yet the content of his poetry is not in the least obscure. It is not a private world of hybrid images expressed by means of symbols that were carefully sifted from the most perplexing bunch that a troubled and putrescent subconscious could come up with. Eliot's poetry is essentially based on a social and universal experience, an experience which on the level of the individual manages to encompass a full perspective of the death of a civilization.

To be explicit about this would, however, have been lacking in refinement, it would have been a betrayal to revered simplicity. Strong inhibitions (due in part, as has been too often insisted upon, to a Puritan upbringing and to the inferiority complex of American highbrows, for whom not having been born an Englishman hurts like an incurable wound7) have come to Eliot's aid and simplified the task of obscuring that which might otherwise have become too obvious. A closer analysis of his poetry shows that his obscurity is all superficial, superimposed, created out of ellipses and silences. The content, the system of symbols with which he works, is remarkably transparent and there is nothing affected or arbitrary about it. Its order and logic are so rigorous that one might classify Eliot's oeuvre as allegory. *The Waste Land* is wholly structured around three fundamental symbols: Humidity, Aridity and Fire.8 These symbols are predominant throughout almost his entire oeuvre. His obscurity is superimposed onto this clear and simple drama. It is above all to be found in the sequence of the images, in this ingenious and confusing poetic 'montage' which brings Eliot close to surrealism – especially to surrealist cinema, of which he is the unacknowledged precursor.

Eliot's poetry is, like all great decadent poetry, at once violently innovative and solidly traditional, retrospective even. One might call the tradition to which he attaches himself that of the English *secentismo*, 10 that influential school which begins with Shakespeare and Chapman, finds its most individual expression in Donne and Webster and, then, after a long period of decline, is briefly revived in the works of Pope. Laforgue chiselled his light irony onto this strong and heavy pillar and Eliot keeps much of this incongruous juxtaposition of *secentist* sonorities placed under the ironic damper of French decadence in his own style – the Eliotic 'montage' owes many of its best effects to these paragraphs of blank verse which are easily mistaken to be Elizabethan at first, but then suddenly broken off by a vulgar modern dissonance.

The power that the English *secentism* has over Eliot is the result of a complex play of attraction and repugnance. Since he is the last poet of the English bourgeoisie, it is only natural he should be drawn to this Golden Age of English poetry. But there is more to it. This golden age had its element of decadence too and this adds to the attraction. It was a time of transition during which a young bourgeois civilization was still caught up in the last forms of medieval decadence. Alongside a truly modern elite, whose most notable names were Bacon and Hobbes, persisted an elite still attached to the Church, the feudal system and whom still considered scholasticism, astrology and alchemy to be relevant disciplines; the most influential and characteristic poet representative of this elite is Donne. Eliot's current position is in several respects similar to that of Donne three hundred years ago. Donne represents something which has been fairly uncommon in the past: a real poet endowed with great poetic power, whose theme is historically viable, but who is nevertheless esoteric rather than popular – which is quite common for poets who belong to a superannuated elite.

But Donne's class was not under threat of the kind of complete extinction that the class which Eliot descends from is under. Donne's class would survive for a while yet, needing only to reject certain outmoded values to be able to adapt itself to a new era with relative ease. And so, while Donne's effort to remain obscure mainly reveals his attachment to everything his class had to abandon in order to survive, Donne introduces the theme of death under very different auspices than Eliot does. These similarities and differences betwixt the two poets are reflected in Eliot's attitude towards Donne, an attitude marked by complexity and ambivalence. Drawn to him by an affinity too great to be ignored, Eliot at the same time fights against that which he finds alien and hostile in the older poet – his disciplined yet ever living flesh, his soul and his psyche, which cannot detach itself from the flesh to become pure spirit, *pneuma*.

The affinity between Eliot and Laforgue is more direct and immediate. In the poetic family-tree, this poet is Eliot's true father: the ties which bind them together manifest themselves above all in Eliot's early poems (those collected in *Prufrock and Other Observations* and *Ara Vos Prec)* only to disappear almost completely in his mature works. Laforgue was not a *poète maudit*. He was only an epigone of Romanticism. In other words, his soul was not laid bare by the crumbling of bourgeois values, but rather directed towards a 'green paradise' to be created after the inferno of capitalism. The true romantic, however, is the petty, degraded bourgeois who still cherishes memories of an idyllic order, still hoping to recover his paradise through a utopian revolution, through faith (Baudelaire on his death-bed), through dreams (like the great opium smokers of English Romanticism), or through a dream-like death. If the romantic tries to escape the bourgeois world, then not because he can see its corruption and has fore-suffered its death. On the contrary, he wishes to escape because he sees that the world is strong and stable and he neither can nor wants to adapt to it, finds it inhospitable.

If we compare the decadent romantics of the *fin de siècle* with the first generation of romantics, we find that the former differ from the latter mainly in that they have much less faith in the reality of a romantic paradise and put far more emphasis on the cult of disease. The first romantics lived in an era when the "dark Satanic Mills" had only just begun invading "England's green and pleasant Land" (Blake). The pre-capitalist idyll was still a reality for them; they believed in something tangible. Besides, their inability to adapt to the capitalist struggle for life was not put down to defects, personal insufficiencies, it was still the sign of a class which would not admit defeat and was full of life, energy. A hundred years later, this ideal remained only in the form of dreams and the inability to adapt was increasingly associated with personal failure, with illness and physical weakness.

Romantic irony was attracted to death as the only possible route of escape to a paradise "where all is but order and beauty", 11 but which is more likely to be a useless "all-inclusive sinecure", such as permeates Laforgue's poetry (this irony also becomes the point of departure for the clownery which is the poet's revenge on the philistine and which also the young Eliot practised, not without success). In Laforgue, the irony is associated with the characteristic behaviour of someone suffering from tuberculosis, not willing to resign himself to death and desperately trying to hold onto life as it slips away from him. There is, in his poetry, an atmosphere of impurity, a permanent itch linked to sexual impotence and an ironic sentimentality which makes fun of that which it cowardly adores in secret.

This Laforguian atmosphere permeates Eliot's early poems and only little by little can one see a completely different kind of poetry stand out against this background, a poetry liberated from the decadent poet's wavering ambiguities, a poetry where irony is slowly eclipsed by tragedy and the consumptive artist's sexual ambivalence is slowly being replaced with the renunciation of the ascetic.

Eliot's critics tend to make much of his romantic irony, these contrasts which repeat the action in two different keys – one sublime, the other sordid. This is the kind of irony which prevails in the satiric poems of *Ara Vos Prec*: in "Sweeney Erect", the banal scene of a man shaving himself peacefully, not paying any attention to the hysterical convulsions of the girl he has just made love to, is compared to the story of Theseus and Ariadne in sublimely declamatory lines; in "Sweeney Among the Nightingales", the shoddy machinations of a Montmartre bar owner and a whore who plan to cheat a customer, evoke images of Clytemnestra's conspiracy against

Agamemnon. Even later, in the famous third part of *The Waste Land*, we find the splendour of Queen Elizabeth and her lover, the Earl of Leicester, sailing down the Thames and the image is juxtaposed with the sordidly tragic loves of the "Thames daughters" who live among "trams and dusty trees" and die among the oil slicks polluting the river and among the tins which litter the popular beaches.

All these episodes should probably be connected to Laforgue and the romanticism of the decadent poets. But in the new context created for them by Eliot, they no longer emboss the irony of contrasts. The opposition between the same situation played out either pleasing or ugly no longer prevails, the pity and horror of the reality of life is now common to both versions. Heroic love is not brought out to enhance its sordid equivalent, nor is sordid love used to ridicule heroic love. The eternal identity of sexual love in all its manifestations – whatever dress it may wear – is what evokes pity and terror. The poet has left the limitations of romanticism behind.

Humidity and Aridity are the two fundamental symbols of the cycle which starts with *Gerontion (Ara Vos Prec)* and to which *The Waste Land* is central. Humidity, whose principle manifestations are water and flowers, stands for life, sex, the eternal return of the seasons, the variety of the carnal and psychic life and the world of passion and of feeling. There is certainly ambivalence in Eliot's attitude towards Humidity; his stance is not so much one of repulsion, but rather, as the fine critic Edmund Wilson rightfully points out when comparing *Prufrock* and *The Waste Land* (especially the first and fourth parts), a youthful renunciation that never again left the poet. We are, however, not interested in the psychoanalysis of the Eliot's character, but in the social and historical range of his sentimental development.

And essential from this point of view is that the nostalgic love dominant in *Prufrock* and occasionally surfacing in later works12 has transformed little by little into a horror of sex and of the vital functions, a deep phobia of life, turning into what one could perhaps best describe as 'complete biological defeatism'. *The Waste Land* is built around a skeleton which derives from comparative religion13 – the animist idea that the seasonal god of life is eternally resurrected.

The first verse gives the tone of the poem: "April is the cruellest month", the cruelest because it conceives, gives birth to and therewith puts an end to the happy illusion of the absence of death in winter. The poem's center is in the third part, at the middle of which we find the synthetic figure of Tirésias, the man who was woman, who knew *utramque venerem, 14* and has thus "fore-suffered" the horror of and pity for the typist, who, after a summary meal, sleeps with her young man on a divan which doubles as a night-time bed15 and who is thus, like all other humans, forced to suffer life and its essential expression, the sex act.

The poet, decadent and defeatist at heart, confronts the horror and vulgarity of triumphant Humidity with dryness and sterility. But the real and concrete dryness and sterility are, unfortunately, nothing but that same Humidity reduced to a negligible and impotent amount.. The king, whose impotence has sterilized the whole kingdom, remains on the Waste Land, this deserted ground, 16 as the "Fisher king", whose unwillingness to resign is to the disgrace of life and all that belongs to it. The foul, half dried-up river, the authentic symbol of the Laforguian attitude, is even more disgusting than the large sea in which Phlébas perishes. The rats and the dry bones are the ever returning symbols of this dryness; which, while being very sterile, very dry, continues to sustain itself on the small quantity of water it still holds. *The hollow men,* the men stuffed with straw, swaying in the wind, exiled in the country of the cactus, dance around the rickly pear – this least humid of plants – at five o'clock in morning, the hour at which human vitality is at its lowest.

These figures from pagan culture are not happier than the typist who "smoothes her hair with automatic hand" or the Highbury girl who "raised her knees supine on the floor of a narrow canoe". And the music to which they dance is hardly more distinguished than the ballad which accompanies the springtime return of Sweeney 17 – the eternal male prefigured by Theseus and [lines lost in French version through printing error, see note]18 there is no choice between this guard of the fig tree and the massive quantities of water which absorb Phlébas. The world is imprisoned by the saps of life and these slight traces19 makes this world's condition even more humiliating and torturing. I. A. Richards recognized this when he praised Eliot for being the only poet who offers us a world without beliefs, without ideals, a world deserted by, or sterile from, values.

But what was a *tabula rasa* for the humanist and positivist Richards, whose scientific mind was free of the prejudices of 'practical reason', 20 and to whom therefore this process was a source of delight, Eliot saw as a horrifying and realistic painting of bourgeois civilization, emptied of faith, of hope and of vitality. Eliot himself tells us not to read *The Waste Land* as a personal and subjective poem, but like the report of a basic experiment, a social experiment, as it were an elegy on the death of the bourgeoisie. In prose, Eliot does not show himself a political animal and his recent love for politics must be considered unfortunate. Even in his poetry, directly political allusions are

- Here we go round the prickly pear
  Prickly pear prickly pear
  Here we go round the prickly pear
  At five o'clock in the morning.
- O the moon shone bright on Mrs. Porter
  And on her daughter.
  They wash their feet in soda water

Often quite foolish, such as the allusion to the Tartar danger in the first version of "The Hollow Men" (in the Chapbook of 1924) and in the notes to *The Waste Land* where he stoops to quote the pompous nonsense of the German *Dostoïevskien* (Herman Hess). But that is hardly surprising: esoteric and obscure as a poet, Eliot is typical of the current state of the bourgeoisie; typical of those who experience this final disease of the bourgeoisie acutely and immediately at a subconscious level, but are unable to speak about it intelligently when they attempt a clear bourgeois rationale.

Eliot's naïve political efforts to fortify the dissolving middle-class are of the same category as the obscurity of his poetry. But the poet has already shown that the middle-class man can only speak ineptitudes: the world to which he has lent his voice is one of the desert cactus only, dry and sterile, but not yet ready to give up the little life which it remains.21

But Eliot did not want to waste time on deserted Earth, nor was he content to remain a hollow man. As heir to the *poets maudits,* he wanted to escape from the desert and, like the Rimbaudian Claudel, he chose religion to be his guiding star. However and this emphasized the superiority of Eliot's integrity over Claudel's, what he sought and found was not a revival of a dead civilization, was not a dressed up positivist system of rusting symbolism, but an escape from a seasonal vicious circle in an unreal dimension.

What Eliot required of religion was an existence which would not hold anything of the life here on earth; it had to be a religion of purity, a spirituality free from any vitality, free from psychology; a purely pneumatic, mystical religion in the strictest sense of the term and one that was severely intellectualist besides. Rejecting any symbolism which set out to sanctify life, Eliot found in Fire the symbol of what he was seeking. He opposed the flowers which make the evil forces of life seem charming, the Aridity which only reduces life to a meaningless struggle, with the Fire that terminates any germ carrying life, smothers any lust whether it is strong or weak, the Fire which is devoid of any attachment to the floods of the phenomenal and personal. Arnaud Daniel, 22 "refined" by the flames of the purgatory becomes the symbol of the rise towards this Shantih, 23 of which "peace which passeth understanding" is only a weak translation.

Already in *The Waste Land* (in spite of what Richards said of it), the symbol of Fire is found to be victorious over the symbols of Humidity and Aridity. Between this poem and the purely religious poems to which Eliot's poetic output was reduced from 1927 onwards, are a group of highly important writings, including the fragments of an unfinished drama (of which *The Hollow Men* originally appears to have formed a part) and writings in prose, the most interesting of which is the essay on the 17th century Anglican preacher Lancelot Andrewes. Andrewes is right up Eliot's street, because it allows him to contrast a purely intellectualist mystic with the carnal and psychological Donne, who confessed himself to be disturbed "by a memory of the pleasures of yesterday..., by a strand of straw under the knee, by a noise in my ear, a light in my eye" at the time of prayer. Donne a very suitable scapegoat for Eliot's wish to demonstrate that religion can only be religious when it is founded, not in the psychological plasma of lust, but in pure, pneumatic fire.

The historical differences between Donne and Eliot which I discussed earlier surface admirably in the contrast between the active asceticism of Donne, an exuberant personality with a robust vitality to fight and overcome and the bloodless asceticism of Eliot, whose fire has only cacti to burn. The essay on Andrewes is certainly the most significant of all Eliot's prose writings; still more interesting is his remarkable *Fragment of an Agon,* where the topic of life is taken up again in an even more realistic and vulgar tone than before. In *Fragment,* Eliot finds a formula expressing the ultimate horror of life with extraordinary force (combining a skilful use of dissonance with a nauseating vulgarity): "birth and copulation and death" – And to leave little doubt concerning the morality of *Fragment,* its epigraph consists of the words of St John of the Cross, on the heart which cannot unite itself with God because it has not yet "divested itself of the love of created beings".

In the religious poems of late, Eliot's style narrows and becomes increasingly "small and dry". The grand symphonic movements of *Gerontion, The Waste Land, The Hollow Men* and *Fragment of an Agon* do not return. The poet's bones are increasingly refined in the purgatorial fire; the air becomes increasingly empty and strange. The life he seeks is most certainly divorced from the carnal life and does not resemble its earthly cousin in any way.

He cannot find the values that must save sterile and dry middle-class man neither in carnal life, nor in historical reality; the kingdom which he seeks is not of this world. Thus speaks

Eliot the poet. Eliot the publicity agent ostentatiously believes in the possibility of integrating life with the value of the spiritualist mystic, to make these two the cause of the ideology to affirm "Classicism in literature, Anglo Catholicism in religion and Royalism in politics" (cf. foreword of the single volume edition of *For Lancelot Andrewes*, 1928). His poetry, however, reveals this ideology to be nothing and adds that the nothing of the fire *che es gli affina* is the better, purer nothing.

Chapter 6

Plot Synopsis

The Cocktail Party is a twentieth century morality play, one that argues that people must accept their burdensome roles as decision makers. Unlike medieval morality plays, which upbraided audiences to choose good deeds and shun evil, *The Cocktail Party* simply places its characters in the crucible of choice and diagnoses their indecision as a malaise. Eliot means to demonstrate that it is the burden of the human race to face tough choices and live with the consequences.

The play centers around the offstage infidelity of Edward Chamberlayne. As the play opens he is hosting his wife Lavinia's cocktail party alone—Lavinia has discovered his affair and has left him. After the party, Edward speaks with a character known as the Unidentified Guest, who seems eerily knowledgeable about Edward's situation and offers much superficially wise advice that only serves to confuse Edward. The Unidentified Guest even offers to bring his wife back to him. Later Edward speaks alone with Celia Coplestone, his mistress and we learn that they planned on being together pending the breakup of his marriage. Yet Edward now seems uncertain about Celia, as if he has a mind to return to his wife.

The next day the Unidentified Guest indeed brings Lavinia home and she and Edward discuss their marital problems and especially Edward's indecisiveness. Edward becomes convinced that his indecision is a mental illness and he seeks treatment, one day ending up in the office of the Unidentified Guest, finally identified as Sir Henry Harcourt-Reilly, a psychologist. Lavinia joins their session and reveals her own affair with Peter Quilpe, another frequent cocktail party guest. Through indirect means, including vague talk about a sanitarium, Reilly convinces the Chamberlaynes to resume their marriage. Then Celia comes in to see Reilly and she later decides to do missionary work.

In the final act, set two years later, the Chamberlaynes are depicted as having a more tranquil marriage and we learn that Celia was killed violently in Kinkanja, where she was doing her missionary work. Despite some characters' shock on hearing the news, most accept her death as natural, perhaps even noble. As the busybody Julia Shuttlethwait sums up for us: "Everyone makes a choice, of one kind or another./And then must take the consequences. Celia chose/A way of which the consequence was crucifixion". Clearly, this is the main idea of the play.

Despite Eliot's own well-known Christianity, *The Cocktail Party* doesn't argue specifically for Christian solutions to the human condition. Celia, endowed by her creator (Eliot) with such character traits as having been a poet and a nurse, is something of a martyr for Christian ideals, as is made clear by her death at least twice being characterized as a crucifixion. But this is seen as but one of several paths; holding cocktail parties may be an equally valid path. No, *The Cocktail Party* is simply an idea play, dramatizing the condition of Man as a moral agent, a chooser.

As an idea play, *The Cocktail Party* has a few things going for it. It is a "well-made" play in the sense that the conflicts spawned from Edward's infidelity are introduced at the beginning and resolved by the play's end. There is a plot that develops. Also, the characters all speak a dry verse, the meter of which helps suggest the lifeless routinization of their lives. Eliot has a gift for this sort of dialogue; many of the characters sound like the defeated narrator of Eliot's early *Love Song of J. Alfred Prufrock*. The dialogue sparkles with intelligence and is what keeps the play going. But its occasional wittiness almost seems out of place embedded within the more somber themes.

But the play suffers from numerous problems. It is difficult to picture Celia participating in an affair with Edward and equally difficult to see Edward initiating such a liaison, especially if he is so passive. Even granting that, it doesn't seem that Edward ever had time to make a conscious choice about whether to choose Celia the day Lavinia left him. He never has a moment to himself before he finds himself hosting a cocktail party. Then he finds himself alone with the sage and slippery Unidentified Guest, who is a master of reverse psychology and also has the mysterious power to bring his wife back. Who knows? If the Unidentified Guest had not intervened, Edward might simply have chosen to marry Celia. But the combination of Lavinia's pre-emptive walk-out and the Unidentified Guest's eerie pronouncements about Edward's indecision stacks the deck against Edward choosing for himself. And then Edward is roundly criticized for his lack of choice.

The workings of the plot are also vague. Julia, Alex and Reilly form a bizarre conspiracy, whose entire existence seems devoted to making people see that they must live with their choices. The three of them perform an esoteric chant at the end of Act Two ("Watch over her in the labyrinth/... Protect her from the Voices/Protect her from the Visions"), which convinces the reader that these characters *represent an idea* rather than function as human characters. Surely few of us have encountered such philanthropy as theirs. Julia sends nearly all the characters mysterious telegrams to meet at the Chamberlayne's, where she has planted a *de facto* spy in Reilly. Reilly as psychologist freely discusses his patients' problems with his Julia and Alex, his co-conspirators. Because these three seem lean on recognizable human motives, these characters exist as cogs in the machinery of the play, only to show the other characters their fates.

Still other developments strain one's credulity. Lavinia's affair with Peter is equally unbelievable; it seems to exist only so that the couples stay on a moral par. They have both sinned, so they both need to forgive each other. Similarly, the love foursome of Edward, Lavinia, Peter and Celia is too symmetrical.

I also am still not sure what to think of Reilly. The fact that he enters the play shrouded in mystery, runs a strange psychological practice and apparently doesn't shy from sending ordinary people to a sanitarium, made Reilly to seem a sinister character for much of the time, especially in light of Eliot's own mental breakdown and suspicions of psychologists. And I wasn't comforted by Reilly's chanting "Protect her from the Voices, " or his admonishment to his patients to "Work out your salvation with diligence." Even though he turns out to have a beneficent influence on the Edward and Lavinia, he remains a shadowy figure at the play's end.

And why all this stuff about choices, about Man-as-Moral-Agent anyway? *The Cocktail Party,* first staged in 1949, seems to be Eliot's reaction to the great intellectual fashion of the 1940s: Existentialism. Jean-Paul Sartre had achieved dazzling fame with such works as the short novel *Nausea* and the play *No Exit,* the moral of which is often summarized as "hell is other people". Sartre's existentialism emphasized man's freedom from the moral certainties of religion, but insisted that this freedom, while man's glory, was also a terrible burden, one that few of us had the strength the bear. *The Cocktail Party* seems informed by a similar spirit. Its characters are indecisive to the point of needing professional help and trapped in a social hell: none of them seem able to be alone for a few minutes. And other people bring no comfort or companionship. Edward echoes Sartre's formula when he says: "What is hell? Hell is oneself, /Hell is alone, the other figures in it/Merely projections".

One senses that Eliot has a whole philosophy of choice and selfhood lurking under here somewhere, one which he may have been better off writing as a philosophical treatise (Eliot earned a Harvard Ph.D. in philosophy before he turned to poetry) or poem, rather than dramatizing as this dry drama. But Eliot was determined to philosophize in a literary mode. We associate Eliot with idea-heavy and nearly unreadable masterpieces such as the long poem *The Wasteland* (a poem that uses six languages along the way) and *The Hollow Men,* which paint a dark vision of man as "broken" because of his lack of faith in God. Eliot, born in St. Louis, went on to accept British citizenship and convert to Anglicanism, but his faith in God never did translate into a rosier view of the human condition. There are religious overtones in *The Cocktail Party*, suggestions that at least for some religion is the right path. That psychologists such as Reilly have taken the role of father-confessors from priests is a well-known twentieth century development. Celia, the play's martyr, describes her plight to Reilly as having a "sense of sin, " and believing that something is wrong with the world itself and that she must "atone" for it. During Celia's confession to Reilly, they converse about the meaninglessness of the human condition and it is here that Eliot is at his eloquent best. Celia: "veryone's alone...They make noises and think they are talking to each other". Reilly: "Both ways avoid the final desolation/Of solitude in the phantasmal world/Of imagination, shuffling memories and desires" —an echo of the first lines of *The Wasteland*, "April is the cruelest month ...mixing/Memory and desire."

Perhaps Eliot's distilled eloquence about Mankind's Plight is best offered in poetry, where the reader is expected to caress every word in search of meaning. As a drama, the characters in *The Cocktail Party* feel like props for Eliot's idea. Celia the martyr. Edward is Eliot's stand-in, existentialist man. Reilly the Freudian father-confessor. Julia the busybody, who seems to have no life of her own other than to help the Chamberlayne's (and perhaps countless others) seek out their "salvation" through Reilly. And Alex the world-traveler with mysterious global connections, always speaking with a knowing air. Peter exists to square off the Edward/Lavinia/Celia love triangle. The characters all speak with intelligence; they just sound too much like Eliot.

Eliot wrote at least one superlative play, his *Murder in Cathedral*. There he was able to follow the historical accounts of the murder of Thomas Beckett and so he started with fully-formed and interesting characters such as Beckett and Henry II and so his focus on writing verse drama paid off. Here Eliot's craftsmanship of writing verse dialogue is impressive, but perhaps it was beyond his powers to create striking characters while writing in such a structured form.

The right theater company could probably stage an

engaging production of *The Cocktail Party*. Certain actors could breathe life into the characters and suggest much of the emotion that is so muted during a reading of the play. In Act II, when the three principals visit Reilly, there is real suspense, (but mainly of how Reilly would treat them; was it all a trap to send a perfectly sane man packing away to the sanitarium?).

But the fundamental problem with this play is with the conception itself. How do you dramatize man "wriggling on a pin?" This is the problem of so much post-war fiction: that anti-heroes who don't *do* anything engage the intellect, but rarely the emotions. We understand the plight of these characters, but because their suffering is expressed only in couch-talk, we cannot empathize. Watching characters *act* — make touch choices, love, fight, defend their actions—stirs up our emotions, our memories of our lives' crossroads. We inhabit the actors' skins and so participate more fully in the drama.

Chapter 7

Complete Text

Persons

EDWARD CHAMBERLAYNE
JULIA (MRS. SHUTTLETHWAITE)
CELIA COPLESTONE
ALEXANDER MACCOLGIE GIBBS
PETER QUILPE
AN UNIDENTIFIED GUEST, *later identified as*
SIR HENRY HARCOURT-REILLY
LAVINIA CHAMBERLAYNE
A NURSE-SECRETARY
CATERER'S MAN

The scene is laid in London

Act I

Scene 1

The drawing room of the Chamberlayne's London flat.

Early evening. Edward chamberlayne, julia shuttlethwaite, celia coplestone, peter quilpe, alexander maccolgie gibbs and an unidentified guest.

ALEX
You've missed the point completely, Julia:
There were no tigers. That was the point.

JULIA
Then what were you doing, up in a tree:
You and the Maharaja?

ALEX
My dear Julia!
It's perfectly hopeless. You haven't been listening.

PETER

You'll have to tell us all over again, Alex.
ALEX
I never tell the same story twice.
JULIA
But I'm still waiting to know what happened.
I know it started as a story about tigers.
ALEX
I said there were no tigers.
CELIA
Oh do stop wrangling,
Both of you. It's your turn, Julia.
Do tell us that story you told the other day, about
Lady Klootz and the wedding cake.
PETER
And how the butler found her in the pantry, rinsing her mouth out with champagne.
I like that story.
CELIA
I love that story.
ALEX
I'm never tired of hearing that story.
JULIA
Well, you all seem to know it.
CELIA
Do we all know it?
But we're never tired of hearing *you* tell it.
I don't believe everyone here knows it.
[*To the* UNIDENTIFIED GUEST]
You don't know it, do you?
UNIDENTIFIED GUEST
No, I've never heard it.
CELIA
Here's one new listener for you, Julia;
And I don't believe that Edward knows it.
EDWARD
I may have heard it, but I don't remember it.
CELIA
And Julia's the only person to tell it.

She's such a good mimic.
JULIA
Am I a good mimic?
PETER
Youare a good mimic. You never miss anything.
ALEX
She never misses anything unless she wants to.
CELIA
Especially the Lithuanian accent.
JULIA
Lithuanian? Lady Klootz?
PETER
I thought she was Belgian
ALEX
Her father belonged to a Baltic family-
One of the oldest Baltic families
With a branch in Sweden and one in Denmark.
There were several very lovely daughters:
I wonder what's become of them now.
JULIA
Lady Klootz was very lovely, once upon a time.
What a life she led! I used to say to her: 'Greta!
You have too much vitality.' But she enjoyed herself.
[To the UNIDENTIFIED GUEST]
Did you know Lady Klootz?
UNIDENTIFIED GUEST
No, I never met her.
CELIA
Go on with the story about the wedding cake.
JULIA
Well, but it really isn't my story.
I heard it first from Delia Verinder
Who was there when it happened.
[To the UNIDENTIFIED GUEST]
Do you know Delia Verinder?
UNIDENTIFIED GUEST
No, I don't know her.
JULIA

Well, one can't be too careful
Before one tells a story.
ALEX
Delia Verinder?
Was she the one who had three brothers?
JULIA
How many brothers? Two, I think.
ALEX
No, there were three, but you wouldn't know the third one:
They kept him rather quiet.
JULIA
Ohl, you mean that one.
ALEX
He was feeble-minded.
JULIA
Oh, not feeble-minded:
He was only harmless.
ALEX
Well then, harmless.
JULIA
He was very clever at repairing clocks;
And he had a remarkable sense of hearing—
The only man I ever met who could hear the cry of bats.
PETER
Hear the cry of bats?
JULIA
He could hear the cry of bats.
CELIA
But how do you know he could hear the cry of bats?
JULIA
Because he said so. And I believed him.
CELIA
But if he was so harmless, how could you believe him?
He might have imagined it.
JULIA
My darling Celia,

You needn't be so sceptical. I stayed there once
At their castle in the North. How he suffered!
They had to find an island for him
Where there were no bats.
ALEX
And is he still there?
Julia is really a mine of information.
CELIA
There isn't much that Julia doesn't know.
PETER
Go on with the story about the wedding cake.
[Edwardleaves the room.]
JULIA
No, we'll wait until Edward comes back into the room.
Now I want to relax. Are there any more cocktails?
PETER
But do go on. Edward wasn't listening anyway.
JULIA .
No, he wasn't listening, but he's such a strain—
Edward without Lavinial He's quite impossible!
Leaving it to me to keep things going.
What a host! And nothing fit to eat!
The only reason for a cocktail party
For a gluttonous old woman like me
Is a really nice tit-bit. I can drink at home.
[Edwardreturns with a tray.]
EDWARD, give me another of those delicious olives.
What's that? Potato crisps? No, I can't endure them.
Well, I started to tell you about Lady Klootz.
It was at the Vincewell wedding. Oh, so many years ago!
[To the UNIDENTIFIED GUEST]
Did you know the Vincewells?
UNIDENTIFIED GUEST
No, I don't know the Vincewells.
JULIA
Oh, they're both dead now. But I wanted to know.
If they'd been friends of yours, I couldn't tell the story.
PETER

Were they the parents of Tony Vincewell?
JULIA
Yes. Tony was the product, but not the solution.
He only made the situation more difficult.
You know Tony Vincewell? You knew him at Oxford?
PETER
No, I never knew him at Oxford:
I came across him last year in California.
JULIA
I've always wanted to go to California.
Do tell us what you were doing in California.
CELIA
Making a film.
PETER
Trying to make a film.
JULIA
Oh, what film was it? I wonder if I've seen it.
PETER
No, you wouldn't have seen it. As a matter of fact
It was never produced. They did a film
But they used a different scenario.
JULIA
Not the one you wrote?
PETER
Not the one I wrote:
But I had a very enjoyable time.
CELIA
Go on with the story about the wedding cake.
JULIA
EDWARD, do sit down for a moment:
I know you're always the perfect host,
But just try to pretend you're another guest
At Lavinia's party. There are so many questions
I want to ask you. It's a golden opportunity
Now Lavinia's away. I've always said:
'If I could only get Edward alone
And have a really serious conversation!'
I said so to Lavinia. She agreed with me.

She said: 'I wish you'd try.' And this is the first time
I've ever seen you without Lavinia
Except for the time she got locked in the lavatory
And couldn't get out. I know what you're thinking!
I know you think I'm a silly old woman
But I'm really very serious. Lavinia takes me seriously.
I believe that's the reason why she went way—
So that I could make you talk. Perhaps she's in the pantry
Listening to all we say!

EDWARD
No, she's not in the pantry.

CELIA
Will she be away for some time, Edward?

EDWARD
I really don't know until I hear from her.
If her aunt is very ill, she may be gone some time.

CELIA
And how will you manage while she is away?

EDWARD
I really don't know. I may go away myself.

CELIA
Go away yourself!

JULIA
Have you an aunt too?

EDWARD
No, I haven't any aunt. But I might go away.

CELIA
But, Edward... what was I going to say?
It's dreadful for old ladies alone in the country,
And almost impossible to get a nurse.

JULIA
Is that her Aunt Laura?

EDWARD
No; another aunt
Whom you wouldn't know. Her mother's sister
And rather a recluse.

JULIA

Her favourite aunt?
EDWARD
Her aunt's favourite niece. And she's rather difficult.
When she's ill, she insists on having Lavinia.
JULIA
I never heard of her being ill before.
EDWARD
No, she's always very strong. That's why when she's ill
She gets into a panic.
JULIA
And sends for Lavinia.
I quite understand. Are there any prospects?
EDWARD
No, I think she put it all into an annuity.
JULIA
So it's very unselfish of Lavinia
Yet very like her. But really, Edward,
Lavinia may be away for weeks,
Or she may come back and be called away again.
I understand these tough old women-
I'm one myself: I feel as if I knew
All about that aunt in Hampshire.
EDWARD
Hampshire?
JULIA
Didn't you say Hampshire?
EDWARD
No, I didn't say Hampshire.
JULIA
Did you say Hampstead?
EDWARD
No, I didn't say Hampstead.
JULIA
But she must live somewhere.
EDWARD
She lives in Essex.
JULIA
Anywhere near Colchester? Lavinia loves oysters.

EDWARD
No. In the depths of Essex.
JULIA
Well, we won't probe into it.
You have the address and the telephone number?
I might run down and see Lavinia
On my way to Cornwall. But let's be sensible:
Now you must let me be your maiden aunt-
Living on an annuity, of course.
I am going to make you dine alone with me
On Friday and talk to me about everything.
EDWARD
Everything?
JULIA
Oh, you know what I mean.
The next election. And the secrets of your cases.
EDWARD
Most of my secrets are quite uninteresting.
JULIA Well, you shan't escape. 'You dine with me on Friday.
I've already chosen the people you're to meet.
EDWARD But you asked me to dine with you alone.
JULIA Yes, alone!
Without Lavinia! You'll like the other people—
But you're to talk to me. So that's all settled.
And now I must be going.
EDWARD Must you be going?
PETER But won't you tell the story about Lady Klootz?
JULIA What Lady Klootz?
CELIA And the wedding cake.
JULIA Wedding cake? I wasn't at her wedding.
Edward, it's been a delightful evening:
The potato crisps were really excellent.
Now let me see. Have I got everything?
It's such a nice party, I hate to leave it.
It's such a nice party, I'd like to repeat it.
Why don't you all come to dinner on Friday?
No, I'm afraid my good Mrs. Batten

Would give me notice. And now I must be going.
ALEX I'm afraid I ought to be going.
PETER
CELIA-
May I walk along with you?
CELIA No, I'm sorry, Peter;
I've got to take a taxi.
JULIA You come with me, Peter:
You can get me a taxi and then I can drop you,
I expect you on Friday, Edward. And Celia-
I must see you very soon. Now don't all go
just because I'm going. Good-bye, Edward.
EDWARD Good-bye, Julia.
[Exeunt Juliaand Peter.]
CELIA Good-bye, Edward.
Shall I see you soon?
EDWARD Perhaps. I don't know.
CELIA Perhaps you don't know? Very well, good-bye.
EDWARD Good-bye, Celia.
ALEX Good-bye, Edward. I do hope
You'll have better news of Levinia's aunt.
EDWARD Oh... yes... thank you. Good-bye, Alex,
It was nice of you to come.
[Exeunt ALEXand CELIA.]
[To the UNIDENTIFIED GUEST]
Don't go yet.
Don't go yet. We'll finish the cocktails.
Or would you rather have whisky?
UNIDENTIFIED GUEST Gin.
EDWARD Anything in it?
UNIDENTIFIED GUEST A drop of water.
EDWARD I want to apologise for this evening.
The fact is, I tried to put off this party:
These were only the people I couldn't put off
Because I couldn't get at them in time;
And I didn't know that you were coming.
I thought that Levinia had told me the names
Of all the people she said she'd invited.

But it's only that dreadful old woman who mattered—
I shouldn't have minded anyone else,
[The bell rings. Edwardgoes to the door, saying:]
But she always turns up when she's least wanted.
[Opens the door]
JULIA!
[Enter Julia.]
JULIA
EDWARD! How lucky that it's raining!
It made me remember my umbrella,
And there it is! Now what are you two plotting?
How very lucky it was my umbrella,
And not Alexander's—he's so inquisitive!
But I never poke into other people's business.
Well, good-bye again. I'm off at last.
[Exit.]
EDWARD I'm sorry. I'm afraid I don't know your name.
UNIDENTIFIED GUEST I ought to be going.
EDWARD Don't go yet.
I very much want to talk to somebody;
And it's easier to talk to a person you don't know.
The fact is, that Levinia has left me.
UNIDENTIFIED GUEST Your wife has left you?
EDWARD Without warning, of course;
Just when she'd arranged a cocktail party.
She'd gone when I came in, this afternoon.
She left a note to say that she was leaving me;
But I don't know where she's gone.
UNIDENTIFIED GUEST This is an occasion
May I take another drink?
EDWARD Whisky?
UNIDENTIFIED GUEST Gin.
EDWARD Anything in it?
UNIDENTIFIED GUEST Nothing but water.
And I recommend you the Same prescription...
Let me prepare it for you, if I may...
Strong... but sip it slowly... and drink it sitting
down.

Breathe deeply and adopt a relaxed position.
There we are. Now for a few questions.
How long married?
EDWARD Five years.
UNIDENTIFIED GUEST Children?
EDWARD No.
UNIDENTIFIED GUEST Then look at the brighter side.
You say you don't know where she's gone?
EDWARD No, I do not.
UNIDENTIFIED GUEST Do you know who the man is?
EDWARD There was no other man—
None that I know of.
UNIDENTIFIED GUEST Or another woman
Of whom she thought she had cause to be jealous?
EDWARD She had nothing to complain of
in my behaviour.
UNIDENTIFIED GUEST Then no doubt it's all for the best.
With another man, she might have made a mistake
And want to come back to you. If another woman,
She might decide to be forgiving
And gain an advantage. If there's no other woman
And no other man, then the reason may be deeper
And you've ground for hope that she won't come back
at all.
If another man, then you'd want to re-marry
To prove to the world that somebody wanted you;
If another woman, you might have to marry her-
You might even imagine that you wanted to marry her.
EDWARD But I want my wife back.
UNIDENTIFIED GUEST That's the natural reaction.
It's embarrassing and inconvenient.
It was inconvenient, having to he about it
Because you can't tell the truth on the telephone.
It will all take time that you can't well spare;
But I put it to you...
EDWARD Don't put it to me.
UNIDENTIFIED GUEST Then I suggest...
EDWARD And please don't suggest.

I have often used these terms in examining witnesses,
So I don't like them. May I put it to you?
I know that I invited this conversation:
But I don't know who you are. This is not what I expected.
I only wanted to relieve my mind
By telling someone what I'd been concealing.
I don't think I want to know who you are;
But, at the same time, unless you know my wife
A good deal better than I thought, or unless you know
A good deal more about us than appears—
I think your speculations rather offensive.
UNIDENTIFIED GUEST I know you as well as I know your wife;
And I knew that all you wanted was the luxury
Of an intimate disclosure to a stranger.
Let me, therefore, remain the stranger.
But let me tell you, that to approach the stranger
Is to invite the unexpected, release a new force,
Or let the genie out of the bottle.
It is to start a train of events
Beyond your control. So let me continue.
I will say then, you experience some relief
Of which you're not aware. It will come to you slowly:
When you wake in the morning, when you go to bed at night,
That you are beginning to enjoy your independence;
Finding your life becoming cosier and cosier
Without the consistent critic, the patient misunderstander
Arranging life a little better than you like it,
Preferring not quite the same friends as yourself,
Or making your friends like her better than you;
And, turning the past over and over,
You'll wonder only that you endured it for so long.
And perhaps at times you will feel a little jealous
That she saw it first and had the courage to break it—
Thus giving herself a permanent advantage.

EDWARD It might turn out so, yet...
UNIDENTIFIED GUEST Are you going to say, you love her?
EDWARD Why, I thought we took each other for granted.
I never thought I should be any happier
With another person. Why speak of love?
We were used to each other. So her going away
At a moment's notice, without explanation,
Only a note to say that she had gone
And was not coming back—well, I can't understand it.
Nobody likes to be left with a mystery:
It's so... unfinished.
UNIDENTIFIED GUEST Yes, it's unfinished;
And nobody likes to be left with a mystery.
But there's more to it than that. There's a loss of personality;
Or rather, you've lost touch with the person
You thought you were. You no longer feel quite human.
You're suddenly reduced to the status of an object—
A living object, but no longer a person.
It's always happening, because one is an object
As well as a person. But we forget about it
As quickly as we can. When you've dressed for a party
And are going downstairs, with everything about you
Arranged to support you in the role you have chosen,
Then sometimes, when you come to the bottom step
There is one step more than your feet expected
And you come down with a jolt. Just for a moment
You have the experience of being an object
At the mercy of a malevolent staircase.
Or, take a surgical operation.
In consultation with the doctor and the surgeon,
In going to bed in the nursing home,
In talking to the matron, you are still the subject,
The centre of reality. But, stretched on the table,
You are a piece of furniture in a repair shop
For those who surround you, the masked actors;
All there is of you is your body

And the 'you' is withdrawn. May I replenish?
EDWARD Oh, I'm sorry. What were you drinking?
Whisky?
UNIDENTIFIED GUEST Gin.
EDWARD Anything with it?
UNIDENTIFIED GUEST Water
EDWARD To what does this lead?
UNIDENTIFIED GUEST To finding out
What you really are. What you really feel.
What you really are among other people.
Most of the time we take ourselves for granted,
As we have to and live on a little knowledge
About ourselves as we were. Who are you now?
You don't know any more than I do,
But rather less. You are nothing but a set
Of obsolete responses. The one thing to do
Is to do nothing. Wait.
EDWARD Wait!
But waiting is the one thing impossible.
Besides, don't you see that it makes me ridiculous?
UNIDENTIFIED GUEST It will do you no harm
to find yourself ridiculous.
Resign yourself to be the fool you are.
That's the best advice that I can give you.
EDWARD But how can I wait, not knowing
what I'm waiting for?
Shall I say to my friends, 'My wife has gone away'?
And they answer 'Where?' and I say 'I don't know';
And they say 'But when will she be back?'
And I reply 'I don't know that she is coming back.'
And they ask 'But what are you going to do?'
And I answer 'Nothing.' They will think me mad
Or simply contemptible.
UNIDENTIFIED GUEST All to the good.
You will find that you survive humiliation.
And that's an experience of incalculable value.
EDWARD Stop! I agree that much of what you've said
Is true enough. But that is not all.

Since I saw her this morning when we had breakfast
I no longer remember what my wife is like.
I am not quite sure that I could describe her
If I had to ask the police to search for her.
I'm sure I don't know what she was wearing
When I saw her last. And yet I want her back.
And I must get her back, to find out what has happened
During the five years that we've been married.
I must find out who she is, to find out who I am.
And what is the use of all your analysis
If I am to remain always lost in the dark?
UNIDENTIFIED GUEST There is certainly no
purpose in remaining in the dark
Except long enough to clear from the mind
The illusion of having ever been in the light.
The fact that you can't give a reason for wanting her
Is the best reason for believing that you want her.
EDWARD want to see her again—here.
UNIDENTIFIED GUEST You shall see her again—here.
EDWARD Do you mean to say that you know
where she is?
UNIDENTIFIED GUEST
That question is not worth the trouble of an answer.
But if I bring her back it must be on one condition:
That you promise to ask her no questions
Of where she has been.
EDWARD I will not ask them.
And yet—it seems to me-when we began to talk
I was not sure I wanted her; and now I want her.
Do I want her? Or is it merely your suggestion?
UNIDENTIFIED GUEST We do not know yet.
In twenty-four hours
She will come to you here. You will be here to meet her.
[The doorbell rings.]
EDWARD I must answer the door.
[Edwardgoes to the door.]
So it's you again, Julia!
[Enter Juliaand Peter.]

JULIA Edward, I'm so glad to find you.
Do you know, I must have left my glasses here,
And I simply can't see a thing without them.
I've been dragging Peter all over town
Looking for them everywhere I've been.
Has anybody found them? You can tell if they're mine-
Some kind of a plastic sort of frame—
I'm afraid I don't remember the colour,
But I'd know them, because one lens is missing.
UNIDENTIFIED GUEST [Sings]
As I was drinkin' gin and water,
And me bein' the One Eyed Riley,
Who came in but the landlord's daughter
And she took my heart entirely.
You will keep our appointment?
EDWARD I shall keep it.
UNIDENTIFIED GUEST [Sings] Tooryooly toory-iley
What's the matter with One Eyed Riley?
[Exit.]
JULIA Edward, who is that dreadful man?
I've never been so insulted in my life.
It's very lucky that I left my spectacles:
This is what I call an adventure!
Tell me about him. You've been drinking together!
So this is the kind of friend you have
When Levinia is out of the way! Who is he?
EDWARD I don't know.
JULIA You don't know?
EDWARD I never saw him before in my life.
JULIA But how did he come here?
EDWARD I don't know.
JULIA You don't know! And what's his name?
Did I hear him say his name was Riley?
EDWARD I don't know his name.
JULIA You don't know his name?
EDWARD I tell you I've no idea who he is
Or how he got here.
JULIA But what did you talk about?

Or were you singing songs all the time?
There's altogether too much mystery
About this place today.
EDWARD I'm very sorry.
JULIA No, I love it. But that reminds me
About my glasses. That's the greatest mystery.
Peter! why aren't you looking for them?
Look on the mantelpiece. Where was I sitting?
Just turn out the bottom of that sofa-
No, this chair. Look under the cushion.
EDWARD Are you quite sure they're not in your bag?
JULIA Why no, of course not: that's where I keep them.
Oh, here they are! Thank you, Edward;
That really was very clever of you;
I'd never have found them but for you.
The next time I lose anything, Edward,
I'll come straight to you, instead of to St. Anthony.
And now I must fly. I've kept the taxi waiting.
Come along, Peter.
PETER I hope you won't mind
If I don't come with you, Julia? On the way back
I remembered something I had to say to Edward...
JULIA Oh, about Levinia?
PETER No, not about Levinia.
It's something I want to consult him about,
And I could do it now.
JULIA Of course I don't mind.
PETER Well, at least you must let. me take
you down in the lift.
JULIA No, you stop and talk to Edward. I'm not
helpless yet.
And besides, I like to manage the machine myself-
In a lift I can meditate. Good-bye then.
And thank you—both of you—very much.
[Exit.]
PETER I hope I'm not disturbing you, Edward.
EDWARD I seem to have been disturbed already;
And I did rather want to be alone.

But what's it all about?
PETER I want your help.
I was going to telephone and try to see you later;
But this seemed an opportunity.
EDWARD And what's your trouble?
PETER This evening I felt I could bear it no longer.
That awful party! I'm sorry, Edward;
Of course it was really a very nice party
For everyone but me. And that wasn't your fault.
I don't suppose you noticed the situation.
EDWARD I did think I noticed one or two things;
But I don't pretend I was aware of everything.
PETER Oh, I'm very glad that you didn't notice:
I must have behaved rather better than I thought.
If you didn't notice, I don't suppose the others did,
Though I'm rather afraid of Julia Shuttlethwaite.
EDWARD Julia is certainly observant
But I think she had some other matter on her mind.
PETER It's about Celia. Myself and Celia.
EDWARD Why, what could there be about
yourself and Celia?
Have you anything in common, do you think?
PETER It seemed to me we had a great deal in common.
We're both of us artists.
EDWARD I never thought of that.
What arts do you practise?
PETER You won't have seen my novel
Though it had some very good reviews.
But it's more the cinema that interests both of us.
EDWARD
A common interest in the moving pictures
Frequently brings young people together.
PETER
Now you're only being sarcastic:
Celia was interested in the art of the film.
EDWARD
As a possible profession?
PETER

She might make it a profession;
Though she had her poetry.
EDWARD
Yes, I've seen her poetry—
Interesting if one is interested in Celia.
Apart, of course, from its literary merit
Which I don't pretend to judge.
PETER
Well, I can judge it,
And I think it's very good. But that's not the point.
The point is, I thought we had a great deal in common
And I think she thought so too.
EDWARD
How did you come to know her?
[Enter ALEX.]
ALEX
Ah, there you are, Edward! Do you know
why I've looked in?
EDWARD
I'd like to know first how you got in, Alex.
ALEX
Why, I came and found that the door was open
And so I thought I'd slip in and see if anyone
was with you.
PETER
Julia must have left it open.
EDWARD
Never mind;
So long as you both shut it when you go out.
ALEX
Ah, but you're coming with me, Edward.
I thought, Edward may be all alone this evening,
And I know that he hates to spend an evening alone,
So you're going to come out and have dinner with me.
EDWARD
That's very thoughtful of you, Alex, I'm sure;
But I rather want to be alone, this evening.
ALEX

But you've got to have some dinner. Are you going out?
Is there anyone here to get dinner for you?
EDWARD
No, I shan't want much and I'll get it myself.
ALEX
Ah, in that case I know what I'll do.
I'm going to give you a little surprise:
You know, I'm rather a famous cook.
I'm going straight to your kitchen now And I shall
prepare you a nice little dinner Which you can have alone.
And then we'll leave you.
Meanwhile, you and Peter can go on talking And
I shan't disturb you.
EDWARD
My dear Alex,
There'll be nothing in the larder worthy of your cooking.
I couldn't think of it.
ALEX
Ah, but that's my special gift—
Concocting a toothsome meal out of nothing.
Any scraps you have will do. I learned that in the East.
With a handful of rice and a little dried fish
I can make half a dozen dishes. Don't say a word.
I shall begin at once.
[Exit to kitchen.]
EDWARD
Well, where did you leave off?
PETER
You asked me how I came to know Celia.
I met her here, about a year ago.
EDWARD
At one of Lavinia's amateur Thursdays?
PETER
A Thursday. Why do you say amateur?
EDWARD
Lavinia's attempts at starting a salon.
Where I entertained the minor guests And
dealt with the misfits, Lavinia's mistakes.

But you were one of the minor successes For a time at least.
PETER
I wouldn't say that.
But Lavinia was awfully kind to me
And I owe her a great deal. And then I met Celia.
She was different from any girl I'd ever known
And not easy to talk to, on that occasion.
EDWARD
Did you see her often?
ALEX'S VOICE
Edward, have you a double boiler?
EDWARD
I suppose there must be a double boiler:
Isn't there one in every kitchen?
ALEX'S VOICE
I can't find it.
Fhere goes that surprise. I must think of another.
PETER
Not very often.
And when I did, I got no chance to talk to her.
EDWARD
You and Celia were asked for different purposes.
Your role was to be one of Lavinia's discoveries;
Celia's, to provide society and fashion.
Lavinia always had the ambition
To establish herself in two worlds at once—
But she herself had to be the link between them.
That is why, I think, her Thursdays were a failure.
PETER
You speak as if everything was finished.
EDWARD
Oh no, no, everything is left unfinished.
But you haven't told me how you came to know Celia.
PETER
I saw her again a few days later
Alone at a concert. And I was alone.
I've always gone to concerts alone—

At first, because I knew no one to go with,
And later, I found I preferred to go alone.
But a girl like Celia, it seemed very strange,
Because I had thought of her merely as a name
In a society column, to find her there alone.
Anyway, we got into conversation
And I found that she went to concerts alone
And to look at pictures. So we often met
In the same way and sometimes went together.
And to be with Celia, that was something different
From company or solitude. And we sometimes had tea
And once or twice dined together.
EDWARD
And after that
Did she ever introduce you to her family
Or to any of her friends?
PETER
No, but once or twice she spoke of them
And about their lack of intellectual interests.
EDWARD
And what happened after that?
PETER
Oh, nothing happened.
But I thought that she really cared about me.
And I was so happy when we were together—
So... contented, so... at peace: I can't express it;
I had never imagined such quiet happiness.
I had only experienced excitement, delirium,
Desire for possession. It was not like that at all.
It was something very strange. There
was such... tranquillity...
EDWARD
And what interrupted this interesting affair?
[Enter ALEX in shirtsleeves and an apron.]
ALEX
Edward, I can't find any curry powder.
EDWARD
There isn't any curry powder. Lavinia hates curry.

ALEX
There goes another surprise, then. I must think.
I didn't expect to find any mangoes,
But I did count upon curry powder.
[Exit.]
PETER
That is exactly what I want to know.
She has simply faded—into some other picture—
Like a film effect. She doesn't want to see me;
Makes excuses, not very plausible,
And when I do see her, she seems preoccupied
With some secret excitement which I cannot share.
EDWARD
Do you think she has simply lost interest in you?
PETER
You put it just wrong. I think of it differently.
It is not her interest in me that I miss—
But those moments in which we seemed to
share some perception,
Some feeling, some indefinable experience
In which we were both unaware of ourselves.
In your terms, perhaps,. she's lost interest in me.
EDWARD
That is all very normal. If you could only know
How lucky you are. In a little while
This might have become an ordinary affair
Like any other. As the fever cooled
You would have found that she was another woman
And that you were another man. I congratulate
you On a timely escape.
PETER
I should prefer to be spared
Your congratulations. I had to talk to someone.
And I have been telling you of something real—
My first experience of reality
And perhaps it is the last. And you don't understand.
EDWARD
My dear Peter, I have only been telling you

What would have happened to you with Celia
In another six months' time. There it is.
You can take it or leave it.
PETER
But what am I to do?
EDWARD
Nothing. Wait. Go back to California.
PETER
But I must see Celia.
EDWARD
Will it be the same Celia?
Better be content with the Celia you remember.
Remember! I say it's already a memory.
PETER
But I must see Celia at least to make her tell me
What has happened, in her terms. Until I know that
I shan't know the truth about even the memory.
Did we really share these interests? Did
we really feel the same
When we heard certain music? Or looked at
certain pictures?
There was something real. But what is the reality...
[The telephone rings.]
EDWARD
Excuse me a moment.
[Into telephone] Hello!... I can't talk now...
Yes, there is.. Well then, I'll ring you
As soon as I can.
I'm sorry. You were saying?
PETER
I was saying, what is the reality
Of experience between two unreal people?
If I can only hold to the memory
I can bear any future. But I must find out
The truth about the past, for the sake of the memory.
EDWARD
There's no memory you can wrap in camphor
But the moths will get in. So you want to see Celia.

I don't know why I should be taking all this trouble
To protect you from the fool you are.
What do you want me to do?
PETER
See Celia for me.
You know her in a different way from me
And you are so much older.
EDWARD
So much older?
PETER
Yes, I'm sure that she would listen to you
As someone disinterested.
EDWARD
Well, I will see Celia.
PETER
Thank you, Edward. It's very good of you.
[Enter ALEX, with his jacket on.]
ALEX
Oh, Edward! I've prepared you such a treat!
I really think that of all my triumphs
This is the greatest. To make something out of nothing!
Never, even when travelling in Albania,
Have I made such a supper out of so few materials
As I found in your refrigerator. But of course
I was lucky to find half-a-dozen eggs.
EDWARD
What! You used all those eggs! Lavinia's aunt
Has just sent them from the country.
ALEX
Ah, so the aunt
Really exists. A substantial proof.
EDWARD
No, no... I mean, this is another aunt.
ALEX
I understand. The real aunt. But you'll be grateful.
There are very few peasants in Montenegro
Who can have the dish that you'll be eating, nowadays.
EDWARD

But what about my breakfast?
ALEX
Don't worry about breakfast.
All you should want is a cup of black coffee
And a little dry toast. I've left it simmering.
Don't leave it longer than another ten minutes.
Now I'll be going and I'll take Peter with me.
PETER
Edward, I've taken too much of your time,
And you want to be alone. Give my love to Lavinia
When she comes back... but, if you don't mind,
I'd rather you didn't tell her what I've told you.
EDWARD
I shall not say anything about it to Lavinia.
PETER
Thank you, Edward. Good night.
EDWARD
Good night, Peter,
And good night, Alex. Oh and if you don't mind,
Please shut the door after you, so it latches.
ALEX
Remember, Edward, not more than ten minutes,
Twenty minutes and my work will be ruined.
[Exeunt ALEXand PETER.]
[EDWARDpicks up the telephone and dials a number.
There is no reply.]
CURTAIN

Act I

Scene 2

The same room a quarter of an hour later. EDWARDis alone, playing Patience. The doorbell rings and he answers it.

CELIA'S VOICE
Are you alone?
[EDWARDreturns with CELIA.]
EDWARD
Celial! Why have you come back?
I said I would telephone as soon as I could:

And I tried to get you a moment ago.
CELIA
If there had happened to be anyone with you
I was going to say I'd come back for my umbrella....
I must say you don't seem very pleased to see me.
Edward, I understand what has happened
But I could not understand your manner on the telephone.
It did not seem like you. So I felt I must see you.
Tell me it's all right and then I'll go.
EDWARD
But how can you say you understand what has happened?
I don't know what has happened, or what is going to happen;
And to try to understand it, I want to be alone.
CELIA
I should have thought it was perfectly simple.
Lavinia has left you.
EDWARD
Yes, that was the situation.
I suppose it was pretty obvious to everyone.
CELIA
It was obvious that the aunt was a pure invention
On the spur of the moment and not a very good one.
You should have been prepared with something better, for Julia;
But it doesn't really matter. They will know soon enough.
Doesn't that settle all our difficulties?
EDWARD
It has only brought to light the real difficulties.
CELIA
But surely, these are only temporary.
You know I accepted the situation
Because a divorce would ruin your career;
And we thought that Lavinia would never want to leave you.
Surely you don't hold to that silly convention
'That the husband must always be the one to be divorced?

And if she chooses to give you the grounds...
EDWARD
I see. But it is not like that at all.
Lavinia is coming back.
CELIA
Lavinia coming back!
Do you mean to say that she's laid a trap for us?
EDWARD
No. If there is a trap, we are all in the trap,
We have set it for ourselves. But I do not know
What kind of a trap it is.
CELIA
Then what has happened?
[The telephone rings.]
EDWARD
Damn the telephone. I suppose I must answer it.
Hello... oh, hello!... No. I mean yes, Alex;
Yes, of course... it was marvellous.
I've never tasted anything like it...
Yes, that's very interesting. But I just wondered
Whether it mightn't be rather indigestible?...
Oh, no, Alex, don't bring me any cheese;
I've got some cheese... No, not Norwegian;
But I don't really want cheese... Slipper what?...
Oh, from Jugoslavia... prunes and alcohol?
No, really, Alex, I don't want anything.
I'm very tired. Thanks awfully, Alex.
Good night.
CELIA
What on earth was that about?
EDWARD
That was Alex.
CELIA
I know it was Alex.
But what was he talking of?
EDWARD
I had quite forgotten.
He made his way in, a little while ago,

And insisted on cooking me something for supper;
And he said I must eat it within ten minutes.
I suppose it's still cooking.
CELIA
You suppose it's still cooking!
I thought I noticed a peculiar smell:
Of course it's still cooking—or doing something.
I must go and investigate.
[Starts to leave the room]
EDWARD
For heaven's sake, don't bother!
[Exit CELIA.]
Suppose someone came and found you in the kitchen?
[EDWARDgoes over to the table and inspects
his game of
Patience. He moves a card. The doorbell rings re-
peatedly. Re-enter CELIA, in an apron.]
CELIA
You'd better answer the door, Edward.
It's the best thing to do. Don't lose your head.
You see, I really did leave my umbrella;
And I'll say I found you here starving and helpless
And had to do something. Anyway, I'm staying
And I'm not going to hide.
[Returns to kitchen. The bell rings again.]
EDWARD
[Goes to front door and is heard to say:]
Julia!
What have you come back for?
[Enter JULIA.]
JULIA
I've had an inspiration!
[Enter CELIAwith saucepan.]
CELIA
Edward, it's ruined!
EDWARD
What a good thing.
CELIA

But it's ruined the saucepan too.

EDWARD

And half a dozen eggs.
I wanted one for breakfast. A boiled egg.
It's the only thing I know how to cook.

JULIA

Celia! I see you've had the same inspiration
That I had. Edward must be fed.
He's under such a strain. We must keep his strength up.
Edward! Don't you realize how lucky you are
To have two Good Samaritans? I never heard of that before.

EDWARD

The man who fell among thieves was luckier than I:
He was left at an inn.

JULIA

Edward, how ungrateful!
What's in that saucepan?

CELIA

Nobody knows.

EDWARD

It's something that Alex came and prepared for me.
He would do it. Three Good Samaritans.
I forgot all about it.

JULIA

But you mustn't touch it.

EDWARD

Of course I shan't touch it.

JULIA

My dear, I should have warned you:
Anything that Alex makes is absolutely deadly.
I could tell such tales of his poisoning people.
Now, my dear, you give me that apron
And we'll see what I can do. You stay and talk to Edward.

[Exit JULIA.]

CELIA

But what has happened, Edward? What has happened?

EDWARD
Lavinia is coming back, I think.
CELIA
You think! don't you know?
EDWARD
No, but I believe it. That man who was here-
CELIA
Yes, who was that man? I was rather afraid of him;
He has some sort of power.
EDWARD
I don't know who he is.
But I had some talk with him, when the rest of you had left,
And he said he would bring Lavinia back, tomorrow.
CELIA
But why should that man want to bring her back—
Unless he is the Devil! I could believe he was.
EDWARD
Because I asked him to.
CELIA
Because you asked him to!
Then he must be the Devil! He must have bewitched you.
How did he persuade you to want her back?
[A popping noise is heard from the kitchen.]
EDWARD
What the devil's that?
[Re-enter JULIA, in apron, with a tray and three glasses.]
JULIA
I've had an inspiration!
There's nothing in the place fit to eat:
I've looked high and low. But I found some champagne
Only a half bottle, to be sure,
And of course it isn't chilled. But it's so refreshing;
And I thought, we are all in need of a stimulant
After this disaster. Now I'll propose a health.
Can you guess whose health I'm going to propose?
EDWARD

No, I can't. But I won't drink to Alex's.
JULIA
Oh, it isn't Alex's. Come, I give you
Lavinia's aunt! You might have guessed it.
EDWARDand CELIA
Lavinia's aunt.
JULIA
Now, the next question
Is, what's to be done. That's very simple.
It's too late, or too early, to go to a restaurant.
You must both come home with me.
EDWARD
No, I'm sorry, Julia.
I'm too tired to go out and I'm not at all hungry.
I shall have a few biscuits.
JULIA
But you, CELIA?
You must come and have a light supper with me--
Something very light.
CELIA
Thank you, Julia.
I think I will, if I may follow you
In about ten minutes? Before I go, there's something
I want to say to Edward.
JULIA
About Lavinia?
Well, come on quickly. And take a taxi.
You know, you're looking absolutely famished.
Good night, Edward.
[Exit JULIA.]
CELIA
Well, how did he persuade you?
EDWARD
How did he persuade me? Did he persuade me?
I have a very clear impression
That he tried to persuade me it was all for the best
That Lavinia had gone; that I ought to be thankful.
He talked as if he thought he knew all about it;

And yet, the effect of all his argument
Was to make me see that I wanted her back.

CELIA
That's the Devil's method! So you want Lavinia back!
Lavinial So the one thing you care about
Is to avoid a break—anything unpleasant!
No, it can't be that. I won't think it's that.
I think it is just a moment of surrender
To fatigue. And panic. You can't face the trouble.

EDWARD
No, it is not that. It is not only that.

CELIA
It cannot be simply a question of vanity:
That you think the world will laugh at you
Because your wife has left you for another man?
I shall soon put that right, Edward,
When you are free.

EDWARD
No, it is not that.
And all these reasons were suggested to me
By the man I call Riley-though his name is not Riley;
It was just a name in a song he sang...

CELIA
He sang you a song about a man named Rileyl!
Really, Edward, I think you are mad—
mean, you're on the edge of a nervous breakdown.
Edward, if I go away now
Will you promise me to see a very great doctor
Whom I have heard of—and his name is Reilly!

EDWARD
It would need someone greater than the greatest doctor
To cure this illness.

CELIA
Edward, if I go now,
Will you assure me that everything is right,
That you do not mean to have Lavinia back
And that you do mean to gain your freedom,
And that everything is all right between us?

That's all that matters. Truly, Edward,
If that is right, everything else will be,
I promise you.
EDWARD
No, CELIA.
It has been very wonderful and I'm very grateful,
And I think you are a very rare person.
But it was too late. And I should have known
That it wasn't fair to you.
CELIA
It wasn't fair to me!
You can stand there and talk about being fair to me!
EDWARD
But for Lavinia leaving, this would never have arisen.
What future had you ever thought there could be?
CELIA
2What had I thought that the future could be?
I abandoned the future before we began,
And after that I lived in a present
Where time was meaningless, a private world of ours,
Where the word 'happiness' had a different meaning
Or so it seemed.
EdWARD
I have heard of that experience.
CELIA
A dream. I was happy in it till today,
And then, when Julia asked about Lavinia
And it came to me that Lavinia had left you
And that you would be free—then I suddenly discovered
That the dream was not enough; that I wanted something more
And I waited and wanted to run to tell you.
Perhaps the dream was better. It seemed the real reality,
And if this is reality, it is very like a dream.
Perhaps it was I who betrayed my own dream
All the while; and to find I wanted
This world as well as that... well, it's humiliating.
EDWARD

There is no reason why you should feel humiliated...
CELIA
Oh, don't think that you can humiliate me!
Humiliation—it's something I've done to myself.
I am not sure even that you seem real enough
To humiliate me. I suppose that most women
Would feel degraded to find that a man
With whom they thought they had shared something wonderful
Had taken them only as a passing diversion.
Oh, I dare say that you deceived yourself;
But that's what it was, no doubt.
EDWARD
I didn't take you as a passing diversion!
If you want to speak of passing diversions
How did you take Peter?
CELIA
Peter? Peter who?
EDWARD
Peter Quilpe, who was here this evening. He was in a dream
And now he is simply unhappy and bewildered.
CELIA
I simply don't know what you are talking about.
Edward, this is really too crude a subterfuge
To justify yourself. There was never anything
Between me and Peter.
EDWARD
Wasn't there? He thought so.
He came back this evening to talk to me about it.
CELIA
But this is ridiculous! I never gave Peter
Any reason to suppose I cared for him.
I thought he had talent; I saw that he was lonely;
I thought that I could help him. I took him to concerts.
But then, as he came to make more acquaintances,
I found him less interesting and rather conceited.
But why should we talk about Peter? All that matters

Is, that you think you want Lavinia.
And if that is the sort of person you are—
Well, you had better have her.
EDWARD
It's not like that.
It is not that I am in love with Lavinia.
I don't think I was ever really in love with her.
If I have ever been in love—and I think that I have—
I have never been in love with anyone but you,
And perhaps I still am. But this can't go on.
It never could have been... a permanent thing:
You should have a man... nearer your own age.
CELIA
I don't think I care for advice from you, Edward.
You are not entitled to take any interest
Now, in my future. I only hope you're competent
To manage your own. But if you are not in love
And never have been in love with Lavinia,
What is it that you want?
EDWARD
I am not sure.
The one thing of which I am relatively certain
Is, that only since this morning
I have met myself as a middle-aged man
Beginning to know what it is to feel old.
That is the worst moment, when you feel that you have lost
The desire for all that was most desirable,
And before you are contented with what you can desire;
Before you know what is left to be desired;
And you go on wishing that you could desire
What desire has left behind. But you cannot understand.
How could you understand what it is to feel old?
CELIA
But I want to understand you. I could understand.
And, Edward, please believe that whatever happens
I shall not loathe you. I shall only feel sorry for you.
It's only myself I am in danger of hating.

But what will your life be? I cannot bear to think of it.
Oh, Edward! Can you be happy with Lavinia?
EDWARD
No—not happy: or, if there is any happiness,
Only the happiness of knowing
That the misery does not feed on the ruin of loveliness,
That the tedium is not the residue of ecstasy.
I see that my life was determined long ago
And that the struggle to escape from it
Is only a make-believe, a pretence
That what is, is not, or could be changed.
The self that can say 'I want this—or want that'—
The self that wills—he is a feeble creature;
He has to come to terms in the end
With the obstinate, the tougher self; who does not speak,
Who never talks, who cannot argue;
And who in some men may be the guardian—
But in men like me, the dull, the implacable,
The indomitable spirit of mediocrity.
The willing self can contrive the disaster
Of this unwilling partnership—but can only flourish
In submission to the rule of the stronger partner.
CELIA
I am not sure, Edward, that I understand you;
And yet I understand as I never did before.
I think—I believe—you are being yourself
As you never were before, with me.
Twice you have changed since I have been looking at
you.
I looked at your face: and I thought that I knew
And loved every contour; and as I looked
It withered, as if I had unwrapped a mummy.
I listened to your voice, that had always thrilled me,
And it became another voice—no, not a voice:
What I heard was only the noise of an insect,
Dry, endless, meaningless, inhuman—
You might have made it by scraping your legs together
Or however grasshoppers do it. I looked,

And listened for your heart, your blood;
And saw only a beetle the size of a man
With nothing more inside it than what comes out
When you tread on a beetle.

EDWARD

Perhaps that is what I am.
Tread on me, if you like.

CELIA

No, I won't tread on you.
That is not what you are. It is only what was left
Of what I had thought you were. I see another person,
I see you as a person whom. I never saw before.
The man I saw before, he was only a projection—
I see that now—of something that I wanted—
No, not wanted—something I aspired to—
Something that I desperately wanted to exist.
It must happen somewhere—but what and where is it?
And I ask you to forgive me.

EDWARD

You... ask me to forgive you!

CELIA

Yes, for two things. First...
[The telephone rings.]

EDWARD

Damn the telephone.
I suppose I had better answer it.

CELIA

Yes, better answer it.

EDWARD

Hello!... Oh, Julia: what is it now?
Your spectacles again... where did you leave them?
Or have we... have I got to hunt all over?
Have you looked in your bag?... Well, don't snap my head off...
You're sure, in the kitchen? Beside the champagne bottle?
You're quite sure?... Very well, hold on if you like;
We... I'll look for them.

CELIA
Yes, you look for them.
I shall never go into your kitchen again.
[Exit EDWARD. He returns with the spectacles and a bottle.]
EDWARD
She was right for once.
CELIA
She is always right.
But why bring an empty champagne bottle?
EDWARD
It isn't empty. It may be a little flat—
But why did she say that it was a half bottle?
It's one of my best: and I have no half bottles.
Well, I hoped that you would drink a final glass with me.
CELIA
What should we drink to?
EDWARD
Whom shall we drink to?
CELIA
To the Guardians.
EDWARD
To the Guardians?
CELIA
To the Guardians. It was you who spoke of guardians.
[They drink.]
It may be that even Julia is a guardian.
Perhaps she is my guardian. Give me the spectacles.
Good night, Edward.
EDWARD
Good night... CELIA.
[Exit CELIA.] Oh!
[He snatches up the receiver.]
Hello, Julia! are you there?...
Well, I'm awfully sorry to have kept you waiting;
But we... I had to hunt for them... No, I found them.
... Yes, she's bringing them now... Good night.

CURTAIN

Act I.

Scene 3

The same room: late afternoon of the next day. EDWARD alone. He goes to the door.

EDWARD: Oh... good evening. [Enter the UNIDENTIFIED GUEST.]

UNIDENTIFIED GUEST Good evening, Mr. Chamberlayne.

EDWARD Well. May I offer you some gin and water?

UNIDENTIFIED GUEST No, thank you. This is a different occasion.

EDWARD I take it that as you have come alone You have been unsuccessful.

UNIDENTIFIED GUEST Not at all. I have come to remind you—you have made a decision.

EDWARD Are you thinking that I may have changed my mind?

UNIDENTIFIED GUEST No. You will not be ready to change your mind Until you recover from having made a decision. No. I have come to tell you that you will change your mind, But that it will not matter. It will be too late.

EDWARD I have half a mind to change my mind now To show you that I am free to change it.

UNIDENTIFIED GUEST You will change your mind, but you are not free. Your moment of freedom was yesterday. You made a decision. You set in motion Forces in your life and in the lives of others Which cannot be reversed. That is one consideration. And another is this: it is a serious matter To bring someone back from the dead.

EDWARD From the dead? That figure of speech is somewhat... dramatic, As it was only yesterday that my wife left me.

UNIDENTIFIED GUEST Ah, but we die to each other daily. What we know of other people Is only our memory of the moments

During which we knew them. And they have changed since then. To pretend that they and we are the same Is a useful and convenient social convention Which must sometimes be broken. We must also remember That at every meeting we are meeting a stranger.

EDWARD So you want me to greet my wife as a stranger? That will not be easy.

UNIDENTIFIED GUEST It is very difficult. But it is perhaps still more difficult To keep up the pretence that you are not strangers. The affectionate ghosts: the grandmother, The lively bachelor uncle at the Christmas party, The beloved nursemaid—those who enfolded Your childhood years in comfort, mirth, security-If they returned, would it not be embarrassing? What would you say to them, or they to you After the first ten minutes? You would find it difficult To treat them as strangers, but still more difficult To pretend that you were not strange to each other.

EDWARD You can hardly expect me to obliterate The last five years.

UNIDENTIFIED GUEST I ask you to forget nothing. To try to forget is to try to conceal.

EDWARD There are certainly things I should like to forget.

UNIDENTIFIED GUEST And persons also. But you must not forget them. You must face them all, but meet them as strangers.

EDWARD Then I myself must also be a stranger.

UNIDENTIFIED GUEST And to yourself as well. But remember, When you see your wife, you must ask no questions And give no explanations. I have said the same to her. Don't strangle each other with knotted memories. Now I shall go.

EDWARD Stop! Will you come back with her?

UNIDENTIFIED GUEST No, I shall not come with her.

EDWARD I don't know why, But I think I should like you to bring her yourself.

UNIDENTIFIED GUEST Yes, I know you would. And for definite reasons Which I am not prepared to explain to you I must ask you not to speak of me to her; And she will not mention me to you.

EDWARD I promise.

UNIDENTIFIED GUEST And now you must await your visitors.

EDWARD Visitors? What visitors?

UNIDENTIFIED GUEST Whoever comes. The strangers. As for myself, I shall take the precaution Of leaving by the service staircase.

EDWARD May I ask one question?

UNIDENTIFIED GUEST You may ask it.

EDWARD Who are you?

UNIDENTIFIED GUEST I also am a stranger. [Exit. A pause. EDWARDmoves about restlessly. The bell rings and he goes to the front door.]

EDWARD Celia! CELIA Has Lavinia arrived?

EDWARD Celia! Why have you come? I expect Lavinia at any moment. You must not be here. Why have you come here?

CELIA Because Lavinia asked me. EDWARD Because Lavinia asked you!

CELIA Well, not directly. Julia had a telegram Asking her to come and to bring me with her. Julia was delayed and sent me on ahead.

EDWARD It seems very odd. And not like Lavinia. I suppose there is nothing to do but wait. Won't you sit down?

CELIA Thank you. [Pause]

EDWARD

Oh, my God, what shall we talk about? We can't sit here in silence.

CELIA Oh, I could. Just looking at you. Edward, forgive my laughing.You look like a little boy who's been sent for To the headmaster's study; and is not quite sure What he's been found out in. I never saw you so before. This is really a ludicrous situation.

EDWARD I'm afraid I can't see the humorous side of it.

CELIA I'm not really laughing at you, Edward. I couldn't have laughed at anything, yesterday; But I've learnt a lot in twenty-four hours. It wasn't a very pleasant experience. Oh, I'm glad I came! I can see you at last as a human being. Can't you see me that way too and laugh about it?

EDWARD I wish I could. I wish I understood anything. I'm completely in the dark.

CELIA But it's all so simple. Can't you see that... [The doorbell rings.]

EDWARD There's Lavinia. [Goes to front door.] Peter! [Enter PETER.]

PETER Where's Lavinia?

EDWARD Don't tell me that Lavinia Sent you a telegram...

PETER No, not to me, But to Alex. She told him to come here And to bring me with him. He'll be here in a minute. Celia! Have you heard from Lavinia too? Or am I interrupting?

CELIA I've just explained to EDWARD-I only got here this moment myself-That she telegraphed to Julia to come and bring me with her.

EDWARD I wonder whom else Lavinia has invited.

PETER Why, I got the impression that Lavinia intended To have yesterday's cocktail party today. So I don't suppose her aunt can have died.

EDWARD What aunt?

PETER The aunt you told us about. But Edward—you remember our conversation yesterday?

EDWARD Of course.

PETER I hope you've done nothing about it.

EDWARD No, I've done nothing.

PETER I'm so glad. Because I've changed my mind. I mean, I've decided That it's all no use. I'm going to California.

CELIA You're going to California!

PETER Yes, I have a new job.

EDWARD And how did that happen, overnight?

PETER Why, it's a man Alex put me in touch with And we settled everything this morning. Alex is a wonderful person to know, Because, you see, he knows everybody, everywhere. So what I've really come for is to say good-bye.

CELIA Well, Peter, I'm awfully glad, for your sake, Though of course we... I shall miss you; You know how I depended on you for concerts and picture exhibitions—more than you realised. It was fun, wasn't it! But now you'll have a chance, I hope, to realise your ambitions. I shall miss you.

PETER It's nice of you to say so; But you'll find someone better, to go about with.

CELIA I don't think that I shall be going to concerts. I am going away too. [LAVINIAlets herself in with a latch-key.]

PETER You're going abroad?

CELIA I don't know. Perhaps.

EDWARD You're both going away! [Enter LAVINIA.]

LAVINIA Who's going away? Well, Celia. Well, Peter. I didn't expect to find either of you here.

PETERand CELIA But the telegram!

LAVINIA What telegram?

CELIA The one you sent to Julia.

PETER And the one you sent to Alex.

LAVINIA I don't know what you mean. Edward, have you been sending telegrams?

EDWARD Of course I haven't sent any telegrams.

LAVINIA This is some of Julia's mischief. And is she coming?

PETER Yes and Alex.

LAVINIA Then I shall ask them for an explanation. Meanwhile, I suppose we might as well sit down. What shall we talk about?

EDWARD Peter's going to America.

PETER Yes and I would have rung you up tomorrow And come in to say good-bye before I left.

LAVINIA And Celia's going too? Was that what I heard? I congratulate you both. To Hollywood, of course? How exciting for you, Celia! Now you'll have a chance At last, to realise your ambitions. You're going together?

PETER We're not going together. CELIA told us she was going away, But I don't know where.

LAVINIA You don't know where? And do you know where you are going, yourself?

PETER Yes, of course, I'm going to California.

LAVINIA Well, Celia, why don't you go to California? Everyone says it's a wonderful climate: The people who go there never want to leave it.

CELIA Lavinia, I think I understand about Peter...

LAVINIA I have no doubt you do.

CELIA And why he is going...

LAVINIA I don't doubt that either.

CELIA And I believe he is right to go.

LAVINIA Oh, so you advised him?

PETER She knew nothing about it.

CELIA But now that I may be going away—somewhere- I should like to say good-bye—as friends.

LAVINIA Why, Celia, but haven't we always been friends? I thought you were one of my dearest friends-At least, in so far as a girl can be a friend Of a woman so much older than herself.

CELIA Lavinia, Don't put me off. I may not see you again. What I want to say is this: I should like you to remember me As someone who wants you and Edward to be happy.

LAVINIA You are very kind, but very mysterious. I'm sure that we shall manage somehow, thank you, As we have in the past.

CELIA Oh, not as in the past! [The doorbell rings and EDWARDgoes to answer it.] Oh, I'm afraid that all this sounds rather silly! But... [EDWARDre-enters with JULIA.]

JULIA There you are, Lavinia! I'm sorry to be late, But your telegram was a bit unexpected. I dropped everything to come. And how is the dear aunt?

LAVINIA So far as I know, she is very well, thank you.

JULIA She must have made a marvellous recovery. I said so to myself, when I got your telegram.

LAVINIA But where, may I ask, was this telegram sent from?

JULIA Why, from Essex, of course.

LAVINIA And why from Essex?

JULIA Because you've been in Essex!

LAVINIA Because I've been in Essex.

JULIA LAVINIA! Don't say you've had a lapse of memory! Then that accounts for the aunt—and the telegram.

LAVINIA Well, perhaps I was in Essex. I really don't know.

JULIA You don't know where you were? Lavinia! Don't

tell me you were abducted! Tell us; I'm thrilled... [The doorbell rings. EDWARDgoes to answer it. Enter ALEX.]

ALEX Has Lavinia arrived?

EDWARD Yes.

ALEX Welcome back, Lavinia! When I got your telegram...

LAVINIA Where from?

ALEX Dedham.

LAVINIA Dedham is in Essex. So it was from Dedham. Edward, have you any friends in Dedham?

EDWARD No, I have no connections in Dedham.

JULIA Well, it's all delightfully mysterious.

ALEX But what is the mystery?

JULIA Alex, don't be inquisitive. Lavinia has had a lapse of memory and so, of course, she sent us telegrams: And now I don't believe she really wants us. I can see that she is quite worn out After her anxiety about her aunt-Who you'll be glad to hear, has quite recovered, Alex-And after that long journey on the old Great Eastern, Waiting at junctions. And I suppose she's famished.

ALEX Ah, in that case I know what I'll do...

JULIA No, Alex. We must leave them alone and let Lavinia rest. Now we'll all go back to my house. Peter, call a taxi. [Exit PETER.] We'll have a cocktail party at my house today.

CELIA Well, I'll go now. Good-bye, Lavinia. Good-bye, Edward.

EDWARD Good-bye, Celia.

CELIA Good-bye, Lavinia.

LAVINIA Good-bye, Celia. [Exit CELIA.]

JULIA And now, Alex, you and I should be going.

EDWARD Are you sure you haven't left anything, Julia?

JULIA Left anything? Oh, you mean my spectacles. No, they're here. Besides, they're no use to me. I'm not coming back again this evening.

LAVINIA Stop! I want you to explain the telegram.

JULIA Explain the telegram? What do you think, Alex?

ALEX No, Julia, we can't explain the telegram.

LAVINIA I am sure that you could explain the telegram. I don't know why. But it seems to me that yesterday I started some machine, that goes on working, And I cannot stop it; no, it's not like a machine-Or if it's a machine, someone else is running it. But who? Somebody is always interfering... I don't feel free... and yet I started it...

JULIA Alex, do you think we could explain anything?

ALEX I think not, Julia. She must find out for herself: That's the only way.

JULIA How right you are! Well, my dears, I shall see you very soon.

EDWARD When shall we see you?

JULIA Did I say you'd see me? Good-bye. I believe... I haven't left anything. [Enter PETER.]

PETER I've got a taxi, Julia.

JULIA Splendid! Good-bye! [Exeunt JULIA, ALEXand PETER.]

LAVINIA I must say, you don't seem very pleased to see me.

EDWARD I can't say that I've had much opportunity To seem anything. But of course I'm glad to see you.

LAVINIA Yes, that was a silly thing to say. Like a schoolgirl. Like Celia. I don't know why I said it. Well, here I am.

EDWARD I am to ask no questions.

LAVINIA And I know I am to give no explanations.

EDWARD And I am to give no explanations.

LAVINIA And I am to ask no questions. And yet... why not?

EDWARD I don't know why not. So what are we to talk about?

LAVINIA There is one thing I ought to know, because of other people And what to do about them. It's about that party. I suppose you won't believe I forgot all about it! I let you down badly. What did you do about it? I only remembered after I had left.

EDWARD I telephoned to everyone I knew was coming But I couldn't get everyone. And so a few came.

LAVINIA Who came?

EDWARD Just those who were here this evening...

LAVINIA That's odd.

EDWARD... and one other. I don't know who he was, But you ought to know.

LAVINIA Yes, I think I know. But I'm puzzled by Julia. That woman is the devil. She knows by instinct when something's going to happen. Trust her not to miss any awkward situation! And what did you tell them!

EDWARD I invented an aunt Who was ill in the country and had sent for you.

LAVINIA Really, Edward! You had better have told the truth: Nothing less than the truth could deceive Julia. But how did the aunt come to live in Essex?

EDWARD Julia compelled me to make her live somewhere.

LAVINIA I see. So Julia made her live in Essex; And made the telegrams come from Essex. Well, I shall have to tell Julia the truth. I shall always tell the truth now. We have wasted such a lot of time in lying.

EDWARD I don't quite know what you mean.

LAVINIA Oh, EDWARD! The point is, that since I've been away I see that I've taken you much too seriously. And now I can see how absurd you are.

EDWARD That is a very serious conclusion To have arrived at in... how many?... thirty-two hours.

LAVINIA Yes, a very important discovery, Finding that you've spent five years of your life With a man who has no sense of humour; And that the effect upon me was That I lost all sense of humour myself. That's what came of always giving in to you.

EDWARD I was unaware that you'd always given in to me. It struck me very differently. As we're on the subject, I thought that it was I who had given in to you.

LAVINIA I know what you mean by giving in to me: You mean, leaving all the practical decisions That you should have made yourself. I remember-Oh, I ought to have realised what was coming, -When we were planning our honeymoon, I couldn't make you say where you wanted to go...

EDWARD But I wanted you to make that decision.

LAVINIA But how could I tell where I wanted to go Unless you suggested some other place first? And I remember that finally in desperation I said: 'I suppose you'd as soon go to Peacehaven'-And you said 'I don't mind.'

EDWARD Of course I didn't mind. I meant it as a compliment.

LAVINIA You meant it as a compliment!

EDWARD It's just that way of taking things that makes you so exasperating.

LAVINIA You were so considerate, people said; And you thought you were unselfish. It was only passivity; You only wanted to be bolstered, encouraged...

EDWARD Encouraged? To what?

LAVINIA To think well of yourself. You know it was I who made you work at the Bar...

EDWARD You nagged me because I didn't get enough work And said that I ought to meet more people: But when the briefs began to come in-And they didn't come through any of your friends-You suddenly found it inconvenient That I should be always too busy or too tired To be of use to you socially...

LAVINIA I never complained.

EDWARD No; and it was perfectly infuriating, The way you didn't complain...

LAVINIA It was you who complained Of seeing nobody but solicitors and clients...

EDWARD And you were never very sympathetic.

LAVINIA Well, but I tried to do something about it. That was why I took so much trouble To have those Thursdays, to give you the chance Of talking to intellectual people...

EDWARD You would have given me about as much opportunity If you had hired me as your butler: Some of your guests may have thought I was the butler.

LAVINIA And on several occasions, when somebody was coming Whom I particularly wanted you to meet, You didn't arrive until just as they were leaving.

EDWARD Well, at least, they can't have thought I was the butler.

LAVINIA Everything I tried only made matters worse and the moment you were offered something that you wanted You wanted something else. I shall treat you very differently In future.

EDWARD Thank you for the warning. But tell me, Since this is how you see me, why did you come back?

LAVINIA Frankly, I don't know. I was warned of the danger, Yet something, or somebody, compelled me to come. And why did you want me?

EDWARD I don't know either. You say you were trying to 'encourage' me: Then why did you always make me feel insignificant? I may not have known what life I wanted, But it wasn't the life you chose for me. You wanted your successful to be successful, You wanted me to supply a public background For your kind of public life. You wished to be a hostess For whom my career would be a support. Well, I tried to be accommodating. But in future, I shall behave, I assure you, very differently.

LAVINIA Bravol This is surprising. Now who could have taught you to answer back like that?

EDWARD I have had quite enough humiliation Lately, to bring me to the point At which humiliation ceases to humiliate. You get to the point at which you cease to feel And then you speak your mind.

LAVINIA That will be a novelty

To find that you have a mind to speak. Anyway, I'm prepared to take you as you are.

EDWARD You mean, you are prepared to take me As I was, or as you think I am. But what do you think I am?

LAVINIA Oh, what you always were. As for me, I'm rather a different person Whom you must get to know.

EDWARD This is very interesting: But you seem to assume that you've done all the changing-Though I haven't yet found it a change for the better. But doesn't it occur to you that possibly I may have changed too?

LAVINIA Oh, Edward, when you were a little boy, I'm sure you were always getting yourself measured To prove how you had grown since the last holidays. You were always intensely concerned with yourself; And if other people grow, well, you want to grow too. In what way have you changed?

EDWARD The change that comes From seeing oneself through the eyes of other people.

LAVINIA That must have been very shattering for you. But never mind, you'll soon get over it And find yourself another little part to play, With another face, to take people in.

EDWARD One of the most infuriating things about you Has always been your perfect assurance That you understood me better than I understood myself.

LAVINIA And the most infuriating thing about you Has always been your placid assumption That I wasn't worth the trouble of understanding.

EDWARD So here we are again. Back in the trap, With only one difference, perhaps—we can fight each other, Instead of each taking his corner of the cage. Well, it's a better way of passing the evening Than listening to the gramophone.

LAVINIA We have very good records; But I always suspected that you really hated music And that the gramophone was only your escape From talking to me when we had to be alone.

EDWARD I've often wondered why you married me.

LAVINIA Well, you really were rather attractive, you know; And you kept on saying that you were in love with me-I believe you were trying to persuade yourself you were. I seemed always on the verge of some wonderful experience And then it never happened. I wonder now How you could have thought you were in love with me.

EDWARD Everybody told me that I was; And they told me how well suited we were.

LAVINIA It's a pity that you had no opinion of your own. Oh, Edward, I should like to be good to you-Or if that's impossible, at least be horrid to you-Anything but nothing, which is all you seem to want of me. But I'm sorry for you...

EDWARD Don't say you are sorry for me! I have had enough of people being sorry for me.

LAVINIA Yes, because they can never be so sorry for you

As you are for yourself. And that's hard to bear. I thought that there might be some way out for you If I went away. I thought that if I died To you, I who had been only a ghost to you, You might be able to find the road back

To a time when you were real—for you must have been real At some time or other, before you ever knew me. Perhaps only when you were a child.

EDWARD I don't want you to make yourself responsible for me: It's only another kind of contempt. And I do not want you to explain me to myself. You're still trying to invent a personality for me Which will only keep me away from myself.

LAVINIA You're complicating what is in fact very simple. But there is one point which I see clearly: We are not to relapse into the kind of life we led Until yesterday morning.

EDWARD There was a door And I could not open it. I could not touch the handle. Why could I not walk out of my prison? What is hell? Hell is oneself, Hell is alone, the other figures in it Merely projections. There is nothing to escape from And nothing to escape to. One is always alone.

LAVINIA Edward, what are you talking about? Talking to yourself. Could you bear, for a moment, To think about me?

EDWARD It was only yesterday That damnation took place. And now I must live with it Day by day, hour by hour, forever and ever.

LAVINIA I think you're on the edge of a nervous breakdown!

EDWARD Don't say that!

LAVINIA I must say it. I know... of a doctor who I think could help you.

EDWARD If I go to a doctor, I shall make my own choice; Not take one whom you choose. How do I know That you wouldn't see him first and tell him all about me From your point of view? But I don't need a doctor. I am simply in hell. Where there are no doctors-At least, not in a professional capacity.

LAVINIA One can be practical, even in hell: And you know I am much more practical than you are.

EDWARD I ought to know by now what you consider

practical. Practical! I remember, on our honeymoon, You were always wrapping things up in tissue paper And then had to unwrap everything again

To find what you wanted. And I never could teach you How to put the cap on a tube of tooth-paste.

LAVINIA Very well then, I shall not try to press you. You're much too divided to know what you want. But, being divided, you will tend to compromise and your sort of compromise will be the old one.

EDWARD You don't understand me. Have I not made it clear That in future you will find me a different person?

LAVINIA Indeed. And has the difference nothing to do With Celia going off to California?

EDWARD Celia? Going to California?

LAVINIA Yes, with Peter. Really, Edward, if you were human You would burst out laughing. But you won't.

EDWARD O God, O God, if I could return to yesterday Before I thought that I had made a decision. What devil left the door on the latch For these doubts to enter? And then you came back, you The angel of destruction—just as I felt sure. In a moment, at your touch, there is nothing but ruin.

O God, what have I done? The python. The octopus. Must I become after all what you would make me?

LAVINIA Well, Edward, as I am unable to make you laugh and as I can't persuade you to see a doctor, There's nothing else at present that I can do about it. I ought to go and have a look in the kitchen. I know there are some eggs. But we must go out for dinner. Meanwhile, my luggage is in the hall downstairs: Will you get the porter to fetch it up for me?

CURTAIN

Act Two

SIR HENRY HARCOURT-REILLY'S consulting room in London. Morning: several weeks later. SIR HENRYalone at his desk. He presses an electric button. The NURSESECRETARY enters, with Appointment Book.

REILLY About those three appointments this morning, Miss Barraway:

I should like to run over my instructions again.
You understand, of course, that it is important
To avoid any meeting?
NURSE-SECRETARY You made that clear, Sir Henry:
The first appointment at eleven o'clock.
He is to be shown into the small waiting room;
And you will see him almost at once.
REILLY I shall see him at once. And the second?
NURSE-SECRETARY The second to be shown into the other room
Just as usual. She arrives at a quarter past;
But you may keep her waiting.
REILLY Or she may keep me waiting;
But I think she will be punctual.
NURSE-SECRETARY I telephone through
The moment she arrives. I leave her there
Until you ring three times.
REILLY And the third patient?
NURSE-SECRETARY The third one to be shown into the small room;
And I need not let you know that she has arrived.
Then, when you ring, I show the others out;
And only after they have left the house....
REILLY Quite right, Miss Barraway. That's all for the moment.
NURSE-SECRETARY Mr. Gibbs is here, Sir Henry.
REILLY Ask him to come straight in.
[Exit NURSE-SECRETARY.]
[ALEXenters almost immediately.]
ALEX When is Chamberlayne's appointment?
REILLY At eleven o'clock,
The conventional hour. We have not much time.
Tell me now, did you have any difficulty
In convincing him I was the man for his case?
ALEX Difficulty? No! He was only impatient
At having to wait four days for the appointment.
REILLY It was necessary to delay his appointment
To lower his resistance. But what I mean is,

Does he trust your judgment?
ALEX Yes, implicitly.
It's not that he regards me as very intelligent,
But he thinks I'm well informed: the sort of person
Who would know the right doctor, as well as the right shops.
Besides, he was ready to consult any doctor
Recommended by anyone except his wife.
REILLY I had already impressed upon her
That she was not to mention my name to him.
ALEX With your usual foresight. Now, he's quite triumphant
Because he thinks he's stolen a march on her.
And when you've sent him to a sanatorium
Where she can't get at him—then, he believes,
She will be very penitent. He's enjoying his illness.
REILLY Illness offers him a double advantage:
To escae from himself—and get the better of his wife.
ALEX Not to escape from her?
REILLY He doesn't want to escape from her.
ALEX He is staying at his club.
REILLY Yes, that is where he wrote from.
[The house-telephone rings.] Hello! yes, show him up.
ALEX You will have a busy morning!
I will go out by the service staircase
And come back when they've gone.
REILLY Yes, when they've gone.
[Exit ALEXby side door.]
[EDWARDis shown in by NURSE-SECRETARY.]
EDWARD Sir Henry Harcourt-Reilly—
[Stops and stares at REILLY]
REILLY [Without looking up from his papers.]
Good morning, Mr. Chamberlayne.
Please sit down. I won't keep you a moment.
—Now, Mr. Chamberlayne?
EDWARD It came into my mind
Before I entered the door, that you might be the same person:

And I dismissed that as just another symptom.
Well, I should have known better than to come here
On the recommendation of a man who did not know you.
But Alex is so plausible. And his recommendations
Of shops have always been satisfactory.
I beg your pardon. But he is a blunderer.
I should like to know... but what is the use!
I suppose I might as well go away at once.
REILLY No. If you please, sit down, Mr. Chamberlayne.
You are not going away, so you might as well sit down.
You were going to ask a question.
EDWARD When you came to my flat
Had you been invited by my wife as a guest
As I supposed...? Or did she send you?
REILLY I cannot say that I had been invited,
And Mrs. Chamberlayne did not know that I was coming.
But I knew you would be there and whom I should find with you.
EDWARD But you had seen my wife?
REILLY Oh yes, I had seen her.
EDWARD So this is a trap!
REILLY Let's not call it a trap.
But if it is a trap, then you cannot escape from it:
And so... you might as well sit down.
I think you will find that chair comfortable.
EDWARD You knew,
Before I began to tell you, what had happened?
REILLY That is so, that is so. But all in good time.
Let us dismiss that question for the moment.
Tell me first, about the difficulties
On which you want my professional opinion.
EDWARD It's not for me to blame you for bringing my wife back,
I suppose. You seemed to be trying to persuade me
That I was better off without her. But didn't you realise
That I was in no state to make a decision?
REILLY If I had not brought your wife back, Mr. Chamberlayne,

Do you suppose that things would be any better—now?
EDWARD I don't know, I'm sure. They could hardly be worse.
REILLY They might be much worse. You might have ruined
three lives
By your indecision. Now there are only two—
Which you still have the chance of redeeming from ruin.
EDWARD You talk as if I was capable of action:
If I were, I should not need to consult you
Or anyone else. I came here as a patient.
If you take no interest in my case, I can go elsewhere.
REILLY You have reason to believe that you are very ill?
EDWARD I should have thought a doctor could see that for himself.
Or at least that he would enquire about the symptoms.
Two people advised me recently,
Almost in the same words, that I ought to see a doctor.
They said—again, in almost the same words—
That I was on the edge of a nervous breakdown.
I didn't know it then myself—but if they saw it
I should have thought that a doctor could see it.
REILLY 'Nervous breakdown' is a term I never use:
It can mean almost anything.
EDWARD And since then, I have realised
That mine is a very unusual case.
REILLY All cases are unique and very similar to others.
EDWARD Is there a sanatorium to which you send such patients
As myself, under your personal observation?
REILLY You are very impetuous, Mr. Chamberlayne.
There are several kinds of sanatoria
For several kinds of patient. And there are also patients
For whom a sanatorium is the worst place possible.
We must first find out what is wrong with you
Before we decide what to do with you.

EDWARD I doubt if you have ever had a case like mine:
I have ceased to believe in my own personality.
REILLY Oh, dear yes; this is serious. A very common malady.
Very prevalent indeed.
EDWARD I remember, in my childhood...
REILLY I always begin from the immediate situation
And then go back as far as I find necessary.
You see, your memories of childhood-
I mean, in your present state of mind—
Would be largely fictitious; and as for your dreams,
You would produce amazing dreams, to oblige me.
I could make you dream any kind of dream I suggested,
And it would only go to flatter your vanity
With the temporary stimulus of feeling interesting.
EDWARD But I am obsessed by the thought of my own insignificance.
REILLY Precisely. And I could make you feel important,
And you would imagine it a marvellous cure;
And you would go on, doing such amount of mischief
As lay within your power—until you came to grief.
Half of the harm that is done in this world
Is due to people who want to feel important.
They don't mean to do harm—but the harm does not interest them.
Or they do not see it, or they justify it
Because they are absorbed in the endless struggle
To think well of themselves.
EDWARD If I am like that
I must have done a great deal of harm.
REILLY Oh, not so much as you would like to think.
Only, shall we say, within your modest capacity.
Try to explain what has happened since I left you.
EDWARD I see now why I wanted my wife to come back.
It was because of what she had made me into.
We had not been alone again for fifteen minutes
Before I felt and still more acutely—
Indeed, acutely, perhaps, for the first time,

The whole oppression, the unreality
Of the role she had always imposed upon me
With the obstinate, unconscious, sub-human strength
That some women have. Without her, it was vacancy.
When I thought she had left me, I began to dissolve,
To cease to exist. That was what she had done to me!
I cannot live with her—that is now intolerable;
I cannot live without her, for she has made me incapable
Of having any existence of my own.
That is what she has done to me in five years together!
She has made the world a place I cannot live in
Except on her terms. I must be alone,
But not in the same world. So I want you to put me
Into your sanatorium. I could be alone there?
[House-telephone rings.]
REILLY [Into telephone] Yes.
[To EDWARD] Yes, you could be alone there.
EDWARD I wonder
If you have understood a word of what I have been saying.
REILLY You must have patience with me, Mr. Chamberlayne:
I learn a good deal by merely observing you,
And letting you talk as long as you please,
And taking note of what you do not say.
EDWARD I once experienced the extreme of physical pain,
And now I know there is suffering worse than that.
It is surprising, if one had time to be surprised:
I am not afraid of the death of the body,
But this death is terrifying. The death of the spirit—
Can you understand what I suffer?
REILLY I understand what you mean.
EDWARD I can no longer act for myself.
Coming to see you—that's the last decision
I was capable of making. I am in your hands.
I cannot take any further responsibility.
REILLY Many patients come in that belief.

EDWARD And now will you send me to the sanatorium?
REILLY You have nothing else to tell me?
EDWARD What else can I tell you?
You don't want to hear about my early history.
REILLY No, I did not want to hear about your early history.
EDWARD And so will you send me to the sanatorium?
I can't go home again. And at my club
They won't let you keep a room for more than seven days;
I haven't the courage to go to a hotel,
And besides, I need more shirts—you can get my wife
To have my things sent on: whatever I shall need.
But of course you mustn't tell her where I am.
Is it far to go?
REILLY You might say, a long journey.
But before I treat a patient like yourself
I need to know a great deal more about him,
Than the patient himself can always tell me.
Indeed, it is often the case that my patients
Are only pieces of a total situation
Which I have to explore. The single patient
Who is ill by himself, is rather the exception.
I have recently had another patient
Whose situation is much the same as your own.
[Presses the bell on his desk three times]
You must accept a rather unusual procedure:
I propose to introduce you to the other patient.
EDWARD What do you mean? Who is this other patient?
I consider this very unprofessional conduct—
I will not discuss my case before another patient.
REILLY On the contrary. That is the only way
In which it can be discussed. You have told me nothing.
You have had the opportunity and you have said enough
To convince me that you have been making up your case
So to speak, as you went along. A barrister
Ought to know his brief before he enters the court.

EDWARD I am at least free to leave. And I propose to do so.
My mind is made up. I shall go to a hotel.
REILLY It is just because you are not free, Mr. Chamberlayne,
That you have come to me. It is for me to give you that—
Your freedom. That is my affair.
[LAVINIAis shown in by the NURSE-SECRETARY.]
But here is the other patient.
EDWARD Lavinia!
LAVINIA Well, Sir Henry!
I said I would come to talk about my husband:
I didn't say I was prepared to meet him.
EDWARD And I did not expect to meet you, Lavinia.
I call this a very dishonourable trick.
REILLY Honesty before honour, Mr. Chamberlayne.
Sit down, please, both of you. Mrs. Chamberlayne,
Your husband wishes to enter a sanatorium,
And that is a question which naturally concerns you.
EDWARD I am not going to any sanatorium.
I am going to a hotel. And I shall ask you, Lavinia,
To be so good as to send me on some clothes.
LAVINIA Oh, to what hotel?
EDWARD I don't know—I mean to say,
That doesn't concern you.
LAVINIA In that case, Edward,
I don't think your clothes concern me either.
[To REILLY]
I presume you will send him to the same sanatorium
To which you sent me? Well, he needs it more than I did.
REILLY I am glad that you have come to see it in that light—
At least, for the moment. But, Mrs. Chamberlayne,
You have never visited my sanatorium.
LAVINIA What do you mean? I asked to be sent
And you took me there. If that was not a sanatorium
What was it?

REILLY A kind of hotel. A retreat
For people who imagine that they need a respite
From everyday life. They return refreshed;
And if they believe it to be a sanatorium
That is good reason for not sending them to one.
The people who need my sort of sanatorium
Are not easily deceived.
LAVINIA Are you a devil
Or merely a lunatic practical joker?
EDWARD I incline to the second explanation
Without the qualification 'lunatic.'
Why should you go to a sanatorium?
I have never known anyone in my life
With fewer mental complications than you;
You're stronger than a... battleship. That's what
drove me mad.
I am the one who needs a sanatorium—
But I'm not going there.
REILLY You are right, Mr. Chamberlayne.
You are no case for my sanatorium:
You are much too ill.
EDWARD Much too ill?
Then I'll go and be ill in a suburban boarding-house.
LAVINIA That would never suit you, Edward. Now I
know of a
hotel
In the New Forest...
EDWARD How like you, Lavinia.
You always know of something better.
LAVINIA It's only that I have a more practical mind
Than you have, Edward. You do know that.
EDWARD Only because you've told me so often.
I'd like to see you filling up an income-tax form.
LAVINIA Don't be silly, Edward. When I say practical,
I mean practical in the things that really matter.
REILLY May I interrupt this interesting discussion?
I say you are both too ill. There are several symptoms
Which must occur together and to a marked degree,

To qualify a patient for my sanatorium:
And one of them is an honest mind.
That is one of the causes of their suffering.
LAVINIA No one can say my husband has an honest mind.
EDWARD And I could not honestly say that of you, Lavinia.
REILLY I congratulate you both on your perspicacity,
But this does not bring us to the heart of the matter.
I do not trouble myself with the common cheat,
Or with the insuperably, innocently dull:
My patients such as you are the self-deceivers
Taking infinite pains, exhausting their energy,
Yet never quite successful. You have both of you pretended
To be consulting me; both, tried to impose upon me
Your own diagnosis and prescribe your own cure.
But when you put yourselves into hands like mine
You surrender a great deal more than you meant to.
This isthe consequence of trying to lie to me.
LAVINIA I did not come here to be insulted.
REILLY You have come where the word 'insult' has no meaning;
And you must put up with that. All that you have told me—
Both of you—was true enough: you described your feelings—
Or some of them—omitting the important facts.
Let me take your husband first.
[TO EDWARD]
You were lying to me
By concealing your relations with Miss Coplestone.
EDWARD This is monstrous! My wife knew nothing about it.
LAVINIA Really, Edward! Even if I'd been blind
There were plenty of people to let me know about it.
I wonder if there was anyone who didn't know.
REILLY There was one, in fact. But you, Mrs. Chamberlayne,

Tried to make me believe that it was this discovery
Precipitated what you called your nervous breakdown.
LAVINIA But it's true! I was completely prostrated;
Even if I have made a partial recovery.
REILLY Certainly, you were completely prostrated,
And certainly, you have somewhat recovered.
But you failed to mention that the cause of your distress
Was the defection of your lover—who suddenly For the first time in his life, fell in love with someone,
And with someone of whom you had reason to be jealous.
EDWARD Really, Lavinia! This is very interesting.
You seem to have been much more successful at concealment
Than I was. Now I wonder who it could have been.
LAVINIA Well, tell him if you like.
REILLY A young man named Peter.
EDWARD Peter? Peter who?
REILLY Mr. Peter Quilpe
Was a frequent guest.
EDWARD Peter Quilpe!
Peter Quilpe! Really Lavinia!
I congratulate you. You could not have chosen
Anyone I was less likely to suspect.
And then he came to me to confide about Celia!
I have never heard anything so utterly ludicrous:
This is the best joke that ever happened.
LAVINIA I never knew you had such a sense of humour.
REILLY It is the first more hopeful symptom.
LAVINIA How did you know all this?
REILLY That I cannot disclose.
I have my own method of collecting information
About my patients. You must not ask me to reveal it—
That is a matter of professional etiquette.
LAVINIA I have not noticed much professional etiquette
About your behaviour today.
REILLY A point well taken.
But permit me to remark that my revelations

About each of you, to one another,
Have not been of anything that you confided to me.
The information I have exchanged between you
Was all obtained from outside sources.
Mrs. Chamberlayne, when you came to me two months ago
I was dissatisfied with your explanation
Of your obvious symptoms of emotional strain
And so I made enquiries.
EDWARD It was two months ago
That your breakdown began! And I never noticed it.
LAVINIA You wouldn't notice anything. You never noticed me.
REILLY Now, I want to point out to both of you
How much you have in common. Indeed, I consider
That you are exceptionally well-suited to each other.
Mr. Chamberlayne, when you thought your wife had left you,
You discovered, to your surprise and consternation,
That you were not really in love with Miss Coplestone...
LAVINIA My husband has never been in love with anybody.
REILLY And were not prepared to make the least sacrifice
On her account. This injured your vanity.
You liked to think of yourself as a passionate lover.
Then you realised, what your wife has justly remarked,
That you had never been in love with anybody;
Which made you suspect that you were incapable
Of loving. To men of a certain type
The suspicion that they are incapable of loving
Is as disturbing to their self-esteem
As, in cruder men, the fear of impotence.
LAVINIA You are cold-hearted, Edward.
REILLY So you say, Mrs. Chamberlayne.
And now, let us turn to your side of the problem.
When you discovered that your young friend
(Though you knew, in your heart, that he was not in love with you,

And were always humiliated by the awareness
That you had forced him into this position)—
When, I say, you discovered that your young friend
Had actually fallen in love with Miss Coplestone,
It took you some time, I have no doubt,
Before you would admit it. Though perhaps you knew it
Before he did. You pretended to yourself,
I suspect and for as long as you could,
That he was aiming at a higher social distinction
Than the honour conferred by being your lover.
When you had to face the fact that his feelings towards her
Were different from any you had aroused in him—
It was a shock. You had wanted to be loved;
You had come to see that no one had ever loved you.
Then you began to fear that no one could love you.
EDWARD I'm beginning to feel very sorry for you, Lavinia.
You know, you really are exceptionally unlovable,
And I never quite knew why. I thought it was my fault.
REILLY And now you begin to see, I hope,
How much you have in common. The same isolation.
A man who finds himself incapable of loving
And a woman who finds that no man can love her.
LAVINIA It seems to me that what we have in common
Might be just enough to make us loathe one another.
REILLY See it rather as the bond which holds you together.
While still in a state of unenlightenment,
You could always say: 'He could not love any woman';
You could always say: 'No man could love her.'
You could accuse each other of your own faults,
And so could avoid understanding each other.
Now, you have only to reverse the propositions
And put them together.
LAVINIA Is that possible?
REILLY If I had sent either of you to the sanatorium
In the state in which you came to me—I tell you this:

It would have been a horror beyond your imagining,
For you would have been left with what you brought with you:
The shadow of desires of desires. A prey
To the devils who arrive at their plenitude of power
When they have you to themselves.
LAVINIA Then what can we do
When we can go neither back nor forward? Edward!
What can we do?
REILLY You have answered your own question,
Though you do not know the meaning of what you have said.
EDWARD Lavinia, we must make the best of a bad job.
That is what he means.
REILLY When you find, Mr. Chamberlayne,
The best of a bad job is all any of us make of it—
Except of course, the saints—such as those who go
To the sanatorium—you will forget this phrase,
And in forgetting it will alter the condition.
LAVINIA Edward, there is that hotel in the New Forest
If you want to go there. The proprietor
Who has just taken over, is a friend of Alex's.
I could go down with you and then leave you there
If you want to be alone...
EDWARD But I can't go away!
I have a case coming on next Monday.
LAVINIA Then will you stop at your club?
EDWARD No, they won't let me.
I must leave tomorrow—but how did you know
I was staying at the club?
LAVINIA Really, Edward!
I have some sense of responsibility.
I was going to leave some shirts there for you.
EDWARD It seems to me that I might as well go home.
LAVINIA Then we can share a taxi and be economical.
Edward, have you anything else to ask him
Before we go?
EDWARD Yes, I have.

But it's difficult to say.
LAVINIA But. I wish you would say it.
At least, there is something I would like you to ask.
EDWARD It's about the future of... the others.
I don't want to build on other people's ruins.
LAVINIA Exactly. And I have a question too.
Sir Henry, was it you who sent those telegrams?
REILLY I think I will dispose of your husband's problem.
[TO EDWARD]
Your business is not to clear your conscience
But to learn how to bear the burdens on your conscience.
With the future of the others you are not concerned.
LAVINIA I think you have answered my question too.
They had to tell us, themselves, that they had made their decision.
EDWARD Have you anything else to say to us, Sir Henry?
REILLY No. Not in this capacity.
[EDWARDtakes out his cheque-book. REILLY raises his hand.]
My secretary will send you my account.
Go in peace. And work out your salvation with diligence.
[Exeunt EDWARDand LAVINIA.]
[REILLYgoes to the couch and lies down. The house-telephone rings. He gets up and answers it.]
REILLY Yes?... Yes. Come in.
[Enter JULIAby side door.]
She's waiting downstairs.
JULIA I know that, Henry. I brought her here myself.
REILLY Oh? You didn't let her know you were seeing me first?
JULIA Of course not. I dropped her at the door
And went on in the taxi, round the comer;
Waited a moment and slipped in by the back way.
I only came to tell you, I am sure she is ready
To make a decision.
REILLY Was she reluctant?
Was that why you brought her?
JULIA Oh no, not reluctant:

Only diffident. She cannot believe
That you will take her seriously.
REILLY That is not uncommon.
JULIA Or that she deserves to be taken seriously.
REILLY That is most uncommon.
JULIA Henry, get up. You can't be as tired as that. I shall wait in the next room,
And come back when she's gone.
REILLY Yes, when she's gone.
JULIA Will Alex be here?
REILLY Yes, he'll be here.
[Exit JULIAby side door.]
[REILLYpresses button.
NURSE-SECRETARY shows in CELIA.]
REILLY Miss Celia Coplestone?... Won't you sit down?
I believe you are a friend of Mrs. Shuttlethwaite.
CELIA Yes, it was Julia... Mrs. Shuttlethwaite
Who advised me to come to you.—But I've met you before,
Haven't I, somewhere?... Oh, of course.
But I didn't know...
REILLY There is nothing you need to know.
I was there at the instance of Mrs. Shuttlethwaite.
CELIA That makes it even more perplexing. However,
I don't want to waste your time. And I'm awfully afraid
That you'll think that I am wasting it anyway.
I suppose most people, when they come to see you,
Are obviously ill, or can give good reasons
For wanting to see you. Well, I can't.
I just came in desperation. And I shan't be offended
If you simply tell me to go away again.
REILLY Most of my patients begin, Miss Coplestone,
By telling me exactly what is the matter with them,
And what I am to do about it. They are quite sure
They have had a nervous breakdown—that is what they call it—
And usually they think that someone else is to blame.
CELIA I at least have no one to blame but myself.

REILLY And after that, the prologue to my treatment
Is to try to show them that they are mistaken
About the nature of their illness and lead them to see
That it's not so interesting as they had imagined.
When I get as far as that, there is something to be done.
CELIA Well, I can't pretend that my trouble is interesting;
But I shan't begin that way. I feel perfectly well.
I could lead an active life—if there's anything to work for;
I don't imagine that I am being persecuted;
I don't hear any voices, I have no delusions—
Except that the world I live in seems all a delusion!
But oughtn't I first to tell you the circumstances?
I'd forgotten that you know nothing about me;
And with what I've been going through, these last weeks,
I somehow took it for granted that I needn't explain myself.
REILLY I know quite enough about you for the moment:
Try first to describe your present state of mind.
CELIA Well, there are two things I can't understand,
Which you might consider symptoms. But first I must tell you
That I should really like to think there's something wrong with me—
Because, if there isn't, then there's something wrong,
Or at least, very different from what it seemed to be,
With the world itself—and that's much more frightening!
That would be terrible. So I'd rather believe
There is something wrong with me, that could be put right.
I'd do anything you told me, to get back to normality.
REILLY We must find out about you, before we decide
What is normality. You say there are two things:
What is the first?
CELIA
An awareness of solitude.
But that sounds so flat. I don't mean simply
That there's been a crash: though indeed there has been.

It isn't simply the end of an illusion
In the ordinary way, or being ditched.
Of course that's something that's always happening
To all sorts of people and they get over it
More or less, or at least they carry on.
No. I mean that what has happened has made me aware
That I've always been alone. That one always is alone.
Not simply the ending of one relationship,
Not even simply finding that it never existed—
But a revelation about my relationship
With everybody. Do you know—
It no longer seems worth while to speak to anyone!
REILLY
And what about your parents?
CELIA
Oh, they live in the country,
Now they can't afford to have a place in town.
It's all they can do to keep the country house going:
But it's been in the family so long, they won't leave it.
REILLY
And you live in London?
CELIA
I share a flat
With a cousin: but she's abroad at the moment,
And my family want me to come down and stay with them.
But I just can't face it.
REILLY
So you want to see no one?
CELIA
No... it isn't that I want to be alone,
But that everyone's alone—or so it seems to me.
They make noises and think they are talking to each other;
They make faces and think they understand each other.
And I'm sure that they don't. Is that a delusion?
REILLY
A delusion is something we must return from.
There are other states of mind, which we take to be delusion,

But which we have to accept and go on from.
And the second symptom?
CELIA
That's stranger still.
It sounds ridiculous—but the only word for it
That I can find, is a sense of sin.
REILLY
You suffer from a sense of sin, Miss Coplestone?
This is most unusual.
CELIA
It seemed to me abnormal.
REILLY
We have yet to find what would be normal
For you, before we use the term 'abnormal.'
Tell me what you mean by a sense of sin.
CELIA
It's much easier to tell you what I don't mean:
I don't mean sin in the ordinary sense.
REILLY
And what, in your opinion, is the ordinary sense?
CELIA
Well... I suppose it's being immoral-
And I don't feel as if I was immoral:
In fact, aren't the people one thinks of as immoral
Just the people who we say have no moral sense?
I've never noticed that immorality
Was accompanied by a sense of sin:
At least, I have never come across it.
I suppose it is wicked to hurt other people
If you know that you're hurting them. I haven't hurt her.
I wasn't taking anything away from her—
Anything she wanted. I may have been a fool:
But I don't mind at all having been a fool.
REILLY
And what is the point of view of your family?
CELIA
Well, my bringing up was pretty conventional—
I had always been taught to disbelieve in sin.

Oh, I don't mean that it was ever mentioned!
But anything wrong, from our point of view,
Was either bad form, or was psychological.
And bad form always led to disaster
Because the people one knew disapproved of it.
I don't worry much about form, myself—
But when everything's bad form, or mental kinks,
You either become bad form and cease to care,
Or else, if you care, you must be kinky.
REILLY
And so you suppose you have what you call a 'kink'?
CELIA
But everything seemed so right, at the time!
I've been thinking about it, over and over;
I can see now, it was all a mistake:
But I don't see why mistakes should make one feel sinful!
And yet I can't find any other word for it.
It must be some kind of hallucination;
Yet, at the same time, I'm frightened by the fear
That it is more real than anything I believed in.
REILLY
What is more real than anything you believed in?
CELIA
It's not the feeling of anything I've ever done,
Which I might get away from, or of anything in me
I could get rid of—but of emptiness, of failure
Towards someone, or something, outside of myself;
And I feel I must... atone-is that the word?
Can you treat a patient for such a state of mind?
REILLY
What had you believed were your relations with this, man?
CELIA
Oh, you'd guessed that, had you? That's clever of you.
No, perhaps I made it obvious. You don't need to know
About him, do you?
REILLY
No.

CELIA
Perhaps I'm only typical.
REILLY
There are different types. Some are rarer than others.
CELIA
Oh, I thought that I was giving him so much!
And he to me—and the giving and the taking
Seemed so right: not in terms of calculation
Of what was good for the persons we had been
But for the new person, us. If I could feel
As I did then, even now it would seem right.
And then I found we were only strangers
And that there had been neither giving nor taking
But that we had merely made use of each other
Each for his purpose. That's horrible. Can we only love
Something created by our own imagination?
Are we all in fact unloving and unlovable?
Then one is alone and if one is alone
Then lover and belovèd are equally unreal
And the dreamer is no more real than his dreams.
REILLY
And this man. What does he now seem like, to you?
CELIA
Like a child who has wandered into a forest
Playing with an imaginary playmate
And suddenly discovers he is only a child
Lost in a forest, wanting to go home.
REILLY
Compassion may be already a clue
Towards finding your own way out of the forest.
CELIA
But even if I find my way out of the forest
I shall be left with the inconsolable memory
Of the treasure I went into the forest to find
And never found and which was not there
And perhaps is not anywhere? But if not anywhere,
Why do I feel guilty at not having found it?
REILLY

Disillusion can become itself an illusion
If we rest in it.
CELIA
cannot argue.
It's not that I'm afraid of being hurt again:
Nothing again can either hurt or heal.
I have thought at moments that the ecstasy is real
Although those who experience it may have no reality.
For what happened is remembered like a dream
In which one is exalted by intensity of loving
In the spirit, a vibration of delight
Without desire, for desire is fulfilled
In the delight of loving. A state one does not know
When awake. But what, or whom I loved,
Or what in me was loving, I do not know.
And if that is all meaningless, I want to be cured
Of a craving for something I cannot find
And of the shame of never finding it.
Can you cure me?
REILLY
The condition is curable.
But the form of treatment must be your own choice:
I cannot choose for you. If that is what you wish,
I can reconcile you to the human condition,
The condition to which some who have gone as far as you
Have succeeded in returning. They may remember
The vision they have had, but they cease to regret it,
Maintain themselves by the common routine,
Learn to avoid excessive expectation,
Become tolerant of themselves and others,
Giving and taking, in the usual actions
What there is to give and take. They do not repine;
Are contented with the morning that separates
And with the evening that brings together
For casual talk before the fire
Two people who know they do not understand each other,
Breeding children whom they do not understand

And who will never understand them.
CELIA
Is that the best life?
REILLY
It is a good life. Though you will not know how good
Till you come to the end. But you will want nothing else
And the other life will be only like a book
You have read once and lost. In a world of lunacy,
Violence, stupidity, greed... it is a good life.
CELIA
I know I ought to be able to accept that
If I might still have it. Yet it leaves me cold.
Perhaps that's just a part of my illness,
But I feel it would be a kind of surrender—
No, not a surrender—more like a betrayal.
You see, I think I really had a vision of something
Though I don't know what it is. I don't want to forget it.
I want to live with it. I could do without everything,
Put up with anything, if I might cherish it.
In fact, I think it would really be dishonest
For me, now, to try to make a life with anybody!
I couldn't give anyone the kind of love—
I wish I could—which belongs to that life.
Oh, I'm afraid this sounds like raving!
Or just cantankerousness... still,
If there's no other way... then I feel just hopeless.
REILLY
There is another way, if you have the courage.
The first I could describe in familiar terms
Because you have seen it, as we all have seen it,
Illustrated, more or less, in lives of those about us.
The second is unknown and so requires faith—
The kind of faith that issues from despair.
The destination cannot be described;
You will know very little until you get there;
You will journey blind. But the way leads towards possession
Of what you have sought for in the wrong place.

CELIA
That sounds like what I want. But what is my duty?
REILLY
Whichever way you choose will prescribe its own duty.
CELIA
Which way is better?
REILLY
Neither way is better.
Both ways are necessary. It is also necessary
To make a choice between them.
CELIA
Then I choose the second.
REILLY
It is a terrifying journey.
CELIA
I am not frightened
But glad. I suppose it is a lonely way?
REILLY
No lonelier than the other. But those who take the other
Can forget their loneliness. You will not forget yours.
Each way means loneliness—and communion.
Both ways avoid the final desolation
Of solitude in the phantasmal world
Of imagination, shuffling memories and desires.
CELIA
That is the hell I have been in.
REILLY
It isn't hell
Till you become incapable of anything else.
Now—do you feel quite sure?
CELIA
I want your second way.
So what am I to do?
REILLY
You will go to the sanatorium.
CELIA
Oh, what an anti-climax! I have known people
Who have been to your sanatorium and come back
again—

I don't mean to say they weren't much better for it—
That's why I came to you. But they returned as...
normal people.
REILLY
True. But the friends you have in mind
Cannot have been to this sanatorium.
I am very careful whom I send there:
Those who go do not come back as these did.
CELIA
It sounds like a prison. But they can't all stay there!
I mean, it would make the place so over-crowded.
REILLY
Not very many go. But I said they did not come back
In the sense in which your friends came back.
I did not say they stayed there.
CELIA
What became of them?
REILLY
They choose, Miss Coplestone. Nothing is forced on them.
Some of them return, in a physical sense;
No one disappears. They lead very active lives
Very often, in the world.
CELIA
How soon will you send me there?
REILLY
How soon will you be ready?
CELIA
Tonight, by nine o'clock.
REILLY
Go home then and make your preparations.
Here is the address for you to give your friends;
[Writes on a slip of paper.]
You had better let your family know at once.
I will send a car for you at nine o'clock.
CELIA
What do I need to take with me?
REILLY
Nothing.

Everything you need will be provided for you.
And you will have no expenses at the sanatorium.
CELIA
I don't in the least know what I am doing
Or why I am doing it. There is nothing else to do:
That is the only reason.
REILLY
It is the best reason.
CELIA
But I know it is I who have made the decision:
I must tell you that. Oh, I almost forgot—
May I ask what your fee is?
REILLY
I have told my secretary
That there is no fee.
CELIA
But...
REILLY
For a case like yours
There is no fee.
[presses button.]
CELIA
You have been very kind.
REILLY
Go in peace, my daughter.
Work out your salvation with diligence.
[NURSE-SECRETARY appears at door. Exit CELIA.
REILLYdials on house-telephone.]
REILLY
[Into telephone]
It is finished. You can come in now.
[Enter JULIAby side door.]
She will go far, that one.
JULIA
Very far, I think.
You do not need to tell me. I knew from the beginning.
REILLY
It's the other ones I am worried about.

JULIA
Nonsense, Henry. I shall keep an eye on them.
REILLY
To send them back: what have they to go back to?
To the stale food mouldering in the larder,
The stale thoughts mouldering in their minds.
Each unable to disguise his own meanness
From himself, because it is known to the other.
It's not the knowledge of the mutual treachery
But the knowledge that the other understands the motive
Mirror to mirror, reflecting vanity.
I have taken a great risk.
JULIA
We must always take risks.
That is our destiny. Since you question the decision
What possible alternative can you imagine?
REILLY
None.
JULIA
Very well then. We must take the risk.
All we could do was to give them the chance.
And now, when they are stripped naked to their souls
And can choose, whether to put on proper costumes
Or huddle quickly into new disguises,
They have, for the first time, somewhere to start from.
Oh, of course, they might just murder each other!
But I don't think they will do that. We shall see.
It's the thought of CELIA that weighs upon my mind.
REILLY
Of CELIA?
JULIA
Of CELIA.
REILLY
But when I said just now
That she would go far, you agreed with me.
JULIA
Oh yes, she will go far. And we know where she is going.
But what do we know of the terrors of the journey?

You and I don't know the process by which the human is
Transhumanised: what do we know
Of the kind of suffering they must undergo
On the way of illumination?
REILLY
Will she be frightened
By the first appearance of projected spirits?
JULIA
Henry, you simply do not understand innocence.
She will be afraid of nothing; she will not even know
That there is anything there to be afraid of.
She is too humble. She will pass between the scolding hills,
Through the valley of derision, like a child sent on an errand
In eagerness and patience. Yet she must suffer.
REILLY
When I express confidence in anything
You always raise doubts; when I am apprehensive
Then you see no reason for anything but confidence.
JULIA
That's one way in which I am so useful to you.
You ought to be grateful.
REILLY
And when I say to one like her,
'Work out your salvation with diligence,' I do not understand
What I myself am saying.
JULIA
You must accept your limitations.
—But how much longer will Alex keep us waiting?
REILLY
He should be here by now. I'll speak to Miss Barraway.
[Takes up house-telephone.]
Miss Barraway, when Mr. Gibbs arrives...
Oh, very good.
[TO JULIA]

He's on his way up.
[Into telephone]
You may bring the tray in now, Miss Barraway.
[Enter ALEX.]
ALEX
Well! Well! and how have we got on?
JULIA
Everything is in order.
ALEX
The Chamberlaynes have chosen?
REILLY
They accept their destiny.
ALEX
And she has made the choice?
REILLY
She will be fetched this evening.
[NURSE-SECRETARY enters with a tray, a decanter and three glasses and exits. REILLYpours drinks.]
And now we are ready to proceed to the libation.
ALEX
The words for the building of the hearth.
[They raise their glasses.]
REILLY
Let them build the hearth
Under the protection of the stars.
ALEX
Let them place a chair each side of it.
JULIA
May the holy ones watch over the roof,
May the Moon herself influence the bed.
[They drink.]
ALEX
The words for those who go upon a journey.
REILLY
Protector of travellers
Bless the road.
ALEX
Watch over her in the desert

Watch over her in the mountain
Watch over her in the labyrinth
Watch over her by the quicksand.
JULIA
Protect her from the Voices
Protect her from the Visions
Protect her in the tumult
Protect her in the silence.
[They drink.]
REILLY
There is one for whom the words cannot be spoken.
ALEX
They cannot be spoken yet.
JULIA
You mean Peter Quilpe.
REILLY
He has not yet come to where the words are valid.
JULIA
Shall we ever speak them?
ALEX
Others, perhaps, will speak them.
You know, I have connections—even in California.
CURTAIN
Act Three.
The drawing room of the Chamberlaynes' London flat. Two years later. A late afternoon in July. A CATERER'S MAN is arranging a buffet table. LAVINIAenters from side door.
CATERER'S MAN
Have you any further orders for us, Madam?
LAVINIA
You could bring in the trolley with the glasses
And leave them ready.
CATERER'S MAN
Very good, Madam.
In
[Exit. LAVINIAlooks about the room critically and moves a bowl of flowers.]

[Re-enter CATERER'S MAN with trolley.]
LAVINIA
There, in that corner. That's the most convenient;
You can get in and out. Is there anything you need
That you can't find in the kitchen?
CATERER'S MAN
Nothing, Madam.
Will there be anything more you require?
LAVINIA
Nothing more, I think, till half past six.
[Exit CATERER'S MAN.]
[EDWARDlets himself in at the front door.]
EDWARD
I'm in good time, I think. I hope you've not been worry-
ing.
LAVINIA
Oh no. I did in fact ring up your chambers,
And your clerk told me you had already left.
But all I rang up for was to reassure you...
EDWARD
[Smiling]
That you hadn't run away?
LAVINIA
Now Edward, that's unfair!
You know that we've given several parties
In the last two years. And I've attended all of them.
I hope you're not too tired?
EDWARD
Oh no, a quiet day.
Two consultations with solicitors
On quite straightforward cases. It's you who should be
tired.
LAVINIA
I'm not tired yet. But I know that I'll be glad
When it's all over.
EDWARD
I like the dress you're wearing:
I'm glad you put on that one.

LAVINIA
Well, Edward!
Do you know it's the first time you've paid me a compliment
Before a party? And that's when one needs them.
EDWARD
Well, you deserve it.—We asked too many people.
LAVINIA
It's true, a great many more accepted
Than we thought would want to come. But what can you do?
There's usually a lot who don't want to come
But all the same would be bitterly offended
To hear we'd given a party without asking them.
EDWARD
Perhaps we ought to have arranged to have two parties
Instead of one.
LAVINIA
Tbat's never satisfactory.
Everyone who's asked to either party
Suspects that the other one was more important.
EDWARD
That's true. You have a very practical mind.
LAVINIA
But you know, I don't think that you need worry:
They won't all come, out of those who accepted.
You know we said, 'We can ask twenty more
Because they will be going to the Gunnings instead.'
EDWARD
I know, that's what we said at the time;
But I'd forgotten what the Gunnings' parties were like.
Their guests will get just enough to make them thirsty;
They'll come on to us later, roaring for drink.
Well, let's hope that those who come to us early
Will be going on to the Gunnings afterwards,
To make room for those who come from the Gunnings.
LAVINIA
And if it's very crowded, they can't get at the cocktails,

And the man won't be able to take the tray about,
So they'll go away again. Anyway, at that stage
There's nothing whatever you can do about it:
And everyone likes to be seen at a party
Where everybody else is, to show they've been invited.
That's what makes it a success. Is that picture straight?
EDWARD
Yes, it is.
LAVINIA
No, it isn't. Do please straighten it.
EDWARD
Is it straight now?
LAVINIA
Too much to the left.
EDWARD
How's that now?
LAVINIA
No, I meant the right.
That will do. I'm too tired to bother.
EDWARD After they're all gone, we will have some champagne,
Just ourselves. You lie down now, LAVINIA.
No one will be coming for at least half an hour;
So just stretch out.
LAVINIA
You must sit beside me,
Then I can relax.
EDWARD
This is the best moment
Of the whole party.
LAVINIA Oh no, EDWARD.
The best moment is the moment it's over;
And then to remember, it's the end of the season
And no more parties.
EDWARD
And no more committees.
LAVINIA
Can we get away soon?

EDWARD
By the end of next week
I shall be quite free.
LAVINIA
And we can be alone.
I love that house being so remote.
EDWARD
That's why we took it. And I'm really thankful
To have that excuse for not seeing people;
And you do need to rest now.
[The doorbell rings.]
LAVINIA
Oh, bother!
Now who would come so early? I simply can't get up.
CATERER'S MAN
Mrs. Shuttlethwaite!
LAVINIA
Oh, it's Julia!
[Enter JULIA. ALEXis seen to enter with her and pass back-stage towards the kitchen.]
JULIA
Well, my dears and here I am!
I seem literally to have caught you napping!
I know I'm much too early; but the fact is, my dears,
That I have to go on to the Gunnings' party—
And you know what they offer in the way of food and drink!
And I've had to miss my tea and I'm simply ravenous
And dying of thirst. What can Parkinson's do for me? Oh yes, I know this is a Parkinson party;
I recognised one of their men at the door—
An old friend of mine, in fact. But I'm forgetting!
I've got a surprise: I've brought Alex with me!
He only got back this morning from somewhere—
One of his mysterious expeditions,
And we're going to get him to tell us all about it.
But what's become of him?
[Enter ALEX.

Alex, where have you been?
ALEX
I thought I would give them a little surprise
And come in unannounced.
EDWARD
Well, Alex!
Where on earth do you turn up from?
ALEX
Where on earth? From the East. From Kinkanja—
An island that you won't have heard of
Yet. Got back this morning. I heard about your party
And, as I thought you might be leaving for the country,
I said, I must not miss the opportunity
To see EDWARD and LAVINIA.
LAVINIA
How are you, Alex?
ALEX
I did try to get you on the telephone
After lunch, but my secretary couldn't get through to you.
Never mind, I said—to myself, not to her—
Never mind: the unexpected guest
Is the one to whom they give the warmest welcome.
I know them well enough for that.
JULIA
But tell us, Alex.
What were you doing in this strange place—
What's it called?
ALEX
Kinkanja.
JULIA
What were you doing
In Kinkanja? Visiting some Sultan?
You were shooting tigers?
ALEX
There are no tigers, Julia,
In Kinkanja. And there are no sultans.
I have been staying with the Governor.
Three of us have been out on a tour of inspection

Of local conditions.
JULIA
What about? Monkey nuts?
ALEX
That was a nearer guess than you think.
No, not monkey nuts. But it had to do with monkeys—
Though whether the monkeys are the core of the problem
Or merely a symptom, I am not so sure.
At least, the monkeys have become the pretext
For general unrest amongst the natives.
EDWARD
But how do the monkeys create unrest?
ALEX
To begin with, the monkeys are very destructive
JULIA
You don't need to tell me that monkeys are destructive...
I shall never forget Mary Mallington's monkey,
The horrid little beast—stole my ticket to Mentone
And I had to travel in a very slow train
And in a couchette. She was very angry
When I told her the creature ought to be destroyed.
LAVINIA
But can't they exterminate these monkeys
If they are a pest?
ALEX
Unfortunately,
The majority of the natives are heathen:
They hold these monkeys in peculiar veneration
And do not want them killed. So they blame the Government
For the damage that the monkeys do.
EDWARD
That seems unreasonable.
ALEX
It is unreasonable,
But characteristic. And that's not the worst of it.
Some of the tribes are Christian converts,
And, naturally, take a different view.

They trap the monkeys. And they eat them.
The young monkeys are extremely palatable:
I've cooked them myself...
EDWARD
And did anybody eat them
When you cooked them?
ALEX
Oh yes, indeed.
I invented for the natives several new recipes.
But you see, what with eating the monkeys
And what with protecting their crops from the monkeys
The Christian natives prosper exceedingly:
And that creates friction between them and the others.
And that's the real problem. I hope I'm not boring you?
EDWARD
No indeed: we are anxious to learn the solution.
ALEX
I'm not sure that there is any solution.
But even this does not bring us to the heart of the matter.
There are also foreign agitators,
Stirring up trouble...
LAVINIA
Why don't you expel them?
ALEX
They are citizens of a friendly neighbouring state
Which we have just recognised. You see, Lavinia,
There are very deep waters.
EDWARD
And the agitators;
How do they agitate?
ALEX
By convincing the heathen
That the slaughter of monkeys has put a curse on them
Which can only be removed by slaughtering the Christians.
They have even been persuading some of the converts—
Who, after all, prefer not to be slaughtered—
To relapse into heathendom. So, instead of eating monkeys

They are eating Christians.
JULIA
Who have eaten monkeys.
ALEX
The native is not, I fear, very logical.
JULIA
I wondered where you were taking us, with your monkeys.
I thought I was going to dine out on those monkeys:
But one can't dine out on eating Christians—
Even among pagans!
ALEX
Not on the whole story.
EDWARD
And have any of the English residents been murdered?
ALEX
Yes, but they are not usually eaten.
When these people have done with a European
He is, as a rule, no longer fit to eat.
EDWARD
And what has your commission accomplished?
ALEX
We have just drawn up an interim report.
EDWARD
Will it be made public?
ALEX
It cannot be, at present:
There are too many international complications.
Eventually, there may be an official publication.
EDWARD
But when?
ALEX
In a year or two.
EDWARD
And meanwhile?
ALEX
Meanwhile the monkeys multiply.
LAVINIA

And the Christians?
ALEX
Ah, the Christiansl Now, I think I ought to tell you
About someone you know—or knew...
JULIA
EDWARD!
Somebody must have walked over my grave:
I'm feeling so chilly. Give me some gin.
Not a cocktail. I'm freezing—in July!
CATERER'S MAN
Mr. Quilpe!
EDWARD
Now who...
[Enter PETER.]
Why, it's Peter!
LAVINIA
Peter!
PETER
Hullo, everybody!
LAVINIA
When did you arrive?
PETER
I flew over from New York last night—
I left Los Angeles three days ago.
I saw Sheila Paisley at lunch today
And she told me you were giving a party—
She's coming on later, after the Gunnings—
So I said, I really must crash in:
It's my only chance to see EDWARD and LAVINIA.
I'm only over for a week, you see,
And I'm driving down to the country this evening,
So I knew you wouldn't mind my looking in so early.
It does seem ages since I last saw any of you!
And how are you, Alex? And dear old Julia!
LAVINIA
So you've just come from New York.
PETER
Yeah, from New York.

The Bologolomskys saw me off.
You remember Princess Bologolomsky
In the old days? We dined the other night
At the Saffron Monkey. That's the place to go now.
ALEX
How very odd. My monkeys are saffron.
PETER
Your monkeys, Alex? I always said
That Alex knew everybody. But I didn't know
That he knew any monkeys.
JULIA
But give us your news;
Give us your news of the world, Peter.
We lead such a quiet life, here in Lonodn.
PETER
You always did enjoy a leg-pull, Julia:
But you all know I'm working for Pan-Am-Eagle?
EDWARD
No. Tell us, what is Pan-Am-Eagle?
PETER
You must have been living a quiet life!
Don't you go to the movies?
LAVINIA
Occasionally.
PETER
Alex knows.
Did you see my last picture, Alex?
ALEX
I knew about it, but I didn't see it.
There is no cinema in Kinkanja.
PETER
Kinkanja? Where's that? They don't have pictures?
Pan-Am-Eagle must look into this.
Perhaps it would be a good place to make one.
—Alex knows all about Pan-Am-Eagle:
It was he who introduced me to the great Bela.
JULIA
And who is the great Bela?

PETER
Why, Bela Szogody—
He's my boss. I thought everyone knew his name.
JULIA
Is he your connection in California, Alex?
ALEX
Yes, we have sometimes obliged each other.
PETER
Well, it was Bela sent me over
Just for a week. And I have my hands full.
I'm going down tonight, to Boltwell.
JULIA
To stay with the Duke?
PETER
And do him a good turn.
We're making a film of English life
And we want to use Boltwell.
JULIA
But I understood that Boltwell
Is in a very decayed condition.
PETER
Exactly. It is. And that's why we're interested.
The most decayed noble mansion in England!
At least, of any that are still inhabited.
We've got a team of experts over
To study the decay, so as to reproduce it.
Then we build another Boltwell in California.
JULIA
But what is your position, Peter?
Have you become an expert on decaying houses?
PETER
Oh dear no! I've written the script of this film,
And Bela is very pleased with it.
He thought I should see the original Boltwell;
And besides, he thought that as I'm English
I ought to know the best way to handle a duke.
Besides that, we've got the casting director:
He's looking for some typical English faces—

Of course, only for minor parts—
And I'll help him decide what faces are typical.
JULIA
Peter, I've thought of a wonderful ideal
I've always wanted to go to California:
Couldn't you persuade your casting director
To take us all over? We're all very typical.
PETER
No, I'm afraid...
CATERER'S MAN
Sir Henry Harcourt-Reilly!
JULIA
Oh, I forgot! I'd another surprise for you.
[Enter REILLY.]
I want you to meet Sir Henry Harcourt-Reilly—
EDWARD
We're delighted to see him. But we have met before.
JULIA
Then if you know him already, you won't be afraid of him.
You know, I was afraid of him at first:
He looks so forbidding...
REILLY
My dear Julia,
You are giving me a very bad introduction—
Supposing that an introduction was necessary.
JULIA
My dear Henry, you are interrupting me.
LAVINIA
If you can interrupt Julia, Sir Henry,
You are the perfect guest we've been waiting for.
REILLY
I should not dream of trying to interrupt Julia...
JULIA
But you're both interrupting!
REILLY
Who is interrupting now?
JULIA
Now my head's fairly spinning. I must have a cocktail.

EDWARD
[To REILLY]
And will you have a cocktail?
REILLY
Might I have a glass of water?
EDWARD
Anything with it?
REILLY
Nothing, thank you.
LAVINIA
May I introduce Mr. Peter Quilpe?
Sir Henry Harcourt-Reilly. Peter's an old friend
Of my husband and myself. Oh, I forgot—
[Turning to ALEX]
I rather assumed that you knew each other—
I don't know why I should. Mr. MacColgie Gibbs.
ALEX
Indeed, yes, we have met.
REILLY
On several commissions.
JULIA
We've been having such an interesting conversation.
Peter's just over from California
Where he's something very important in films.
He's making a film of English life
And he's going to find parts for all of us. Think of it!
PETER
But, JULIA, I was just about to explain—
I'm afraid I can't find parts for anybody
In this film-it's not my business;
And that's not the way we do it.
JULIA
But, Peter;
If you're taking Boltwell to California
Why can't you take me? It's very much cheaper.
PETER
We're not taking Boltwell. We reconstruct a Boltwell.
JULIA

Well, why can't you reconstruct me? Oh, dear,
I can see you're determined not to have me:
So good-bye to my hopes of seeing California.
PETER
You know you'd never come if we invited you.
But there's someone I wanted to ask about,
Who did really want to get into films,
And I always thought she could make a success of it
If she only got the chance. It's Celia Coplestone.
She always wanted to. And now I could help her.
I've already spoken to Bela about her,
And I want to introduce her to our casting director.
I've got an idea for another film.
Can you tell me where she is? I couldn't find her
In the telephone directory.
JULIA
Not in the directory,
Or in any directory. You can tell them now, Alex.
LAVINIA
What does Julia mean?
ALEX
I was about to speak of her
When you came in, Peter. I'm afraid you can't have Celia.
PETER
Oh... Is she married?
ALEX
Not married, but dead.
LAVINIA
Celia?
ALEX
Dead.
PETER
Dead. That knocks the bottom out of it.
EDWARD
Celia dead.
JULIA
You had better tell them, Alex,
The news that you bring back from Kinkanja.

LAVINIA
Kinkanja? What was Celia doing in Kinkanja?
We heard that she had joined some nursing order...
ALEX
She had joined an order. A very austere one.
And as she already had experience of nursing...
LAVINIA
Yes, she had been a V.A.D. I remember.
ALEX
She was directed to Kinkanja,
Where there are various endemic diseases
Besides, of course, those brought by Europeans,
And where the conditions are favourable to plague.
EDWARD
Go on.
ALEX
It seems that there were three of them—
Three sisters at this station, in a Christian village;
And half the natives were dying of pestilence.
They must have been overworked for weeks.
EDWARD
And then?
ALEX
And then, the insurrection broke out
Among the heathen, of which I was telling you.
They knew of it, but would not leave the dying natives.
Eventually, two of them escaped:
One died in the jungle and the other
Will never be fit for normal life again.
But Celia Coplestone, she was taken.
When our people got there, they questioned the villagers—
Those who survived. And then they found her body,
Or at least, they found the traces of it.
EDWARD
But before that...
ALEX
It was difficult to tell.

But from what we know of local practices
It would seem that she must have been crucified
Very near an ant-hill.
LAVINIA
But Celia!... of all people...
EDWARD
And just for a handful of plague-stricken natives
Who would have died anyway.
And half the natives were dying of pestilence.
They must have been overworked for weeks.
EDWARD
And then?
ALEX
And then, the insurrection broke out
Among the heathen, of which I was telling you.
They knew of it, but would not leave the dying natives.
Eventually, two of them escaped:
One died in the jungle and the other
Will never be fit for normal life again.
But Celia Coplestone, she was taken.
When our people got there, they questioned the villagers—
Those who survived. And then they found her body,
Or at least, they found the traces of it.
EDWARD
But before that...
ALEX
It was difficult to tell.
But from what we know of local practices
It would seem that she must have been crucified
Very near an ant-hill.
LAVINIA
But Celia!... of all people...
EDWARD
And just for a handful of plague-stricken natives
Who would have died anyway.
JULIA
Two years ago.

PETER
Two years ago! I tried to forget about her,
Until I began to think myself a success
And got a little more self-confidence;
And then I thought about her again. More and more
At first I did not want to know about Celia
And so I never asked. Then I wanted to know
And did not dare to ask. It took all my courage
To ask you about her just now; but I never thought
Of anything like this. I suppose I didn't know her,
I didn't understand her. I understand nothing.
REILLY
You understand your metier, Mr. Quilpe—
Which is the most that any of us can ask for.
PETER
And what a metier! I've tried to believe in it
So that I might believe in myself.
I thought I had ideas to make a revolution
In the cinema, that no one could ignore—
And here I am, making a second-rate film!
But I thought it was going to lead to something better,
And that seemed possible, while Celia was alive.
I wanted it, believed in it, for Celia.
And, of course, I wanted to do something for Gelia—
But what mattered was, that Celia was alive.
And now it's all worthless. Celia's not alive.
LAVINIA
No, it's not all worthless, Peter. You've only just begun.
I mean, this only brings you to the point
At which you must begin. You were saying just now
That you never knew Celia. We none of us did.
What you've been living on is an image of Celia
Which you made for yourself, to meet your own needs.
Peter, please don't think I'm being unkind...
PETER
No, I don't think you're being unkind, LAVINIA:
You're telling me what I ought to know about myself.
LAVINIA

No, but what I'm saying is something I've been learning.
That's how I know that your picture of Celia
Was only a substitute for another picture—
That of yourself as a famous novelist.
It was bound to come a crash—better sooner than later!
I'm not very clever at explaining...

PETER
But I know that you're right.

LAVINIA
And perhaps what I've been saying
Will seem less unkind if I can make you understand
That in fact I've been talking about myself.

EDWARD
Lavina is right. This is where you start from.
If you find out now, Peter, things about yourself
That you don't like to face: well, just remember
That some men have to learn much worse things
About themselves and learn them later
When it's harder to recover and make a new beginning.
It's not so hard for you. You're naturally good.

PETER
I'm sorry. I don't believe I've taken in
All that you've been saying. But I'm grateful all the same.
You know, all the time that you've been talking,
One thought has been going round and round in my head—
That I've only been interested in myself:
And that isn't good enough for Celia.

JULIA
You must have learned how to look at people, Peter,
When you look at them with an eye for the films:
That is, when you're not concerned with yourself
But just being an eye. You will come to think of Celia
Like that, some day. And then you'll understand her
And be reconciled and be happy in the thought of her.
And now I'm going to change the subject.
Celia chose a road that led her to Kinkanja;
You have chosen one that leads you to Boltwell—

And you've got to go there.
PETER
Oh. I'm glad you reminded me.
The car will be waiting. I mustn't keep them.
Yes, I'm off to Boltwell—with a team of experts.
So now I'll be going.
EDWARD
Shall we see you again, Peter,
Before you leave England?
LAVINIA
Do try to come to see us.
You know, I think it would do us all good—
You and me and EDWARD... to talk about Celia.
PETER
Thanks very much. But not this time—
I simply shan't be able to.
EDWARD
But on your next visit?
PETER
The next time I come to England, I promise you.
I really do want to see you both, very much.
Good-bye, Julia. Good-bye, Alex. Good-bye, Sir Henry.
[Exit.]
LAVINIA
Sir Henry, there is something I want to say to you
Now that Peter's left us.
REILLY
That young man
Is very intelligent. He should go far—
Along his own lines.
ALEX
Yes, I was well advised
To put him in the hands of Bela Szogody.
LAVINIA
It came to me, when Alex told about Celia
And I looked at your face. It seemed to convey to me
That the way in which she died was not important
Or the fact that she died because she would not leave

A few dying natives.
REILLY
Who knows, Mrs. Chamberlayne,
The difference that made to the natives who were dying
Or the state of mind in which they died?
LAVINIA
I'm willing to grant that. What struck me, though,
Was that your face showed no surprise or horror
At the way in which she died. I don't know if you knew her.
I suspect you did. In any case you know about her.
Yet I thought your expression was one of... satisfaction!
Interest, Yes, but not in the details.
ALEX
There's one detail which is rather interesting
And rather touching, too. We found that the natives,
After we'd re-occupied the village
Had erected a sort of shrine for Celia
Where they brought offerings of fruit and flowers,
Fowls and even sucking pigs.
They seemed to think that by propitiating Celia
They might insure themselves against further misfortune.
We left that problem for the Bishop to wrestle with.
REILLY
Yes, the Bishop's problem is certainly a detail.
—Mrs. Chamberlayne, I must be very transparent
Or else you are very perceptive.
JULIA
Oh, Henry!
LAVINIA is much more observant than you think.
I believe, Henry, if I may put it vulgarly,
That Lavinia has forced you to a show-down.
REILLY
You state the position correctly, Julia.
Do you mind if I quote poetry, Mrs. Chamberlayne?
LAVINIA
Oh no, I should love to hear you speaking poetry...
JULIA

She has made a point, Henry.
LAVINIA
... if it answers my question.
REILLY
Ere Babylon was dust
The magus Zoroaster, my dead child,
Met his own image walking in the garden.
That apparition, sole of men, he saw.
For know there are two worlds of life and death:
One that which thou beholdest; but the other
Is underneath the grave, where do inhabit
The shadows of all forms that think and live
Till death unite them and they part no more.
—When I first met Miss Coplestone, in this room,
I saw the image, standing behind her chair,
Of a Celia Coplestone whose face showed the
 astonishment
Of the first five minutes after a violent death.
If this strains your credulity, Mrs. Chamberlayne,
I ask you only to entertain the suggestion
That a sudden intuition, in certain minds,
May tend to express itself at once in a picture.
That happens to me, sometimes. So it was obvious
That here was a woman under sentence of death.
That was her destiny. The only question
Then was, what sort of death? I could not know;
Because it was for her to choose the way of life
To lead to death and, without knowing the end
Yet choose the form of death. We know the death she
chose. I did not know that she would die in this way,
She did not know. So all that I could do
Was to direct her in the way of preparation.
That way, which she accepted, led to this death.
And if that is not a happy death, what death is happy?
EDWARD
Do you mean that having chosen this form of death
She did not suffer as ordinary people suffer?
REILLY

Not at all what I mean. Rather the contrary.
I'd say that she suffered all that we should suffer
In fear and pain and loathing—all these together—
And reluctance of the body to become a thing.
I'd say she suffered more, because more conscious
Than the rest of us. She paid the highest price
In suffering. That is part of the design.

LAVINIA

Perhaps she had been through greater agony beforehand.
I mean—I know nothing of her last two years.

REILLY

That shows some insight on your part, Mrs. Chamberlayne;
But such experience can only be hinted at
In myths and images. To speak about it
We talk of darkness, labyrinths, Minotaur terrors.
But that world does not take the place of this one.
Do you imagine that the Saint in the desert
With spiritual evil always at his shoulder
Suffered any less from hunger, damp, exposure,
Bowel trouble and the fear of lions,
Cold of the night and heat of the day, than we should?

EDWARD

Sir Henry, you only make the horrible more horrible;
Yet I think I begin to see your point of view.
But if this was right—if this was right for Celia—
There must be something else that is terribly wrong,
And the rest of us are somehow involved in the wrong.
I should only speak for myself. I'm sure that I am.

REILLY

Let me free your mind from one impediment:
You must try to detach yourself from what you still feel
As your responsibility.

EDWARD

I cannot help the feeling
That, in some way, my responsibility
Is greater than that of a band of half-crazed savages.

LAVINIA

Oh, Edward, I knew! I knew what you were thinking!
Doesn't it help you, that I feel guilty too?

REILLY

If we all were judged according to the consequences
Of all our words and deeds, beyond the intention
And beyond our limited understanding
Of ourselves and others, we should all be condemned.
Mrs. Chamberlayne, I often have to make a decision
Which may mean restoration or ruin to a patient—
And sometimes I have made the wrong decision.
As for Miss Coplestone, because you think her death was waste
You blame yourselves and because you blame yourselves
You think her life was wasted. It was triumphant.
But I am no more responsible for the triumph—
And just as responsible for her death as you are.

LAVINIA

Yet I know I shall go on blaming myself
For being so unkind to her... so spiteful.
I shall go on seeing her at the moment
When she said good-bye to us, two years ago.

EDWARD

Your responsibility is nothing to mine, Lavinia.

LAVINIA

I'm not sure about that. If I had understood you
Then I might not have misunderstood Celia.

REILLY

You will have to live with these memories and make them
Into something new. Only by acceptance
Of the past will you alter its meaning.

JULIA

Henry, I think it is time that I said something:
So please don't interrupt.

REILLY

I won't interrupt you.

JULIA

Everyone makes a choice, of one kind or another,

And then must take the consequences. Celia chose
A way of which the consequence was crucifixion;
Peter Quilpe chose a way that takes him to Boltwell;
And now the consequence of the Chamberlaynes' choice
Is a cocktail party. They must be ready for it.
Their guests may be arriving at any moment.
[ALEXleaves the room.]
REILLY
Julia, you are right. It is also right
That the Chamberlaynes should now be giving a party.
LAVINIA
And I have been thinking, for these last five minutes,
How I could face my guests. I wish it was over.
I mean... I am glad you came... I am glad Alex told us...
And Peter had to know...
EDWARD
Now I think I understand...
LAVINIA
Then I hope you will explain it to me!
EDWARD
Oh, it isn't much
That I understand yet! But Sir Henry has been saying,
I think, that every moment is a fresh beginning;
And Julia, that life is only keeping on;
And somehow, the two ideas seem to fit together.
LAVINIA
But all the same... I don't want to see these people.
REILLY
It is your appointed burden. And as for the party,
I am sure it will be a success.
[Re-enter ALEX.]
JULIA
And I think, Henry,
That we should leave before the party begins.
They will get on better without us. You too, Alex.
ALEX
Just a moment, Julia. There is one brief ceremony
Before we go...

[Enter CATERER'S MAN with a tray and five glasses.] I took the liberty Of bringing a bottle of my own champagne—
I thought it should be mine, for this occasion—
And giving instructions at the door as I came in.
I wish to propose a toast.
[They all rise.]
EDWARD
[Absently]
To the Guardians.
ALEX
>To one particular Guardian, whom you have forgotten.
I give you—Lavinia's Aunt!
ALL
Lavinia's Aunt!
[They drink and the CATERER'S MAN takes out the tray.]
JULIA
Now, Henry. Now, Alex.
JULIA, REILLYand ALEX
We're going to the Gunnings'.
[Exeunt JULIA, REILLYand ALEX.]
LAVINIA
Edward, how am I looking?
EDWARD
Very well.
I might almost say, your best. But you always look your best.
LAVINIA
Oh, Edward, that spoils it. No woman can believe
That she always looks her best. You're rather transparent,
You know, when you're trying to cheer me up.
To say I always look my best can only mean the worst.
EDWARD
I never shall learn how to pay a compliment.
LAVINIA
What you should have done was to admire my dress.
EDWARD

But I've already told you how much I like it.
LAVINIA
But so much has happened since then. And besides,
One sometimes likes to hear the same compliment twice.
EDWARD
And now for the party.
LAVINIA
Now for the party.
EDWARD
It will soon be over.
LAVINIA
I wish it would begin.
EDWARD
There's the doorbell.
LAVINIA
Oh, I'm glad. It's begun.
CURTAIN

Chapter 8

Study Questions

Q. Discuss the Images of Defective Senses in T.S. Eliot's The Cocktail Party.

Or

Q. *Do you agree that* the muddle of reality and illusion confounds the main characters and their attempts to escape drive the plot. Comment

"You and I don't know the process by which the human is Transhumanized: what do we know Of the kind of suffering they must undergo On the way of illumination?"

"The way of illumination"—a path leads to light, out of darkness. T.S. Eliot's play *The Cocktail Party*, among all its banal or peculiar occurrences, is laced with images of defective senses and perception, particularly of sight. Within five lines of the play's beginning we are confronted with defective senses: "You haven't been listening, " complains Alex to the confused Julia when she asks about the tigers in his story. Julia exhibits another confused faculty, that of taste: at first she claims "What's that? Potato crisps? No, I simply can't endure them, ", but later says "The potato crisps were really excellent". Soon she adds sight to the list: "I must have left my glasses here, /And I simply can't see a thing without them..../I'm afraid I don't remember the colour, /But I'd know them, because one lens is missing". Even with her glasses, Julia's sight will be impaired. And the glasses turn out to have been in her handbag all along. Yet Julia's glasses, though often lost, through their very existence allow her to see better. The spectacles may indeed be a symbol for the play's theme of blindness, but for Julia they provide an excuse to "see" more—to spy on her companions, as she admits when she says "Left anything? Oh, you mean my spectacles./No, they're here. Besides, they're no use to me./I'm not coming back again this evening".

The other characters of Eliot's play all exhibit their own failings of perception. Alex finds no mangoes or curry powder in Edward's kitchen, only eggs—no exotic or intense tastes, only the bland and prosaic. Alex says of his egg concoction that "of all my triumphs/This is the greatest", but Julia later dismisses it with the warning that "anything that Alex makes is absolutely deadly". His tastes, presumably, do not agree with the majority of his friends—they are "defective."

Julia, in turn, opens a champagne bottle (the stage directions specifically mention "a popping noise... heard from the kitchen") and then claims "I found some champagne—/ Only a half bottle, to be sure, /And of course it isn't chilled". Neither Edward nor Celia take any notice of the noise or of Julia's actions: they do not hear or connect reality with her lie. Edward's hearing also fails when he forgets Julia is waiting on the telephone and three times asks his "Unidentified Guest" if he wants whiskey, only to be told to get gin. And Harcourt-Reilly himself, of course, belts out his drinking song about badly-sighted "One-Eyed Riley".

Edward and Lavinia's first meeting in the play is full of mis-sensings. Edward does at last remember Harcourt-Reilly's gin and water, only to be rebuffed. Lavinia refuses to listen to Celia, clouding the issue with diplomatic niceties, until Celia corrals her with "Don't put me off". And Edward and Lavinia's opening spat concerns their conflicting images of each other, mis-hearings and mis-seeings. Edward, at least, has learned from his talk with Celia about "seeing oneself through the eyes of other people". And he no longer uses "the gramaphone... only your escape/From talking to [Lavinia] when we had to be alone"—their fight is out in the open, with no distracting music to prevent listening to each other.

The cinema is a major image in *The Cocktail Party*, both because of the leisurely, intellectual life of the characters and because of Peter and Celia's mutual interest in it. And what is the cinema but falseness caused by inadequate sight? Our eyes are not quick enough to detect the individual frames of film, so a series of still images create the illusion of motion. That illusion is exactly what afflicts the characters of Eliot's play: they live static, unfulfilled lives, though in seeing each other only infrequently, after many "frames, " they seem to be out doing new and remarkable things. Their life is a facade, like the reconstructed Boltwell Castle that Peter plans to build in California—a creation without substance. "Hell is oneself, /Hell is alone, the other figures in it/Merely projections", shadow-puppets of idealized personality. Indeed, in Peter's world, the absent Celia "has simply faded—into some other picture—/ Like a film effect".

Sir Henry Harcourt-Reilly's object is to remove these illusions and repair these faulty senses. Edward has long since stopped seeing his wife as she is, for within a day after her departure, he says, "I no longer remember what my wife is like./I am not quite sure that I could describe her/If I had to ask the police to search for her./I'm sure I don't know what she was wearing/When I saw her last.... And what is the use of all your analysis/If I am to remain always lost in the dark?". And Harcourt-Reilly's rhetoric only reminds Edward that he has "often used these terms in examining witnesses"—but "examining" all too easily takes on a non-legal meaning with a doctor in attendance and a maelstrom of other visual terms swirling about the drama. Edward rejects Harcourt-Reilly's probes, any speculation about Lavinia, or even about Reilly's own identity: metaphorically, he closes his eyes in the hope that no-one else will see him. But Reilly persists in "finding out/What you really are. What you really feel.".

And Reilly's efforts succeed. His initial setup, with his "usual foresight", separates his three patients (Edward, Lavinia and Celia) until he can reveal the feuding husband and wife to each other. Reilly sees and senses, their genuine problems instead of the self-involved twaddle most of his patients believe they see: Edward complains "I would have thought a doctor could see for himself.... Two people advised me recently.... If they saw it/I should have thought that a doctor could see it." and Reilly's calm ripostes convince us that he does see and much more clearly than poor Edward. Edward complains "I wonder/If you have understood a word of what I have been saying" but Reilly learns by closely observing and listening, especially by "taking note of what you do not say"—a deeper vision. Edward never noticed his wife's "breakdown"—"You wouldn't notice anything. You never noticed me" she retorts—for he has only andstrong;the shadow of desires of desires". Like one of Plato's prisoners before the cave, he sees only vague flickerings, shadows and illusions, but never the real substance—only the fakery of Peter's cinema effects.

Edward responds to treatment: his sense and senses, improve. Harcourt-Reilly worries that Edward and Lavinia will end up as nothing but "mirror to mirror, reflecting vanity, " but Julia assures him "I shall keep an eye on them". And in Act III, two years later, their "vision" seems much improved. Lavinia, as we might expect, is meticulous in arranging the house for the upcoming party (she "looks about the room critically and moves a bowl of flowers"). But she and Edward also take the time to ask after each other, to ensure that the other is neither "worrying" nor "tired" and work together to straighten a picture on the wall. Edward even compliments Lavinia's dress, a triumph of vision and perception! And the two of them help to reconcile Peter to Celia's death, pointing out to the young cinematographer that "what you've been living on is an image of Celia".

Indeed, Celia best represents Eliot's ideas of human blindness. Even by Act I, Scene 2, we see her vision clarify, when she sees Edward as a dessicated mummy, hears him as a lonely droning insect—"I see another person, /I see you as a person whom I never saw before./The man I saw before, he was only a projection... something that I desperately wanted to exist.". Celia, troubled, visits Reilly and claims "I don't hear any voices, I have no delusions—/Except that the world I live in seems all a delusion!". She has seen through the senseless and sense-less facade of the world, for she sees that people "make noises and think they are talking to each other;/They make faces and think they understand each other, /And I'm sure that they don't.". Reilly warns Celia that those who are "cured" back into innocent obliviousness "may remember the vision they have had"—but is "vision" here an apparition or a way of seeing? Do those who retreat from Celia's discovery abandon a dream, or an entire sense? Reilly claims the retreat to normal life "I could describe in familiar terms/Because you have seen it, as we all have seen it", but, if Celia presses on, "the destination cannot be described.... You will journey blind"—our normal senses fail us, for we need some higher perception. An illusion or mirage is a failure of vision, so what of vision and mortal existence, whose illusion Celia has pierced? Such higher senses, perhaps, belong to the Guardians of Eliot's half-hidden mythos. True sight may be granted only through travel "on the way of illumination".

Q. Present your views on T.S. Eliot as a Pioneer of Modernism.

A poet is not one who can compose poetry—called by some the highest and noblest art form—but one who is so exalted that he can passionately feel what can be beautifully expressed as a poem. Anyone who seeks can find moments of beauty, love, harmony and meaning through poetry on dull days. And good poetry never fails.

Poetry, said Thomas Stearns Eliot, "may make us from time to time a little more aware of the deeper, unnamed feelings which form the substratum of our being, to which we rarely penetrate; for our lives are mostly constant evasions of ourselves and an evasion of the visible world."

Eliot (1888-1965), better known as T.S. Eliot, was an American-English poet, playwright, editor, literary critic and a leader of the modernist movement in literature. He was born in St. Louis, Missouri, the seventh and youngest child of a prominent family of New England origin. His family tree included the Reverend William Greenleaf Eliot, founder of Washington University in St. Louis and on his mother's side, Isaac Stearns, one of the original settlers of the Massachusetts Bay Colony. Eliot's father was an affluent industrialist and his mother was a writer, who produced among other works, the biography of William Greenleaf Eliot.

T.S. Eliot was privileged to receive the extensive education available in his time due to a very supportive family. He almost had no pressure from his father to be "practical" or to go into business. That helped him climb the academic ladder quickly. From Smith Academy in St. Louis he went to Milton, in Massachusetts; from Milton, he entered Harvard in 1906; he received a B.A. in 1909, after three instead of the usual four years. In the academic year 1909-10 he also was an assistant in philosophy at Harvard.

A few men who influenced this young man at Harvard included George Santayana, the philosopher and poet and the critic Irving Babbitt. Eliot derived an anti-Romantic attitude from Babbitt that was augmented by his later reading of British philosophers F.H. Bradley and T.E. Hulme. The influence lasted through his life.

Eliot was an accomplished sailor because of his keen interest in crabs from an early age. He traded the Mississippi River in the warm months for the rocky shoals of Cape Ann. With an early exposure to adventure he developed an alienation from both of the regions he once called home. He often mentioned he felt like a New Englander in the Southwest and a Southwesterner in New England. Despite his sense of detachments to both the regions, Eliot was surprisingly at social ease when he began his studies at Harvard in the fall of 1906.

Among many other influences, there was a book Eliot found in the Harvard Union library in 1908, which changed his life. Arthur Symons's The Symbolist Movement in Literature introduced him to the poetry of Jules Laforgue and Laforgue's combination of ironic elegance and psychological nuance gave his yet immature literary efforts a voice. By 1909-1910, however, he was a confirmed poet by any standard. He joined the board and as a secretary of Harvard's literary magazine, the Advocate and developed a lifelong friendship with Conrad Aiken.

In 1910 and 1911 Eliot established himself as a poet by copying into a leather notebook the poems: "The Love Song of J. Alfred Prufrock, " "Portrait of a Lady, " "La Figlia Che

Piange, " "Preludes, " and "Rhapsody on a Windy Night." Developing a style of his own and dexterously combining some of the boldness of Robert Browning's monologues with the natural elegance of symbolist verse, he mixed Laforgue's poetry of alienation with the moral earnestness of what he once called "Boston doubt." These poems venture into the subtleties of the unconscious with a scathing wit. Their effect was both unique and convincing and their sense of assurance surprised his contemporaries who were the first ones to read them in manuscript.

Eliot's stay in France in 1910-11 while attending Henri Bergson's lectures in philosophy at the Sorbonne and reading poetry with Alain-Fournier also helped him develop a style. His residence in Paris at 151 bis rue St. Jacques, close to the Sorbonne, was instrumental in his close friendship with a fellow lodger, Jean Verdenal, a medical student who later died in the battle of the Dardenelles and to whom Eliot dedicated "The Love Song of J. Alfred Prufrock."

With Verdenal, Eliot entered the intellectual life of France. That provided him ample chances to be around the figures of Emile Durkheim, Paul Janet, Remy de Gourmont, Pablo Picasso and Henri Bergson. He attended Bergson's lectures at the College de France and was briefly taken by Bergson's philosophical interest in the progressive evolution of consciousness. It did not stop the young poet gravitating toward the politically conservative, neoclassical and Catholic writing of Charles Maurras. These conflicting opposite views helped his enthusiasms work toward a professional interest in philosophy and propelling him back to a doctoral program at Harvard the next year.

Until the fall of 1911, Eliot remained as preoccupied with ideas as with literature. He was fortunate to be a student in the so-called golden age of Harvard philosophy. His association with William James, the visiting Bertrand Russell and Josiah Royce influenced him a great deal. Under Royce's instruction, Eliot wrote a dissertation on Bergson's neoidealist critic F. H. Bradley and brought out a searching philosophical critique of the psychology of consciousness. He also started taking interest in anthropology and religion and attended almost as many courses in Sanskrit and Hindu thought as he did in philosophy. By 1914, while leaving on a traveling fellowship to Europe, he assured a number of Harvard's philosophers that he would be coming back as a potential colleague.

Meanwhile Eliot still was working on his style, studied poetry of Dante, English writers John Webster and John Donne and French Symbolist Jules Laforgue, which further helped him in finding his own unique style. In 1913 he read Bradley's Appearance and Reality, which influenced him so much that he decided to study in the fall at Merton College, Oxford, with Harold Joachim, Bradley's colleague and successor.

After spending beginning of summer of 1914 at a seminar in Marburg, Germany, Eliot had to cut short his plans due to looming World War I clouds. He returned to London with Aiken in the late summer and established his residence in England by fall of 1914. Aiken showed Eliot's manuscript poems to Ezra Pound. Pound was not easily impressed, but nonetheless agreed to meet Eliot. Pound wrote to Harriet Monroe at Poetry magazine that Eliot had "actually trained himself and modernized himself on his own." That was the beginning of a collaboration that would change Anglo-American poetry, but that was after Eliot had established deep English roots. It was a mutually benefited association, while Eliot began to reform poetic diction with Pound; Pound helped him in getting his early poems into print. Pound had privately published a small book, A Lume Spento, as early as 1908, that did do well and "Prufrock" turned out to be the first poem by either of these literary revolutionaries to go beyond any tests to achieve perfection. "The Love Song of J. Alfred Prufrock" was not only his first important publication, but the first masterpiece of "modernism" in English, in which, he examines, through the introspections of the narrator, the emptiness and soulless quality of the bleak social world surrounding him.

Let us go then, you and I,
When the evening is spread out against the sky
Like a patient etherized upon a table....

Publication of Prufrock and Other Observations in 1917 by the Egoist, with the silent financial support of Ezra and Dorothy Pound, brought Eliot success and fame and it became a turning point in his literary career as it marked the maturity of the twentieth-century poetic revolution.

Eliot then taught French and Latin at the Highgate School. Soon after he had a brief stint as a bank clerk in Lloyds Bank Ltd., which gave him the security he needed to turn back to poetry. Meanwhile, he continued to write reviews and essays in both literary criticism and technical philosophy.

It was almost when serious poetry was about to be overshadowed by fiction that T. S. Eliot again provided the stark salvation of The Waste Land (1922), his most critically acclaimed work which describes the journey of the human soul searching for redemption. The publication of his poem The Waste Land won Eliot an international reputation and until today it remains his most famous and also most controversial one. Written when he was thirty-four, the long blank verse poem speaks about a cultural and spiritual crisis, which is resonated in its use of fragmentation and discontinuity. Divided into five sections, it is in a series of vignettes, loosely linked by the legend of the search for the Grail, a dense chorus of voices and historical quotations that dissolve one into another. The poem expresses the disenchantment, disillusionment and disgust of the period after World War I. Eliot eruditely combines slang with scholarly language. Grail story, the legend of the Fisher King, Sir James George Frazer's Golden Bough and Dante's Commedia were the main source of material for this great work. The poem's original manuscript of about 800 lines was cut down to 433 at the suggestion of Ezra Pound. The Waste Land is not Eliot's greatest poem, though it is his most famous.

April is the cruelest month, breeding
Lilacs out of the dead land, mixing
Memory and desire, stirring
Dull roots with spring rain.

Eliot's criticism and poetry are often interwoven. The great essay on Dante appeared two years after Eliot was confirmed in the Church of England (1927); in that year he also became a British subject, after spending more than a decade in UK.

Eliot's masterpiece is The Four Quartets, which won him the Nobel Prize for Literature in 1948. It was issued as a book in 1943, though each "quartet" is a complete poem. The first of the quartets, "Burnt Norton, " had appeared in the Collected Poems of 1936. It is a witty meditation on the nature of time and its relation to eternity. This work made a deep impression on his readers and even those who were unable to accept the poems' Christian beliefs recognized the intellectual integrity with which Eliot pursued his high theme, the originality of the form and the technical mastery of his verse.

We shall not cease from exploration
And the end of all our exploring
Will be to arrive where we started

And know the place for the first time. ("Little Gidding, " the last of his Four Quartets) Eliot later tried his hand at plays, beginning with Sweeney Agonistes (published 1926; first performed in 1934) and ending with The Elder Statesman (first performed 1958; published 1959). Most of his plays, with the exception of Murder in the Cathedral (published and performed 1935), are no comparison to the lyric and meditative poetry. Eliot's argument was that even secular drama attracts people who instinctively seek a religion. He even put drama above all other forms of poetry. After World War II, Eliot returned to writing comedies with The Cocktail Party in 1949, The Confidential Clerk in 1953 and The Elder Statesman in 1958. Writing in a blank verse of his own invention, in which the metrical effect is not deviated from the sense his plays, brought "poetic drama" back to the popular stage.

Eliot always kept his private life rigorously in the background. In early spring of 1915, Eliot's old Milton Academy and Harvard friend Scofield Thayer, later editor of the Dial and then also at Oxford, introduced Eliot to Vivien Haigh-Wood, a dancer and a friend of Thayer's sister. Eliot was drawn immediately to Vivien's openness. He gave up his habitual tentativeness with women and married Vivien in June 1915 at the Hampstead Registry Office. His parents were not happy when they learnt about Vivien's history of emotional and physical problems. The marriage nearly caused a family break, but with that Eliot began his English life. Vivien was not wiling to cross the Atlantic in wartime and that forced Eliot to take his place in literary London. They were to have no children. After 1933, they lived apart and Vivien died in 1947.

In January 1957 he married his secretary, Valerie Fletcher. Eliot and his wife at first turned to Bertrand Russell, who shared with them both his London flat and his considerable social resources. Russell and Vivien, however, became briefly involved and the arrangement soured.

Eliot was an incurable joker and among his many pranks was to seat visiting authors in chairs with whoopee cushions and offers them exploding cigars. To the poet's pleasure, the American comedian Groucho Marx was his great fan. In 1964 he wrote to Groucho: "The picture of you in the newspaper saying that, amongst other reasons, you have come to London to see me has greatly enchanted my credit line in the neighborhood and particularly with the greengrocer across the street." Old Possum's Book of Practical Cats (1939), Eliot's classical book of verse for children, has achieved a considerable world success in the musical adaptation Cats. His most influential exercise in social criticism was Notes toward a Definition of Culture (1948).

In the 60 years from 1905 to his death, Eliot published some 600 articles and reviews. Eliot's principal purpose in his literary-critical essays was "the elucidation of works of art and the correction of taste."

Eliot exercised a strong influence on Anglo-American culture from the 1920s until late in the century. His experiments in diction, style and versification revitalized English poetry and in a series of critical essays he shattered old orthodoxies and erected new ones. His fame has also been shadowed by accusations of racism, misogynism, fascism, emotional coldness and anti-Semitism, which has made him unpleasant for many readers. However, the publication of The Four Quartets (1943) silenced his critics, which led to his recognition as the greatest living English poet and man of letters and in 1948 he was awarded both the Order of Merit and the Nobel Prize for Literature.

Among his many careers his employment with the publishing house of Faber and Faber was the longest one. He was a "director, " or working editor, of the publishing firm of Faber and Faber, Ltd. from the early 1920s until his death and as such was a liberal and generous patron of young poets.

If one categorized Eliot's careers, he would probably be regarded as editor, dramatist, literary critic and philosophical poet. He would also be remembered as the most erudite poet of his time in the English language. His undergraduate poems were "literary" and conventional. In an attempt to keep poetry alive he gave the world extraordinary works of literature. With his intense personal experiences, Eliot tried to express general truths. His vast knowledge of world literature, especially those in ancient Sanskrit, was instrumental in providing him with universal thought process. His poetry broke all barriers and touched its readers everywhere so profoundly.

What helped Eliot in becoming a celebrated writer and poet is rather difficult to say precisely, although there are certain clear patterns. As with most writers, Eliot had a complex personality, which was often misunderstood by his contemporaries. One of the reasons was his very perplexed nature and he often took his life too seriously.

As J. Alfred Prufrock explains, "I have measured out my life with coffee spoons."He once spoke of a lifetime burning in every moment. He had the mind to conceive a perfect life and he also had the honesty to admit that he could not meet it. Often torn between the life of a saint and a sinner, Eliot will always remain the greatest poet of the twentieth century. Eliot died in London on January 4, 1965 and, according to his own instructions, his ashes were interred in the church of St. Michael's in East Coker. A commemorative plaque on the church wall bears his chosen epitaph—lines chosen from Four Quartets: "In my beginning is my end. In my end is my beginning."

Q. What do you Understand by the Term Blank Verse?

Or

Q. Discuss Blank Verse with Reference to Eliot's The Cocktail Party.

Blank Verse is any verse comprised of unrhymed lines all in the same meter, usually *iambic pentameter.* It was developed in Italy and became widely used during the Renaissance because it resembled classical, unrhymed poetry. Marlowe's "mighty line, " which demonstrated blank verse's range and flexibility, made blank verse the standard for many English writers, including both Shakespeare and Milton and it remained a very practiced form up until the twentieth century when Modernism rebelled and openly experimented with the tradition. Regardless, blank verse was embraced by Yeats, Pound, Frost and Stevens who skillfully brought the tradition through this century. While it may not be as common as open form, it retains an important role in the world of poetry.

Blank verse can be composed in any meter and with any amount of feet per line, though the iamb is generally the predominant foot. Along with the iamb are 3 other standard feet and a number of variations that can be employed in a blank verse poem. It is difficult—almost impossible—to write a blank verse poem consisting of all iambs and other types of feet get used more often than one may think. These are:

- Lamb-two syllables, unstressed-stressed, as in "today".
- Trochee-two syllables, stressed-unstressed, as in "standard".
- Anapest-three syllables, unstressed-unstressed-stressed, as in "disengage"
- Dactyl-three syllables, stressed-unstressed-unstressed, as in "probably".

Variations include:

- Headless Iamb or Tailess Trochee-one stressed syllable. Labeling the foot depends on where it is located in the line.
- Spondee-two stressed syllables, as in "hot dog"
- Amphibrach-three syllables, unstressed-stressed-unstressed, as in "forgetful"
- Double Iamb-four sylalbles, unstressed-unstressed-

stressed-stressed, as in "will you eat it?" A double iamb is counted as two feet.

Blank verse can be written with any combination of the above feet. The name of the dominant foot coupled with the number of feet in the line provide the name of a poem's meter. For example, the dominant foot in Robert Frost's "Mending Wall" is the iamb and there are five feet per line. Thus, the poem is written in iambic pentameter. Notice, however, that not each foot is an iamb, but Frost mixes up the feet, as in the first few lines of the poem.

Something there is that doesn't love a wall,
That sends the frozen-ground-swell under it,
And spills the upper boulders in the sun

When you read the words, the natural rhythm is not de-dum, de-dum, de-dum—it is not strictly iambic. The first line, for example, scans as a trochee and four iambs. *Scansion,* by the way is how poets demonstrate the meter of a poem using accents to show the stressed syllables. With scanning, one can tell if a poem is metered or not and, if so, what kind of meter is present, as in "Mending Wall:"

Sómething there ís that dóesn't lóve a wáll.

Of course, how a person scans a single line or an entire poem depends on the reader's natural rhythms and inclinations and, while there may be better ways to scan a poem, there is not always a single correct scan. In the first line of "Mending Wall", for instance, the first iamb *could* be read as a trochee, with the stress falling on "there" instead of "is."

How to and Examples

One way to write in blank verse is to take an old poem and turn the existing lines into ten-syllable lines. Then, modify the diction and the syntax (be careful not Yoda always try to sound) in such a way that the iamb becomes the predominant foot. Remember, the poem should be read naturally without forcing the meter onto the rhythm. Each line does not need to read "de-dum, de-dum, de-dum, de-dum, de-dum" but, rather, that that meter can be over-imposed onto the natural rhythm of the line. As well, the poem should be read in sentences, not by line break. Line breaks should be determined by the meter. Allow the meter of the poem to drive you as you write it. Let it decide where the line length and line breaks should be without imposing your own natural habits. This can be very difficult to do if you have never tried writing blank verse before and I have found the above method does not work best for me. A second way is to simply write in pentameter by using roughly ten syllable lines, then, going back and changing syntax and diction to emphasize the iamb. With a little practice the meter will soon be controlling the way the line moves and sounds and it will modify your natural rhytms to adhere with the pattern. What does blank verse do to the line? It lengthens it, of course, but the meter also pushes the line into the next line and so on, giving blank verse a strong, narrative pull. I find blank verse makes my own poems long winded, the meter drives me to keep writing and I feel a narrative voice emerging that I don't feel in a shorter-lined poem. Blank verse can be very helpful in that way, particularly if you feel you don't know what to write. The meter and long line demand words to fulfill its requirements, which makes blank verse a decent exercise for escaping writer's block.Examples of blank verse include: "Mending Wall"-Robert Frost (almost anything by Frost will be a solid example)

Q. A poet's choice of a prosody obviously depends on what his language and tradition afford; these are primary considerations. Do you find these in Eliot.?

The anonymous author of the Old English poem *Deor* used the conventional four-stress metric available to him; but he punctuated groups of lines with a refrain: Þaes ofereode: Þisses swa maeg! (that passed away: this also may!)

The refrain adds something to the prosodic conventions of regulated stress, alliteration and medial pause: a sense of a smaller and sharper rhythmic unit within the larger rhythms of the given metre. While the poet accepts from history his language and from poetic convention the structure of his metre, he shapes his own style through individual modifications of the carrying rhythms. When critics speak of a poet's "voice, " his personal tone, they are also speaking of his prosodic style.

Prosodic style must be achieved through a sense of tension; it is no accident that the great masters of poetic rhythm work against the discipline of a given metrical form. In his sonnets, Shakespeare may proceed in solemn iambic regularity, creating an effect of measured progression through time and its legacy of suffering and despair:

No longer mourn for me when I am dead
Than you shall hear the surly sullen bell
Give warning to the world that I am fled....
"Sonnet 71"

Or he may wrench the metre and allow the reader to feel the sudden violence of his feelings, the power of a conviction raised to a command:

The first two feet of the first line are trochaic reversals; the last two feet comprise a characteristic pyrrhic-spondaic formation. A trochaic substitution is quite normal in the first foot of an iambic pentameter line; a trochaic substitution in the second foot, however, creates a marked disturbance in the rhythm. There is only one "normal" iambic foot in the first line; this line runs over (or is enjambed) to the second line with its three consecutive iambic feet followed by a strong caesura and reversed fourth foot. These lines are, in Gerard Manley Hopkins' terms, metrically "counter-pointed"; trochees, spondees and pyrrhics are heard against a ground rhythm of regular iambics. Without the ground rhythm, Shakespeare's expressive departures would not be possible.

A poet's prosodic style may show all of the earmarks of revolt against prevailing metrical practice. Whitman's celebrated "free verse" marks a dramatic break with the syllable-stress tradition; he normally does not count syllables, stresses, or feet in his long sweeping lines. Much of his prosody is rhetorical; that is, Whitman urges his language into rhythm by such means as anaphora (*i.e.*, repetition at the beginning of successive verses) and the repetition of syntactical units. He derives many of his techniques from the example of biblical verses, with their line of various types of parallelism. But he often moves toward traditional rhythms; lines fall into conventional parameters:

O past! O happy life! O songs of joy!
"Out of the Cradle Endlessly Rocking" (1859)
Or they fall more often into disyllabic hexameters:
Borne through the smoke of the battles and pierc'd with missiles I saw them....
"When Lilacs Last in the Dooryard Bloom'd" (1865–66)

Despite the frequent appearance of regular metrical sequences, Whitman's lines cannot be scanned by the usual graphic method of marking syllables and feet; his prosody, however, is fully available to analysis. The shape on the page of the lines below (they comprise a single strophe or verse unit) should be noted, specifically the gradual elongation and sudden diminution of line length. Equally noteworthy are the repetition of the key word *carols*, the alliteration of the *s* sounds and the use of words in falling (trochaic) rhythm, "lagging," "yellow," "waning":

Shake out carols!
Solitary here, the night's carols!
Carols of lonesome love! death's carols!
Carols under that lagging, yellow, waning moon!
O under that moon where she droops almost down into the sea!
O reckless despairing carols.
"Out of the Cradle"

No regular metre moves these lines; but a clearly articulated rhythm—produced by shape, thematic repetitions, sound effects and patterns of stress and pause—defines a prosody.

Whitman's prosody marks a clear break with previous metrical practices. Often a new prosody modifies an existing metrical form or revives an obsolete one. In "Gerontion" (1920), T.S. Eliot adjusted the blank-verse line to the emotionally charged, prophetic utterance of his persona, a spiritually arid old man:

After such knowledge, what forgiveness? Think now
History has many cunning passages, contrived corridors
And issues, deceives with whispering ambitions,
Guides us by vanities. Think now...

(From T.S. Eliot, *Collected Poems 1909–1962*, Harcourt Brace Jovanovich, Inc.)

The first three lines expand the pentameter line beyond its normal complement of stressed and unstressed syllables; the fourth line contracts, intensifying the arc of feeling. Both Pound and Eliot used stress prosodies. Pound counted out four strong beats and used alliteration in his brilliant adaptation of the old English poem "The Seafarer" (1912):

Chill its chains are; chafing sighs
Hew my heart round and hunger begot
Mere-weary mood. Lest man known not
That he on dry land loveliest liveth...

(From Ezra Pound, *Personae*, Copyright 1926 by Ezra Pound. Reprinted by permission of New Directions Publishing Corporation.)

He uses a similar metric for the energetic opening of his "Canto I." Eliot mutes the obvious elements of the form in the celebrated opening of *The Waste Land* (1922):

April is the cruellest month, breeding
Lilacs out of the dead land, mixing
Memory and desire, stirring
Dull roots with spring rain.

(From T.S. Eliot, *Collected Poems 1909–1962*, Harcourt Brace Jovanovich, Inc.)

Here is the "native metre" with its falling rhythm, elegiac tone, strong pauses and variably placed stresses. If this is free verse, its freedoms are most carefully controlled. "No verse is free, " said Eliot, "for the man who wants to do a good job."

The prosodic styles of Whitman, Pound and Eliot—though clearly linked to various historical antecedents—are innovative expressions of their individual talents. In a sense, the prosody of every poet of genius is unique; rhythm is perhaps the most personal element of the poet's expressive equipment. Alfred Lord Tennyson and Robert Browning, English poets who shared the intellectual and spiritual concerns of the Victorian age, are miles apart in their prosodies. Both used blank verse for their dramatic lyrics, poems that purport to render the accents of real men speaking. The blank verse of Tennyson's

"Ulysses" (1842) offers smoothly modulated vowel music, carefully spaced spondaic substitutions and unambiguous pentameter regularity:

The long day wanes; the slow moon climbs; the deep
Moans round with many voices. Come, my friends,
'Tis not too late to seek a newer world.

Browning's blank verse aims at colloquial vigour; its "irregularity" is a function not of any gross metrical violation—it always obeys the letter of the metrical law—but of the adjustment of abstract metrical pattern to the rhythms of dramatic speech. If Tennyson's ultimate model is Milton's Baroque prosody with its oratorical rhythms, Browning's model was the quick and nervous blank verse of the later Elizabethan dramatists. Characteristic of Browning's blank verse are the strong accents, involuted syntax, pregnant caesuras and headlong energy in "The Bishop Orders His Tomb at St. Praxed's Church" (1845):

Vanity, saith the preacher, vanity!
Draw round my bed: is Anselm keeping back?
Nephews—sons mine... ah God, I know not! Well—
She, men would have to be your mother once,
Old Gandolf envied me, so fair she was!

Chapter 9

Critical Essays

The Politics of T.S. Eliot

One hundred years ago, Thomas Steams Eliot was born into an intelligently conservative family in St. Louis. His grandfather, a Unitarian minister and a man of mark, founded the Church of the Messiah and Washington University; the Eliots of St. Louis were Republican reformers, active in good causes, pillars of order. If one visits St. Louis today and searches for Eliot's birthplace, one is oppressed by a sense of the vanity of human wishes. The Eliot house vanished long ago; the Church of the Messiah, too, vanished long ago; the whole quarter, once elegant, where the Eliots lived is devastated and depopulated.

No memorial to the great poet of the 20th century stands in the city where he was bom. Nor in London, except for the memorial stone in Westminster Abbey, does one encounter any visible trace of Eliot, who never owned a house. The expectation of change, in the 20th century, has been greater than the expectation of continuity, nearly everywhere. And the permanent things, as Eliot called them-those enduring truths and ways of life and standards of order-are awash in the flood of sensual appetite and ideological passion. As Eliot expressed this phenomenon of decadence, referring to standards of education, in his book Notes towards the Definition of Culture, we are "destroying our ancient edifices to make ready the ground upon which the barbarian nomads of the future will encamp in their mechanised caravans." From his youth, Eliot took up the defense of the permanent things, with some boldness. A great innovator in poetry, he became a great conservative in morals and politics, so that my book on conservative thought begins with Burke and ends with Eliot. At no time in his life was he afflicted by political radicalism. After a decade of residence in London, he announced that he was a classicist in literature, a royalist in politics and Anglo-Catholic in religion. "I am aware that the second term is at present without definition, " he wrote, "and easily lends itself to what is almost worse than clap-trap, I mean temperate conservatism...... He would have despised the current American political label "moderate": the Conservative Party of England was not nearly conservative enough for T.S. Eliot. Affirming Tradition.

In 1922, poor and overworked in London, he founded a magazine, 77te Criterion, which endured until January 1939 when Europe was about to erupt. The magazine was intended to work among the educated classes of Europe "an affirmation and development of tradition, " as opposed to the dissemination of Marxism and other ideologies among the intelligentsia. Also, though not quite avowedly, the review was meant to work a political resurrection, touching often upon political theory and institutions. Its circulation never exceeded 800 copies. George Orwell would have liked to buy it, but lacked the purchase price-yet it published the writing of men and women of very high talent and the bound volumes of this periodical remain worth reading earnestly, if need be to the exclusion of any magazine of our own day.

Russell Kirk is a Distinguished Scholar at The Heritage Foundation. He spoke at The Heritage Foundation on February 9, 1989. ISSN 0272-1155. 01989 by The Heritage Foundation.

In Eliot's editorial "Commentaries" in that magazine will be found many shrewd or wise observations about politics—short pieces never reprinted. In such observations he impartially scourged the leaders of all political factions in Britain—with the partial exception of Stanley Baldwin, because Baldwin was something of a classical scholar as well as an honest man. Although a high Tory in English political tradition, he never participated in the action of the

Conservative Party—except, late in life, to lecture to the London Conservative Union, in 1955, concerning which memorable lecture, more presently. Two of Eliot's slim books are concerned in part with political questions: The Idea of a Christian Society, published just after the Second World War and Notes towards the Definition of Culture, published when socialism had descended upon Britain shortly after that war. Eliot wrote one political or quasi-political poem, Coriolan. I have reprinted in The Portable Conservative Reader his succinct, mordant remarks on Marxist critics of literature.

Other Eliot observations on politics may be found in certain of his literary essays, notably those on William Bram'hall, Charles Whibley and Machiavelli. Now this may seem, bibliographically, rather a slight bulk of literary production to justify Eliot's eminence as a leader of conservative opinion. Permit me, then, to explain why Eliot is so much read and so much respected, by men and women attached to the "permanent things." Thinkers and Actors. In his lecture on'The literature of Politics, " published in his collection To Criticize the Critic, Eliot refers to an essay by your servant, in which I mentioned, as American conservative thinkers, Paul Elmer More, Irving Babbitt, Bernard Iddings Bell and Robert Nisbet-none of whom had plunged into the hufly-burly of practical politics. Eliot comments upon this separation of serious political writing from political action, This is not a very healthy state of affairs, unless the views of such writers become more widely diffused and translated, modified, adapted, even adulterated, into action.

It-seems to me that in a healthy society, there will be a gradation of types between thought and action; at one extreme the detached contemplative, the critical mind which is concerned with the discovery of truth, not with its promulgation and still less with its translation into action and at the other extreme, the N.C.O. of politics, the man who in spite of relative indifference to general ideas, is equipped with native good sense, right feeling and character, supported by discipline and education. Between these two extremes there is room for several varieties and several kinds of political thinking; but there should be no breach of continuity between them. A little later in the same lecture, Eliot adds, 'To go more directly to the point, a political tradition in which the doctrinaire dominates the man of action and a tradition in which political philosophy is formulated or re-codified to suit the requirements and justify the conduct of a ruling clique, may be equally disastrous." Penetrating to the Core. Eliot concludes his lecture by remarking that he is not concerned with those temporary writers of alleged influence, "or with those publicists who have impressed their names upon the public by catching the morning tide and rowing very fast in the direction in which the current was flowing." Rather, he says "there should always

- Be a few writers preoccupied in penetrating to the core of the matter, in trying to arrive at the truth and to set it forth, without too much hope, without ambition to alter the immediate course of affairs and without being downcast or defeated when nothing appears to ensue." Now Eliot was himself one of those few writers, alluded to by him, who have endeavored to get at the political truth, or a more general truth in which political order is involved and to set it forth: men of talent who labor intellectually in what Eliot called the "pre-political" area. Eliot's moral imagination, his broad learning and his poetic talents enabled him indeed to penetrate to the core of the matter, when he touched upon the civil social order and that order's relationships to a transcendent order. Conservatively inclined people on either side of the Atlantic and farther afield than that, therefore often turn to Eliot's prose and not infrequently to his verse, for light. In short, Eliot's seminal mind, with its keen perceptions—Eliot's armed vision—opened the way for seekers after intellectual order and moral order and social order to penetrate beyond the cant and slogan of the hour. Slamming Shaw. For when Eliot in his writings touches upon Hobbes, or Freud, or Marx, or Mannheim, or Shaw, or H.G.

Wells, he punctures balloons as deftly as, two centuries earlier, did a very different man of letters, David Hume. Take, for instance, another passage from his lecture on the literature of politics. Eliot remarks that sometimes one is tempted to suspect "that the profounder and wiser the man, the less likely is his influence to be discernible." Then he goes on to give a tremendous knock to George Bernard Shaw: Yet the immediate influence of—shall we say—Mr. Bernard Shaw in the period of his most potent influence, I suppose, at the beginning of this century, must have been more appreciable and more widely diffused, than that of much finer minds; and one is compelled to admire a man of such verbal agility as not only to conceal from his readers and audiences the shallowness of his own thought, but to persuade them that in admiring his work they were giving evidence of their own intelligence as well. I do not say that Shaw could have succeeded alone, without the more plodding and laborious minds with which he associated himself, but by persuading low-brows that they were high-brows and that high-brows must be socialists, he contributed greatly to the prestige of socialism. But between the influence of a Bernard Shaw or an H.G. Wells and the influence of a Coleridge or a Newman, I can conceive no common scale of measurement. What Eliot gives us is not the posturing glibness of Shaw, but wisdom after the mode of Samuel Taylor Coleridge and John Henry Newman. Incidentally, or accidentally, by showing that a famous innovating poet could reject ideology—socialist, communist, or fascist ideology—Eliot contributed greatly to the prestige of conservatism, in the better sense of that abused word. Saving the World from Suicide. Now in remarking that Eliot was pre-political in the sense that he concerned himself principally with ultimate questions, I do not mean that he took little thought for the political exigencies in his era. On the contrary, Eliot was most earnestly and sorrowfully, concerned with the disasters and the grim prospects of our bent world. His commentaries in Ae Ctiterion often bore directly on political questions and men of the hour; and indeed a fundamental purpose of his review was to save the world

- From suicide through joining together writers and public men of intelligence, in Britain, Europe and America. Aspiring Toward a Healthy Democracy. During the years when we met occasionally and exchanged lengthy letters, he was possessed of a good knowledge of practical politics in the United States—always thinking of himself as an American—as well as a lively familiarity with matters of state in Britain and the Continent. During the 1950s though alarmed at educational follies in Britain and America, he was not so depressed by public affairs as he had been while editing 7"he Criterion, between the World Wars. In December 1928, Eliot published in his magazine his essay'The Literature of Fascisand'—which he rejected, along with the literature of Communism. "A new school of political thought is needed, " he wrote, "which might learn from political thought abroad, but not from political practice. Both Russian communism and Italian fascism seem to me to have died as political ideas, in becoming political facts." He was no enthusiast for an abstract democracy, an ideology of democratism; but a healthy democracy, rooted in old institutions, he aspired to restore. He continued in his article on Fascism, It is one thing to say what is sadly certain, that democratic government has been watered down to almost nothing.... But it is another thing to ridicule the idea of democracy.... A real democracy is always a restricted democracy and can only flourish with some limitation by hereditary rights and responsibilities.... The modern question as popularly put is: 'democracy is dead, what is to replace it?' whereas it should be: 'the frame of democracy has been destroyed; how can we, out of the materials at hand, build anew structure in which democracy can live?' Eleven years later, in his little book 7he Idea of a Christian Society, Eliot exhorted liberals and socialists, as war with the Axis powers was imminent, tbat'The term 'democracy'...does not contain enough positive content to stand alone against the forces that you dislike—it can easily be transformed by them. If you will not have God (and He is a jealous God) you should pay your respects to Hitler or Stalin." Question of Questions. For behind the virulent ideologies—substitutes for religion—in the 20th century, behind the feeble politics of liberalism, behind the ineffectuality of conservatives, Eliot perceived, lay a refusal to admit ethics and theology to political thinking. As he would conclude his lecture on the literature of politics in 1957:-"For the question of questions, which no political philosophy can escape and by the right answer to which all political thinking must in the end be judged, is simply this: What is Man? what are his limitations? what is his misery and what his greatness? and what, finally, his destiny?" I need hardly remark to you, ladies and gentlemen, that such principles of politics provoked wrath and ridicule among the intelligentsia of Bloomsbury in Eliot's time—even though Eliot's overwhelming reputation as a poet and the strength of his personality somewhat muted outcries against his Toryism. In recent years, most critics have endeavored to ignore Eliot's politics altogether as irrelevant; while some have reproached him venomously as an enemy of democracy and equality of condition. It is mildly amusing to find Eliot denounced for his Christian faith and his "feudalisf' politics by tenured professors of English, some of them enjoying salaries in excess of one hundred thousand dollars, comforted and cosseted by serried ranks of word-processor

- Operators and go-fers, amply provided with funds for travel and somewhat dubious "research, " generously pensioned when they retire from their occasional teaching of a seminar or two—these scholars and gentlemen who preach egalitarian doctrines; these unimaginative pedants who, should a socialist regime ever come to this land, would be mightily reduced in their circumstances and privileges. Eliot was hard pressed for money until late years; and when at length he was awarded the Nobel Prize, the only substantial sum received by him in a lifetime, he was promptly deprived of the lion's share of it by the Inland Revenue.

Ile Pope of Russell Square, as some called him, from his little office at the firm of Faber and Faber—where I called upon him occasionally in the 1950s—looked down with some contempt upon the crowd of literati of the Left, some of them political simpletons, others unscrupulous opportunists. All that could be said for the London crowd was that they were less silly than the Manhattan crowd of writers or would-be-writers; as Eliot put it, 'The worst form of expatriation for an American writer is residence in New York City." It is so still. New York Intellectuals. "It is natural and not necessarily convincing, " he wrote mordantly in 1933 in the pages of The Criterion, "to find young intellectuals in New York turning to communism and turning their communism to literary account. The literary profession is not only, in all countries, overcrowded and underpaid... it has much ado to maintain its dignity as a profession at all." Marxism might provide the aspiring writer with both a new creed and an assured income. "It is not always easy, of course, in the ebullitions of a new movement, to distinguish the man who has received the living word from the man whose access of energy is the result of being relieved of the necessity of thinking for himself. Men who have stopped thinking make a powerful force. There are obvious inducements, besides that—never wholly absent—of simple conversion, to entice the man of letters into political and social theory which he then employs to revive his sinking fires and rehabilitate his profession." Eliot lifelong refused to run with these hounds; he subscribed his name to no ideological protests and manifestos; he rejected root and branch British socialism, not to speak of communism, fascism and Naziism (which Hannah Arendt calls "an ideology in embryo"). But this repudiation of collectivist ideology aside, to what political convictions, realistically speaking, did Eliot adhere? Did his politics consist merely of negotiations? Not at all. There are two aspects, or perhaps jurisdictions, of Eliot's practical politics: his British views and his American views. Permit me first to say something about his American politics, that being the briefer subject. Rooted in New England. Eliot wrote to me once that the America for which his family stood had ended with the defeat of John Quincy Adams by Andrew Jackson in the presidential contest of 1828. (Eliot's distant kinsman Henry Adams made a similar observation.) So one may say that the politics of the Eliot family had been very like the politics of their kinfolk of the Adams family: Federalist so long as a Federalist party cohered, suspicious of leveling democracy, austerely moral, rooted in the culture of New England. These political views and habits were transferred by William Greenleaf Eliot, T.S. Eliot's grandfather, to Missouri. If I may take the liberty of quoting from my own works, a paragraph from my book about Eliot is pertinent here:

- The political exemplar of Eliot's youth had been a gentleman as real to the St. Louis boy as if he still had sat at the head of the dining table on Locust

Street: the grandfather he never actually saw, the Reverend William Greenleaf Eliot, 'the nineteenth-century descendant of Chaucer's parson.' That grandfather bad been a Christian hero—and a pillar of the visible community, a reforming conservative, as well as a buttress of the community of souls. In St. Louis he had reformed the schools; founded the university; become the apostle of gradual emancipation of the slaves, the champion of national union, the leader in a dozen other turbulent causes of reform—but always in the light of the permanent things.... His grandfather's notion of perfectibility and some others beliefs (among them the grandfather's zeal for prohibiting strong drink), T.S. Eliot would discard; and yet a grandfather like that must weigh more lifelong, for an adherent of Tradition, than all the political metaphysicians in the books.

I having been blessed with a grandfather rather like Eliot's, we got on well when we talked about American politics, Eliot and I. Eliot's profession of royalism, by the way, signified mostly that he supported the English throne, having become a British subject and that he approved of long-established monarchies elsewhere—such of them as had survived the tooth of time and the frenzy of revolutionaries that had followed hard upon both World Wars. He had not the faintest intention of saddling the United States with a monarch, any more than had his ancestor John Adams (who, nevertheless, had been accused of just such a design): in America, a royal house would have been an unnatural and untenable imposition. Little on America's Politics. Eliot having written next to nothing about America's practical politics, it is unnecessary here to go farther into his American views, except to remark in passing that he entertained a low opinion of Franklin Roosevelt and a good opinion of the elder Senator Robert Taft. He sympathized strongly with the group called the Southern Agrarians and among them was well acquainted with Allen Tate, a frequent contributor to The Criterion; he had been influenced by the conservative political convictions of Irving Babbitt and Paul Elmer More, the chief humanist critics; he shared their misgivings as to the tendencies of the American democracy, but proposed no alteration of the constitutional framework; so far as he touched upon American remedies, his hope lay in the restoration of learning—a subject he discussed at some length in a series of lectures at the University of Chicago during 1950.

(These "Aims of Education" lectures are included in his collection To Criticize the Critic.) A journal published by the Committee on Social Thought at the University of Chicago, Measure, published Eliot's lectures on education shortly after their delivery. Robert Hutchins, then chancellor of the University of Chicago, published in a following number of Measure a rather sharp rejoinder, in which Hutchins said, among other things, that "the only difference between Edmund Burke and T.S. Eliot is that Eliot is a democrat and Burke was not." When next in Chicago, Eliot found himself at a party in his honor with Robert Hutchins as a guest. Seeking Hutchins out, Eliot inquired of him, in his accustomed very civil manner, "Dr. Hutchins, I am grateful for your trouble in commenting upon my lectures on education; but I am puzzled by your remark about Burke and me. I never have called myself a democrat; and I suppose that Burke in his age, was more of a democrat than I am in my age. So could you tell me what you meant?

"But Mr. Hutchins turned his back and walked away. Why did he do that, Dr. Kirk?" "Because he never had read Burke, " I replied. "Hutchins once signed his name to an article attacking Burke that was published in 77ze 77tomist; but the article was written entirely by someone else; and that is all that Hutchins knows about Burke You had unveiled his abysmal ignorance of much." Like many other people in universities, Robert Hutchins was an egalitarian democrat in theory and an exacting autocrat in practice. Eliot had a talent for vexing such people. Consistent Tory. As for English politics, Eliot was a consistent Tory, rather than a regular Conservative. (The two partisan labels are not identical: Disraeli thought of changing the party's name back to Tory, after Peel had made it the Conservative party; but Metternich, in exile, dissuaded Disraeli.)

Toryism means loyalty to King and Church; the Tories are bound up with the Church of England—and, at least in times past, with the squirearchy, the smaller landed proprietors. So it was with Eliot: he had declared himself a royalist (though, for that matter, nine out of ten English subjects approve of the royal family); he was a most devout communicant of the Church of England and for some years a churchwarden in London; and he believed that the class of the old county families of England supplied the nation with leaders, in many walks of life, who ought not be supplanted by an elite, an alleged meritocracy. Yet the political thinkers and leaders he most admired included the great Whig Edmund Burke—whose name appears more frequently in Eliot's lectures after, on his decision, Faber and Faber published my book Ae Conservative Mind. Both in his early essay on Charles Whibley and his late lecture on the literature of politics, Eliot comments on four political writers, masters of literary style, who clearly have influenced his own views: Bolingbroke, Burke, Coleridge and Disraeli.

(In his essay on Whibley, he mentions also Lord Halifax.) Eliot's political thought, in considerable part, is descended from those great conservatives; it more nearly approximates that of Coleridge, whom

Eliot recognizes as "a man of my own type." Conservative Hollow Man. So there is nothing very exotic about Eliot's political principles: they are bound up with English history, the English constitution and the great divines of the Church of England. Those very principles dissuaded him from praising the Conservative Party of his day.

In June 1929, when MacDonald and Labour won the general election, forcing out of office Baldwin's Conservative government (even though the Conservatives had obtained a plurality of the popular vote) Eliot found that the new Lib-Lab cabinet had not one new idea among them. What might be done, in an hour when fascists and communists grew in influence among the intellectuals and among the mass of voters? He wrote in The Criterion: This is of course a great opportunity—for the Conservative Party, an opportunity which we are quite sure it will fail to seize. It is the opportunity of thinking in leisure and of appreciating the efforts of private persons who have committed some thinking already. 'Me Labour Party is a capitalist party in the sense that it is living on the reputation of thinking done by the Fabians of a generation ago.... The Conservative Party has a great opportunity in the fact that within the memory of no living man under sixty, has it acknowledged any contact with intelligence. It has, what no other political party at present

Enjoys, a complete mental vacuum: a vacancy that might be filled with anything, even with something valuable. The leaders of the Conservatives were Hollow Men. Eliot feared that the political and social institutions of Britain were giving way; that feeble politicians, belligerent trade unions, a cumbersome bureaucracy, an apathetic public, a Church that no longer held meaning for most English people, an obsession with getting and spending—these phenomena and circumstances were eroding irrevocably the England that Eliot had come to love. For the most part, Eliot's vaticinations would be justified by subsequent events. Seeldng to Retain a Humane Society. Like my friend Wilhelm R6thou, ladies and gentlemen and do likewise. You will find therein, for one thing, a demolition of Karl Mannheim's proposals for a planned society—indeed, for universal planning. "For one thing to avoid is a universalized planning, " Eliot writes; "one thing to ascertain is the limits of the plannable."

Probably Eliot would have said, if asked, that the most important passage in this last slim book of his is one concerned with the dependence of our culture, or of any culture, upon religious belief. Here is that passage, in part: I do not believe that the culture of Europe could survive the complete disappearance of the Christian Faith. And I am convinced of that, not merely because I am a Christian myself, but as a student of social biology. If Christianity goes, the whole of our culture goes. Then you must start painfully again and you cannot put on a new culture ready made. You must wait for the grass to grow to feed the sheep to give the wool out of which your new coat will be made.

You must pass through many centuries of barbarism. We should not live to see the new culture, nor would our great-great-great-grandchildren; and if we did, not one of us would be happy in it. Continued Decay. Since Eliot's death, many unhappy choices have been made in Britain and the decay that he lamented has continued apace, in several ways—though not in all. The deliberate lowering of intellectual standards in British schools and universities and formal protestations of disbelief by eminent bishops and archbishops, have been among those dismaying phenomena. Yet it is not possible, Eliot instructs us, to measure the long-run influence of a poet or a philosopher. In the fullness of time, perhaps it will

be found that Eliot sowed better than he knew and that his political and cultural writings will endure along with his great poems and bear some fruit. We must be very patient, said Eliot, awaiting the dissolution liberalism and the recovery of tradition. My friend Eliot did not expect to turn back the clock by any social or literary magic; nor did he fancy that we would be pleased by the result, even were it possible; for we all are creatures of the age into which we have been born. As he expressed this hard truth in 'Uttle Gidding"-We cannot restore old policies Orfollow an antique drum. Reading Eliot will not tell us how to balance the federal budget and reduce the national debt—even though the poet of 77te Waste Land was a banker for some years. But his poetry tells us much about the human condition, in its splendor and its misery; and his prose
Makes us acutely aware of the permanent things. I knew Eliot somewhat during his later years and understand him better now that his ashes lie in the medieval church of East Coker. For, as Eliot wrote, also in "Little Gidding"—And what the dead had no speech for, when living, They can tell you, being dead. the communication q the dead is tongued with the fire beyond the language of the living.

T. S. Eliot as Conservative Mentor

T. S. Eliot was indisputably the greatest poet writing in English in the twentieth century. He was also the most revolutionary Anglophone literary critic since Samuel Johnson and the most influential religious thinker in the Anglican tradition since the Wesleyan movement. His social and political vision is contained in all his writings and has been absorbed and reabsorbed by generations of English and American readers, upon whom it exerts an almost mystical fascination—even when they are moved, as many are, to reject it. Without Eliot, the philosophy of Toryism would have lost all substance during the last century. And while not explicitly intending it, Eliot set this philosophy on a higher plane, intellectually, spiritually and stylistically, than has ever been reached by the adherents of the socialist idea.

Eliot attempted to shape a philosophy for our times that would be richer and more true to the complexity of human needs than the free-market panaceas that have so often dominated the thinking of conservatives in government. He assigned a central place in his social thinking to high culture. He was a thorough traditionalist in his beliefs but an adventurous modernist in his art, holding artistic modernism and social traditionalism to be different facets of a common enterprise. Modernism in art was, for Eliot, an attempt to salvage and fortify a living artistic tradition in the face of the corruption and decay of popular culture.

Eliot was born in St Louis, Missouri, in 1888 and educated at Harvard, the Sorbonne and Merton College, Oxford, where he wrote a doctoral thesis on the philosophy of F. H. Bradley, whose Hegelian vision of society exerted a profound influence over him. He came, as did so many educated Americans of his generation, from a profoundly religious and public-spirited background, although his early poems suggest a bleak and despairing agnosticism, which he only gradually and painfully overcame. In 1914 he met Ezra Pound, who encouraged him to settle in England. He married during the following year, which also saw the publication of his first successful poem, "The Love Song of J. Alfred Prufrock." This work, together with the other short poems that were published along with it as Prufrock and Other Observations in 1917, profoundly altered the course of English literature. They were the first truly modernist works in English, although the most visible influences on their imagery and diction were not English but French—specifically, the fin-de-siècle irony of Laforgue and the symbolism of Rimbaud, Mallarmé and Verlaine. They were also social poems, concerned to express a prevailing collective mood, even when dressed in the words of a specific protagonist. The wartime generation found themselves in these poems, in a way that they had not found themselves in the pseudo-romantic literature of the Edwardian period.

Shortly afterwards Eliot published a book of essays, The Sacred Wood, which was to be as influential as the early poetry. In these essays, Eliot presented his new and exacting theory of the role of criticism, of the necessity for criticism if our literary culture is to survive. For Eliot, it is no accident that criticism and poetry so often come together in the same intelligence—as in his own case and the case of Coleridge, whom he singled out as the finest of English critics. For the critic, like the poet, is concerned to develop the "sensibility" of his reader—by which term Eliot meant a kind of intelligent observation of the human world. Critics do not abstract or generalize: they look and record what they see. But in doing so, they also convey a sense of what matters in human experience, distinguishing the false from the genuine emotion. While Eliot was to spell out only gradually and obscurely over many years just what he meant by "sensibility, " his elevated conception of the critic's role struck a chord in many of his readers. Furthermore, *The Sacred Wood* contained essays that were to revolutionize literary taste. The authoritative tone of these essays gave rise to the impression that the modern world was at last making itself heard in literature—and that its voice was T. S. Eliot's.

The Sacred Wood turned the attention of the literary world to the "metaphysical poets" of the sixteenth and seventeenth centuries and to the Elizabethan dramatists—the lesser predecessors and the heirs of Shakespeare, whose raw language, rich with the sensation of the thing described, provided a telling contrast to the sentimental sweetness that Eliot condemned in his immediate contemporaries. There is also an essay on Dante, discussing a question that was frequently to trouble Eliot—that of the relationship between poetry and belief. To what extent could one appreciate the poetry of the *Divine Comedy* while rejecting the doctrine that had inspired it? This question was a real one for Eliot, for several reasons.

Eliot was—like his fellow modernists and contemporaries, Ezra Pound and James Joyce—profoundly influenced by Dante, whose limpid verse-form, colloquial style and solemn philosophy created a vision of the ideal in poetry. At the same time, he rejected the theological vision of the *Divine Comedy*—rejected it with a deep sense of loss. Yet in his own poetry the voice of Dante would constantly return, offering him turns of phrase, lightning flashes of thought and—most of all—a vision of the modern world from a point of view outside it, a point of view irradiated by an experience of holiness (albeit an experience that he did not then share). And when Eliot did finally come to share in this vision, he wrote, in the last of the *Four Quartets*, the most brilliant of all imitations of Dante in English—an imitation which is something far finer than an imitation, in which the religious vision of Dante is transported and translated into the world of modern England.

One other essay in *The Sacred Wood* deserves mention—"Tradition and the Individual Talent, " in which Eliot introduces the term which best summarizes his contribution to the political consciousness of the twentieth century: tradition. In this essay Eliot argues that true originality is possible only within a tradition—and further, that every tradition must be remade by the genuine artist, in the very act of creating something new. A tradition is a living thing and just as each writer is judged in terms of those who went before, so does the meaning of the tradition change as new works are added to it. It was this literary idea of a living tradition that was gradually to permeate Eliot's thinking and to form the core of his social and political philosophy.

Prufrock and *The Sacred Wood* already help us to understand the paradox of T. S. Eliot—that our greatest literary modernist should also be our greatest modern conservative. The man who overthrew the nineteenth century in literature and inaugurated the age of free verse, alienation and experiment was also the man who, in 1928, was to describe himself as "classical in literature, royalist in politics and Anglo-Catholic in religion." This seeming paradox contains a clue to Eliot's greatness as a social and political thinker. For Eliot recognized that it is precisely in modern conditions—conditions of fragmentation, heresy and unbelief—that the conservative project acquires its sense. Conservatism is itself a modernism and in this fact lies the secret of its success. What distinguishes Burke from the French revolutionaries is not his attachment to things past, but rather his desire to live fully in the concrete present, to understand the present in all its imperfections and to accept the present as the only reality that is offered to us. Like Burke, Eliot recognized the distinction between a backward-looking nostalgia, which is but another form of modern sentimentality and a genuine tradition, which grants us the courage and the vision with which to live in the modern world.

In 1922 Eliot founded *The Criterion,* a literary quarterly which he continued to edit until 1939, when he discontinued the journal under the pressure of "depression of spirits" induced by "the present state of public affairs." As the title of the journal suggests, the project was animated by Eliot's sense of the importance of criticism and of the futility of modernist experiments when not informed by literary judgement and moral seriousness. The journal also contained social philosophy of a conservative persuasion—although Eliot preferred the word "classicism" as a description of its political outlook.

The Criterion was the forum in which much of our modernist literature was first published, including the poetry of Pound, Empson, Auden and Spender. Its first issue contained the work which established Eliot himself as the greatest poet of his generation: *The Waste Land*. This poem seemed to its first readers to capture completely the disillusionment and emptiness that followed the hollow victory of the First World War—the conflict in which European civilization had committed suicide, just as Greek civilization had done in the Peloponnesian War. Yet the poem hardly mentioned the war, had none of the vivid imagery of battle that English readers knew from the works of Wilfrid Owen and Siegfried Sassoon and was choc-a-bloc with references to and quotations from a scholar's library. Its ostensible subject-matter was drawn from works of armchair anthropology—in particular, from Sir James Frazer's *Golden Bough,* a work which had also provided the title of *The Sacred Wood*.

The Waste Land was later republished with notes in which Eliot explained some of his references and allusions, such as that contained in the title, which alludes to the Fisher King of the Parsifal legend and *The Waste Land* over which he presides, awaiting the hero who will ask the questions that will destroy winter's bleak enchantment and renew the world. The allegory of modern civilization contained in this reference to the medieval fertility cults and their literary transformation in Arthurian romance, was not lost on Eliot's readers. Nor was it the first time that these symbols and legends of medieval romance had been put to such a use—witness Wagner's *Parsifal*, to which Eliot refers obliquely, by quoting from Verlaine's poem.

Nevertheless, there was a peculiar poignancy in the very erudition of the poem, as though the whole of Western culture were being brought to bear on the desert landscape of the modern city in a last effort to encompass it, to internalize it and to understand its meaning. The use of anthropological conceptions parallels Wagner's use of the Teutonic myths. (In *The Waste Land* there are more quotations from Wagner than from any other poet.) Eliot is invoking the religious worldview—and in particular the sense that life's renewal depends upon supernatural forces—but as a fact about human consciousness, rather than an item of religious belief. In this way, he was able to avail himself of religious ideas and imagery without committing himself to any religious belief. As he was rapidly discovering, without religious ideas the true condition of the modern world cannot be described. Only by describing modernity from a point of view outside of history can we grasp the extent of our spiritual loss.

After *The Waste Land* Eliot continued to write poetry inspired by the agonizing dissociation, as he saw it, between the sensibility of our culture and the available experience of the modern world. This phase of his development culminated in a profound Christian statement—the poem Ash Wednesday, in which he abandoned his anthropological manner and announced his conversion to the Anglo-Catholic faith. By now Eliot was ready to take up his own peculiar cross: the cross of membership. No longer playing the part of spiritual and political exile, he threw in his lot with the tradition to which his favorite authors had belonged. He became a British citizen, joined the Anglican Church and wrote his great verse drama, *Murder in the Cathedral*. In a series of essays, he praised the writings of sixteenth-century Anglican divines and attacked the secular heresies of his time.

This phase of Eliot's development at length led to *After Strange Gods*, a "primer of modern heresy, " in which he expressed his conservative antipathy to secular doctrine. It was Eliot's first of several attempts at social philosophy, of which the two most famous are *The Idea of a Christian Society* (1940) and *Notes Towards the Definition of Culture* (1948). Both these works are marked by a tentativeness and anxiety about the new condition of Europe, which make them far less clear guides to Eliot's vision than the great poem which he wrote at the same time, a poem which has been, for many of my generation, the essential account of our spiritual crisis—and the greatest message of hope that has been given to us. *Four Quartets* is a profound exploration of spiritual possibilities, in which the poet seeks and finds the vision outside time in which time and history are redeemed. It is a religious work and at the same time a work of extraordinary lyric power, like the Cimetière marin of Valéry, but vastly more mature in its underlying philosophy.

Eliot's life began with a question: the question of modern life and its meaning. His literary work was a long, studious and sincere attempt to provide an answer. In the course of this enterprise, Eliot re-shaped the English language, changed the forms of English verse and produced some of the most memorable utterances in our literature. Although an impressive scholar, with a mastery of languages and literatures that he reveals but does not dwell upon in his writings, Eliot was also a man of the world. He worked first as a teacher, then in a London bank and then in the publishing house of Faber and Faber, which he made into the foremost publisher of poetry and criticism in its day. His unhappy first marriage did not impede his active participation in the literary life of

London, over which he exerted an influence every bit as great as André Breton over the literary life of Paris.

His refusal, through all this, to adopt the mantle of the bohemian, to claim the tinsel crown of artist, or to mock the "bourgeois" lifestyle, sets him apart from the continental tradition which he otherwise did so much to promote. He realised that the true task of the artist in the modern world is one not of repudiation but of reconciliation. For Eliot, the artist inherits, in heightened and self-conscious form, the very same anxieties that are the stuff of ordinary experience. The poet who takes his words seriously is the voice of mankind, interceding for those who live around him and gaining on their behalf the gift of consciousness with which to overcome the wretchedness of secular life. He too is an ordinary bourgeois and his highest prize is to live unnoticed amidst those who know nothing of his art—as the saint may live unnoticed among those for whom he dies.

To find the roots of Eliot's political thinking, we must go back to the modernism that found such striking expression in *The Waste Land*. English literature in the early part of the twentieth century was to a great extent captured by pre-modern imagery, by references to a form of life (such as we find in Thomas Hardy) that had vanished forever and by verse forms which derived from the repertoire of romantic isolation.

It had not undergone that extraordinary education which Baudelaire and his successors had imposed upon the French—in which antiquated forms like the sonnet were wrenched free of their pastoral and religious connotations and fitted out with the language of the modern city, in order to convey the new and hallucinatory sense of an irreparable fault, whereby modern man is divided from all that has preceded him. Eliot's admiration for Baudelaire arose from his desire to write verse that was as true to the experience of the modern city as Baudelaire's had been to the experience of Paris. Eliot also recognized in Baudelaire the new character of the religious impulse under the conditions of modern life: "The important fact about Baudelaire," he wrote, "is that he was essentially a Christian, born out of his due time and a classicist, born out of his due time." Eliot's indictment the neo-romantic literature of his day was not merely a literary complaint. He believed that his contemporaries' use of worn-out poetic diction and lilting rhythms betrayed a serious moral weakness: a failure to observe life as it really is, a failure to feel what must be felt towards the experience that is inescapably ours. And this failure is not confined, he believed, to literature, but runs through the whole of modern life. The search for a new literary idiom is therefore part of a larger search—for the reality of modern experience. Only then can we confront our situation and ask ourselves what should be done about it.

Eliot's deep distrust of secular humanism—and of the socialist and democratic ideas of society which he believed to stem from it—reflected his critique of the neo-romantics. The humanist, with his myth of man's goodness, is taking refuge in an easy falsehood. He is living in a world of make-believe, trying to avoid the real emotional cost of seeing things as they are. His vice is the vice of Edwardian and "Georgian" poetry—the vice of sentimentality, which causes us not merely to speak and write in clichés, but to feel in clichés too, lest we should be troubled by the truth of our condition. The task of the artistic modernist, as Eliot later expressed it, borrowing a phrase from Mallarmé, is "to purify the dialect of the tribe": that is, to find the words, rhythms and artistic forms that would make contact again with our experience—not my experience, or yours, but our experience, the experience that unites us as living here and now. And it is only because he had captured this experience—in particular, in the bleak vision of *The Waste Land*—that Eliot was able to find a path to its meaning.

He summarizes his attitude to the everyday language of modern life and politics in his essay on the Anglican bishop Lancelot Andrewes and it is worth quoting the passage in full:

> To persons whose minds are habituated to feed on the vague jargon of our time, when we have a vocabulary for everything and exact ideas about nothing—when a word half-understood, torn from its place in some alien or half-formed science, as of psychology, conceals from both writer and reader the utter meaninglessness of a statement, when all dogma is

in doubt except the dogmas of sciences of which we have read in the newspapers, when the language of theology itself, under the influence of an undisciplined mysticism of popular philosophy, tends to become a language of tergiversation—Andrewes may seem pedantic and verbose. It is only when we have saturated ourselves in his prose, followed the movement of his thought, that we find his examination of words terminating in the ecstasy of assent. Andrewes takes a word and derives the world from it....

For Eliot, words had begun to lose their precision—not in spite of science, but because of it; not in spite of the loss of true religious belief, but because of it; not in spite of the proliferation of technical terms, but because of it. Our modern ways of speaking no longer enable us to "take a word and derive the world from it": on the contrary, they veil the world, since they convey no lived response to it. They are mere counters in a game of cliché, designed to fill up the silence, to conceal the void which has come upon us as the old gods have departed from their haunts among us.

That is why modern ways of thinking are not, as a rule, orthodoxies, but heresies—a heresy being a truth that has been exaggerated into falsehood, a truth in which we have taken refuge, so to speak, investing in it all our unexamined anxieties and expecting from it answers to questions which we have not troubled ourselves to understand. In the philosophies that prevail in modern life—utilitarianism, pragmatism, behaviorism—we find that "words have a habit of changing their meaning...or else they are made, in a most ruthless and piratical manner, to walk the plank." The same is true, Eliot implies, whenever the humanist heresy takes over: whenever we treat man as God and so believe that our thoughts and our words need be measured by no other standard but themselves.

Eliot was brought up in a democracy. He inherited that great fund of public spirit which is the gift of American democracy to the modern world and the cause of so much ignorant hatred of America. But he was not a democrat in his sensibility. Eliot believed that culture could not be entrusted to the democratic process precisely because of the carelessness with words, this habit of unthinking cliché, which would always arise when every person is regarded as having an equal right to express himself. In *The Use of Poetry and the Use of Criticism* he writes:

> When the poet finds himself in an age in which there is no intellectual aristocracy, when power is in the hands of a class so democratised that while still a class it represents itself to be the whole nation; when the only alternatives seem to be to talk to a coterie or soliloquize, the difficulties of the poet and the necessity of criticism become greater.

Hence, the critic has, for Eliot, an enhanced significance in the modern, democratic world. It is he who must act to restore what the aristocratic ideal of taste would have spontaneously generated—a language in which words are used with their full meaning and in order to show the world as it is. Those nurtured on empty sentiment have no weapons with which to deal with the reality of a god-forsaken world. They fall at once from sentimentality into cynicism and so lose the power either to experience life or to live with its imperfection.

Eliot therefore perceived an enormous danger in the liberal and "scientific" humanism which was offered by the prophets of his day. This liberalism seemed to him to be the avatar of moral chaos, since it would permit any sentiment to flourish and would deaden all critical judgement with the idea of a democratic right to speak—which becomes, insensibly, a democratic right to feel. Although "human kind cannot bear very much reality"—as he expresses the point, first in *Murder in the Cathedral* and then in *Four Quartets*—the purpose of a culture is to retain that elusive thing called "sensibility": the habit of right feeling. Barbarism ensues, not because people have lost their skills and scientific knowledge, nor is it averted by retaining those things; rather, barbarism comes through a loss of culture, since it is only through culture that the important realities can be truly perceived.

Eliot's thought here is difficult to state precisely. And it is worth drawing a parallel with a thinker whom he disliked: Friedrich Nietzsche. For Nietzsche, the crisis of modernity had come about because of the loss of the Christian faith. This loss of faith is the inevitable result of science and the growth of knowledge. At the same time, it is not possible for mankind really to live without faith; and for us, who have inherited all the habits and concepts of a Christian culture, that faith must be Christianity. Take away the faith and you do not take away a body of doctrine only, nor do you leave a clear, uncluttered landscape in which man at last is visible for what he is. Rather, you take away the power to perceive other and more important truths, truths about our condition which cannot, without the benefit of faith, be properly confronted—such as the truth of our mortality.

The solution that Nietzsche impetuously embraced in this quandary was to deny the sovereignty of truth altogether—to say that "there are no truths," and to build a philosophy of life on the ruins of both science and religion in the name of a purely aesthetic ideal. Eliot saw the absurdity of that response. Yet the paradox remains. The truths that mattered to Eliot are truths of feeling, truths about the weight of human life. Science does not make these truths more easily perceivable: on the contrary, it releases into the human psyche a flock of fantasies—liberalism, humanism, utilitarianism and the rest—which distract it with the futile hope for a scientific morality.

The result is a corruption of the very language of feeling, a decline from sensibility to sentimentality and a veiling of the human world. The paradox, then, is this: the falsehoods of religious faith enable us to perceive the truths that matter. The truths of science, endowed with an absolute authority, hide the truths that matter and make human reality imperceivable. Eliot's solution to the paradox was compelled by the path that he had taken to its discovery—the path of poetry, with the agonizing examples of poets whose precision, perception and sincerity were the effects of Christian belief. The solution was to embrace the Christian faith—not, as Tertullian did, because of the paradox, but rather in spite of it.

This explains Eliot's growing conviction that culture and religion are in the last analysis indissoluble. The disease of sentimentality could be overcome, he believed, only by a high culture in which the work of purification was constantly carried on. This is the task of the critic and the artist and it is a hard task:

And so each venture
Is a new beginning, a raid on the inarticulate
With shabby equipment always deteriorating
In the general mess of imprecision of feeling,

Undisciplined squads of emotion. And what there is to conquer By strength and submission, has already been discovered Once or twice, or several times, by men whom one cannot hope To emulate—but there is no competition—

There is only the fight to recover what has been lost

And found and lost again and again: and now, under conditions That seem unpropitious....

This work of purification is a dialogue across the generations with those who belong to the tradition: only the few can take part in it, while the mass of mankind stays below, assailed by those "undisciplined squads of emotion." The high culture of the few is, however, a moral necessity for the many, for it permits human reality to show itself and so to guide our conduct.

But why should the mass of mankind, lost as they are in bathos, "distracted from distraction by distraction, " be guided by "those who know" (to use Dante's pregnant phrase)? The answer must lie in religion and in particular in the common language which a traditional religion bestows, both on the high culture of art and on the common culture of a people. Religion is the life-blood of a culture. It provides the store of symbols, stories and doctrines that enable us to communicate about our destiny. It forms, through the sacred texts and liturgies, the constant point to which the poet and the critic can return—the language alike of ordinary believers and of the poets who must confront the ever-new conditions of life in the aftermath of knowledge, of life in a fallen world.

For Eliot, however, religion in general and the Christian religion in particular, should not be seen merely in Platonic terms as an attitude towards what is eternal and unchanging. The truth of our condition is that we are historical beings who find whatever consolation and knowledge is vouchsafed to us in time. The consolations of religion come to us in temporal costume, through institutions that are alive with the spirit of history. To rediscover our religion is not to rise free from the temporal order; it is not to deny history and corruption, in order to contemplate the timeless truths. On the contrary, it is to enter more deeply into history, so as to find in the merely transitory the mark and the sign of that which never passes: it is to discover the "point of intersection of the timeless with time, " which is, according to *Four Quartets*, the occupation of the saint.

Thus there emerges the strangest and most compelling of parallels: that between the saint and martyr of *Murder in the Cathedral* and the meditating poet of *Four Quartets*. Just as the first brings, through his martyrdom, the light of eternity into the darkness of the people of Canterbury (represented as a chorus of women), so does the poet "redeem the time, " by finding in the stream of time those timeless moments which point beyond time. And the attempt by the poet to rediscover and belong to a tradition that will give sense and meaning to his language is one with the attempt to find a tradition of belief, of behavior and of historical allegiance, that will give sense and meaning to the community. The real significance of a religion lies less in the abstract doctrine than in the institutions which cause it to endure. It lies also in the sacraments and ceremonies, in which the eternal becomes present and what might have been coincides with what is.

For Eliot, therefore, conversion was not a matter merely of acknowledging the truth of Christ. It involved a conscious gesture of belonging, whereby he united his poetical labors with the perpetual labor of the Anglican church. For the Anglican church is peculiar in this: that it has never defined itself as "protestant"; that it has always sought to accept rather than protest against its inheritance, while embracing the daring belief that the truths of Christianity have been offered in a local form to the people of England. It is a church which takes its historical nature seriously, acknowledging that its duty is less to spread the gospel among mankind than to sanctify a specific community. And in order to fit itself for this role, the Anglican church has, through its divines and liturgists, shaped the English language according to the Christian message, while also bringing that message into the here and now of England. In "Little Gidding, " the last of the *Four Quartets*, the poet finds himself in the village retreat where an Anglican saint had retired to pray with his family. He conveys what to many is the eternal truth of the Anglican confession, in lines which are among the most famous that have ever been written in English:

If you came this way,
Taking any route, starting from anywhere,
At any time or at any season,
It would always be the same: you would have to put off
Sense and notion. You are not here to verify,
Instruct yourself, or inform curiosity
Or carry report. You are here to kneel
Where prayer has been valid. And prayer is more
Than an order of words, the conscious occupation
Of the praying mind, or the sound of the voice praying.
And what the dead had no speech for, when living,
They can tell you, being dead: the communication
Of the dead is tongued with fire beyond the language of the living.
Here, the intersection of the timeless moment
Is England and nowhere. Never and always.

Later, returning to this theme of communication with the dead—our dead—and referring to those brief moments of meaning which are the only sure gift of sensibility, Eliot completes the thought:

We are born with the dead:
See, they return and bring us with them.
The moment of the rose and the moment of the yew-tree
Are of equal duration. A people without history
Is not redeemed from time, for history is a pattern
Of timeless moments. So, while the light fails
On a winter's afternoon, in a secluded chapel
History is now and England.

Much has been written about "Little Gidding, " the

atmosphere of which stays in the mind of every cultivated Englishman who reads it. What is important, however, is less the atmosphere of the poem than the thought which advances through it. For here Eliot achieves that for which he envies Dante—namely, a poetry of belief, in which belief and words are one and in which the thought cannot be prized free from the controlled and beautiful language. Moreover, there is one influence throughout which is inescapable—the King James Bible and the Anglican liturgy that grew alongside it. Without being consciously biblical and while using only modern and colloquial English, Eliot endows his verse with the authority of liturgy and with the resonance of faith.

These lines take us back to the core belief of modern conservatism, which Burke expressed in the following terms: Society, he wrote, is indeed a contract; but not a contract among the living only; rather, it is a partnership between the living, the dead and those yet to be born. And, he argued, only those who listen to the dead are fit custodians of future generations. Eliot's complex theory of tradition gives sense and form to this idea. For he makes clear that the most important thing that future generations can inherit from us is our culture. Culture is the repository of an experience which is at once local and placeless, present and timeless, the experience of a community as sanctified by time.

This we can pass on only if we too inherit it. Therefore, we must listen to the voices of the dead and capture their meaning in those brief, elusive moments when "History is now and England." In a religious community, such moments are a part of everyday life. For us, in the modern world, religion and culture are both to be gained through a work of sacrifice. But it is a sacrifice upon which everything depends. Hence, by an extraordinary route, the modernist poet becomes the traditionalist priest: and the stylistic achievement of the first is one with the spiritual achievement of the second.

To many people, Eliot's theory of culture and tradition is too arduous, imposing an impossible duty upon the educated elite. To others, however, it has been a vital inspiration. For let us ask ourselves just what is required of "one who knows."

Should he, in the modern world, devote himself like Sartre or Foucault to undermining the "structures" of bourgeois society, to scoffing at manners and morals and ruining the institutions upon which he depends for his exalted status?

Should he play the part of a modern Socrates, questioning everything and affirming nothing? Should he go along with the mindless culture of play, the post-modernist fantasy world in which all is permitted since neither permission nor interdiction have any sense? To answer yes to any of those questions is in effect to live by negation, to grant nothing to human life beyond the mockery of it. It is to inaugurate and endorse the new world of "transgression, " a world which will not reproduce itself, since it will undermine the very motive which causes a society to reproduce. The conservative response to modernity is to embrace it, but to embrace it critically, in full consciousness that human achievements are rare and precarious, that we have no God-given right to destroy our inheritance, but must always patiently submit to the voice of order and set an example of orderly living. The future of mankind, for the socialist, is simple: pull down the existing order and allow the future to emerge. But it will not emerge, as we know. These philosophies of the "new world" are lies and delusions, products of a sentimentality which has veiled the facts of human nature.

We can do nothing unless we first amend ourselves. The task is to rediscover the world which made us, to see ourselves as part of something greater, which depends upon us for its survival—and which still can live in us, if we can achieve that "condition of complete simplicity/(Costing not less than everything), " to which Eliot directs us.

We shall not cease from exploration
And the end of all our exploring
Will be to arrive where we started
And know the place for the first time.

Such is the conservative message for our time. It is a message beyond politics, a message of liturgical weight and authority. But it is a message which must be received, if humane and moderate politics is to remain a possibility.

'Where are the Eagles and the Trumpets?': the Strange Case of Eliot's Missing Quatrains T.S. Eliot

T. S. Eliot rated the quatrain poems he wrote between 1917 and 1919 among his best and most important work. Shortly after the publication of The Waste Land, for example, he wrote to his brother, Henry: "I consider my Sweeney poems as serious as anything I have ever written, in fact much more serious and more mature than the early poems but I do not know anyone who agrees with me on this point except William Butler Yeats and Vivienne who have both said much the same thing about them".

Further evidence of his high regard for them can be found in the two selected editions published in his lifetime—the contents of both of which he chose. In the first small selection in 1940 he included "Sweeney among the Nightingales" rather than "Portrait of a Lady, " and in the second and fuller selection he made eight years later (which remains the standard selected edition), he included all seven of the English quatrains. However, his opinion has not been endorsed by academic criticism.

One of the most striking aspects of this criticism until recently is the unquestioned and unquestioning organic narrative that is used to chart Eliot's poetic career. In this narrative the quatrains are located between on the one hand the greatness of the two "central" early poems, "The Love Song of J. Alfred Prufrock" and "Portrait of a Lady, " and on the other the work that is depicted as the fulfillment of his "first period": The Waste Land. Ronald Bush, for example, uses just such an organizing structure, asserting that "the causes of [Eliot's] evolution were there from the beginning" and spends five pages out of three hundred on the quatrains.

Grover Smith uses a similar rhetorical strategy but is prepared to be more blunt about his antipathy toward the poems: "From 1917 to 1919 he based his technique more on Gautier than anyone else. Pound having disastrously encouraged him to study Gautier's Emaux et camees, he set to work being amusing". Periodical criticism shows a similar lack of balance, as essays on the quatrains are few and far between and those that do exist are normally either short, allusion-hunting pieces or are primarily biographical.

Even while this imbalance appears to be changing in two recent books (Robert Crawford and Kinley E. Roby), the quatrain poems, when they have been considered at all, have generally been portrayed as only useful stepping stones in Eliot's development as a poet. F. B. Pinion is exemplary in this regard: "Though [Eliot's allegiance to Gautier] produced a number of poems which excited the younger generation with their daring and wit, the Gautier period must be regarded as temporizing and preparatory". By using the term the "Gautier period, " Pinion rhetorically intimates that they were too derivative, influenced only by Gautier. Yet there is also the paradoxical admission that they were perceived in very different terms at the time—they "excited the younger generation with their daring and wit." The use of the word "wit" is particularly problematic here, since critics, including Pinion himself, generally valorize the term by using Eliot's definition of it (which he formulated in some of the theoretical essays he was writing at the time) to explain the power of the later poems, especially The Waste Land.

Indeed, Eliot's assertion in the letter to his brother that no one liked the quatrains apart from himself, his wife and Yeats is certainly not true, as Pinion points out. Angus Calder, however, is more explicit about whom of the "younger generation" the quatrains "excited, " although he too exemplifies the typical critical approach to Eliot's quatrains: "Most of the poems in English were written in quatrains, " he writes, " Pound's Mauberley sequence at the same time was largely composed of not dissimilar verses. Their retreat from vers libre towards an erudite formality is an interesting reaction". Calder sets the work of the two poets during this period in opposition to the "reality" of the trenches and postwar "working-class agitation" and so charges "reaction" with a double-edged signification: a conservative recoil from vers libre and a reactionary response to the politics of the time. He then criticizes them for being too artificial, for displaying too much formal ingenuity, for not being "real" enough: " | Art,

' or we might say not unfairly, ǀartiness, ' provided a fortress to which they could retreat". After arguing that they were too "art, " too arid, Calder asserts that they also reveal Eliot's "routine middle-class WASP anti-semitism" and "right wing political reflexes, " which enables him not only to minimize the importance of the sentiments and the quatrains, but also to disown them both on his own behalf and, even more insidiously, on Eliot's behalf as well. Having put the poems in their minor place, Calder in the next sentence reveals that it was these same poems that made Eliot's name: "Eliot's quatrains captivated amongst others the Sitwells... and clearly intrigued a major writer, Hugh MacDiarmid... refers casually to ǀBurbank' as if the poems were common knowledge and actually parodies Eliot's already parodic ǀSweeney' poems. Extracting witty new life from the quatrain, an easy ǀtraditional' form, Eliot educated the generation of Auden and Betjeman and Stevie Smith, born in the century's first decade". After this extraordinary passage, Calder then blithely says that the poem that Ara Vos Prec was really "about" is and was "Gerontion."

What is particularly revealing about the pattern of showing the quatrains' influence and then denying their importance is that their influence seems to have been creative, their lack of importance academic. The people who are ritually shown to have been impressed by the quatrains are poets themselves, whereas academic criticism disowns them. This dichotomy seems to have been operative even in the early twenties: when W. H. Auden is quoting the Sweeney poems, F. W. Bateson is reading The Sacred Wood, This would seem to suggest that there is something about the poems that is resistant (or even antipathetic) to literary criticism as it had been institutionalized and was practiced in the Anglophone world until recently. Clearly, one aspect of this general critical agreement is the easy susceptibility of poems like "The Love Song of J. Alfred Prufrock, " "Portrait of a Lady, " and "Gerontion" to being fitted into certain comfortable paradigms about the reading process that were quickly developed in the 1920s by the academy. They appear to have an overall self who speaks—however fragmented that self might appear—and they seem to have a meaning that can be plumbed. On a certain level, as with The Waste Land, a hermeneutical reading can be constructed without seeming particularly forced: there is general agreement as to what these texts are "about, " an aboutness within which and around which the critical arguments are contained. The quatrains, on the other hand, are far more resistant to the possibility of any such satisfying, closed hermeneutical reading; critics are still arguing over what the quatrains are about, what is happening, who is being portrayed. That is to say, using Paul de Man's later formulations, the quatrains foreground the questions of what one is reading, of how one reads, "questions all belonging to the realm of empirical poetics... rather than hermeneutics (what is the truth of the text)".

Although the production of strange narratives has been endemic in Eliot criticism as a whole, the bizarre nature of those engendered by the quatrains is on a level all its own. As Christopher Ricks comments: "Most critics of poetry are poets manque, but many critics of Eliot are novelists manques". To a certain extent this is an inevitable result of Eliot's poetic technique: his poetry, with its ellipses, allusions, jumps, successions of images that seem to interrelate, creates a need to provide links, the connecting tissue. As Eliot famously wrote in his preface to his translation of St John Perse's Anabase:

Any obscurity of the poem, on first readings, is due to the suppression of "links in the chain, " of explanatory and connecting matter and not to incoherence, or to the love of cryptogram.... The sequence of images coincides and concentrates into one intense impression.... The reader has to allow the images to fall into his memory successively without questioning the reasonableness of each at the moment; so that, at the end, a total effect is produced.

Peter Ackroyd agrees that the quatrains are particularly opaque in this way, but then, like a number of critics, suggests that the solution is a biographical one, revolving around Eliot's marriage: "The poems are difficult principally because although they seem to work in objective or dramatic terms—

with the titles setting the ‘scene’, as it were—their transitions and imagery come from some private source of feeling which is either concealed or obscure and unarticulated”. On the other hand, in reading Eliot's criticism of the time it becomes clear that he himself deliberately wanted to create this effect. This is not to deny that biographical and psychological concerns are operative in the poetry, but rather to insist that the driving metaphors of surface and depth are extremely problematic when dealing with these poems. Eliot's relationship with his wife does not offer the solution to these poems but instead offers a key that can be turned in the lock to reveal not the true garden, but a different one.

Ronald Schuchard also reads the quatrains biographically, not as the general product of an unhappy marriage but as the direct result of Eliot's knowledge of his wife's affair with Bertrand Russell. He argues that Eliot's “vision of sexual humanity was terribly darkened, ” and consequently the poetry of this period necessarily and inevitably evinces disgust at human sexuality (1988, 211). Aside from the lack of evidence that the affair took place (the only evidence is a letter of Russell's) or that if it took place Eliot knew about it, the only trouble with this argument is that Eliot's poetry from its inception betrayed a horror and fear of sexuality, particularly female sexuality. According to Ackroyd, the poems that Eliot wrote in Paris in 1910 and 1911 all evoke and show this fear and horror: “[In a poem] dated March 1911, the ‘Absolute'... is depicted as a female syphilitic spider.

Even in the more achieved poetry, the images of women are of those who destroy his self-possession and elicit from him feelings of self-disgust”. The critics who wish to read the 1917 to 1919 poems biographically generally emphasize the “Ode” which Eliot published in the 1920 English edition and then cut from the American. It depicts a sordid and repulsive marriage night with one stanza ending with the phrase: “succuba eviscerate, ” a phrase (one can hardly call it an image) clearly linked to the 1911 syphilitic female spider. The poem that replaced “Ode” in the American edition, “Hysteria, ” also evinces fear and disgust at female sexuality and was originally published in 1915, just before his marriage to Vivienne. The frequent occurrence of this theme and motif long before Eliot met Vivienne brings into question any straight correspondence between Eliot's marriage, "Ode, " and the rest of these poems. In addition, this sort of biographical reading of the poems is complicated by the fact that Eliot showed Vivienne his work and seemed to have listened to her criticism. In The Waste Land manuscript, for example, Vivienne has written "wonderful" next to the passage that begins, "My nerves are bad tonight. Yes, bad. Stay with me"—a passage which has usually been perceived as representing their marriage. Indeed, she even suggested an extra line which Eliot inserted into the final copy: "What you get married for if you don't want children" (Waste Land Facsimile, 11, 15).

Rather than excluding "Ode" simply because of Vivienne, it seems more likely that Eliot excised it for other personal as well as political reasons. Its full title was "Ode, On Independence Day, July 4th 1918, " a title that would clearly have more resonance in America than in England. He was concerned as it was that he would simply be regarded as "disgusting" by American reviewers but in addition he obviously worried about how his mother would react to his work. As he wrote to his brother.

I sent you a few days ago by registered post... a copy of my Limited Edition. I have not sent this to Mother or told her about it. I thought of cutting out the page on which occurs a poem called "Ode" and sending the book as if there had been an error and an extra page put in.... The "ode" is not in the edition that Knopf is publishing, all the others are. And I suppose she will have to see that book. Do you think that "Sweeney Erect" will shock her?

In sum, rather than simply looking at the quatrains in relation to either Eliot's career as a whole or in terms of his marriage, it is far more productive to view the poems of 1917 to 1919 as a discrete body of work. Doing so helps elucidate not only Eliot's own writing, but also the period as a whole, for this work, both poetry and criticism, which culminated in 1920 with the publication of Poems and The Sacred Wood, was intended and planned as a significant intervention into the culture of the time. Their form and style, unlike those of the earlier poems and later The Waste Land, were chosen and worked on as a direct critical response to the contemporary artistic and cultural scene. As Eliot remembered in 1959, the form came first: " studied Gautier's poems and then we thought, |Have I anything to say in which this form will be useful?' and we experimented. The form gave impetus to the content". Pound's own earlier reminiscence in the July 1932 Criterion makes the political nature of the intervention much clearer:

> [In 1917] two authors, neither engaged in picking the other's pocket, decided that the dilution of vers libre, Amygism, Lee Masterism, general floppiness had gone too far and that some counter-current must be set going.... Remedy prescribed:
>
> "Emaux et Camees" (or the Bay State Hymn Book). Rhyme and regular strophes.
>
> Result: Poems in Mr. Eliot's second volume not contained in his first... also Hugh Selwyn Mauberley.

It is no coincidence that Eliot's first major piece of literary criticism in 1917, "Reflections on Vers Libre, " was an attack on Amy Lowell and Imagism. And by June 1917 Pound had engineered it so that Eliot was Assistant Editor of The Egoist and able to review and comment on whatever he liked.

If we take 1921 to 1922 as the annus mirabilis of modernism, after which it was unignorable and rapidly institutionalized in the literary academy, then what is happening between 1917 and 1920 looks very different. It is a space of fluidity and flux, when earlier formations are breaking down and new ones are only just emerging. During these three years Eliot was formulating many of the theoretical ideas that came to underpin the New Criticism, which, paradoxically, ignored not only the creative work he was producing during this period but also much of the work of other writers whom he was influenced by and praised. In particular it ignores the crucial figure of Wyndham Lewis: Tarr was being serialized in The Egoist from 1916 to 1919 and, when it was released as a novel Eliot reviewed it there. Indeed, what Fredric Jameson says about Lewis in the "Prologue" to his Fables of Aggression is strikingly applicable to Eliot's poetry of this period as well. Jameson argues that Tarr can electrify new readers and that its style, its reinvention" of the sentence, demands "new reading habits for which we are less and less prepared". The reason for this, he says, is that "Anglo-American modernism has... traditionally been dominated by an impressionistic aesthetic" and "the most influential formal impulses of canonical modernism have been strategies of inwardness, which set out to reappropriate an alienated universe by transforming it into personal styles and private languages". As a consequence, "such wills to style have seemed in retrospect to reconfirm the very privatization and fragmentation of social life against which they meant to protest". This is a useful summary of the type of readings the pre-conversion Eliot poems, in particular, have generally elicited. Jameson goes on to argue that, as a consequence of this retrospective, inward, alienated individualistic reading,

> The initial, passionately subversive force of the modernist symbolic act is ever fainter and more distant for the contemporary reader... and this not least because the modernist canon has itself become classical, institutionalized within the university.
>
> If it is ideal to deplore... the loss or repression of that original antisocial resonance of the great modernisms, it is on the other hand a matter of some historical gratification to come upon a modernism which is still extant and breathing. The neglect of Lewis is thus a happy accident for us, who can then, as from out of a time capsule, once more sense that freshness and virulence of modernizing stylization less and less accessible in the faded text of his contemporaries. Except for his 1917 to 1919 poetry written under the pressure of Lewis's presence. Eliot's work became an integral part of that canonical modernism from which Lewis was excluded. However, the quatrains exist in a similar "time capsule" as Lewis's work and have the same "freshness" and "virulence." Furthermore, Jameson's sense of Lewis's mechanized language, of its

metonymic impulse that Lewis acknowledges yet seeks to contain within larger formal structures, is strikingly apt for the quatrain poems, where the allusive content fissures uncontrollably within a strict rhyme and strophe scheme.

Eliot's criticism of this period repeatedly emphasizes the mechanical technical, professional aspect of writing "good" poetry. The articles he wrote for The Egoist consistently attack the notion of inspiration, " which he perceives as a particularly English disease. In "Professionalism or..., " for example, he takes to task the Times Literary Supplement's criticism of professionalism in the arts, arguing that the "British worship of inspiration... in literature is merely an avoidance of comparison with foreign literatures, a dodging of standards". Instead of considering the professional the enemy, Eliot identifies him as the "man of mixed motives" exemplified by the figures of the "Victorian epoch." Contra the TLS, what causes degeneration, decline, decadence, in the arts is "mixed motives": the writing such motives produce is not, cannot be, coherent or ordered since it seeks to be something other than a work of art. He ends the article with an assertion that poetry is hard work, a craft that must be learned in a professional manner: "Technique is more volatile; it can only be learned, the more difficult part of it by absorption. Try to put into a sequence of simple quatrains the continuous syntactic variety of Gautier or Blake, or compare these two with A. E. Housman. Surely professionalism in art is hard work on style with singleness of purpose."

Eliot's attempt to create the "continuous syntactic variety" in the quatrains took time. In the first, "The Hippopotamus" (1917), there is no syntactical run-on between stanzas and, with the exception of the seventh and eighth, they divide up equally: the first two lines of the stanza describe "the hippopotamus" and the last two the "True Church." By the time he wrote "Sweeney Erect" in 1919, however, his technical control was secure. The first stanza divides at the end of the second line, but the repetition of "Paint me" means that it is not an oppositional divide. The second strophe has no division, the third divides after the second line with a full stop and all three stanzas are end-stopped. The fourth stanza divides at the third line, which ends with a colon, followed by a sentence that runs on into the next stanza, one without any division. The sixth stanza returns to being end-stopped with no oppositional division. The next varies again, since, to be understood, the first line has to be run into the next ("The lengthened shadow of a man/Is history")—until here all the lines are complete clauses in themselves: they could be separated from those preceding or succeeding and still make sense. The eighth stanza then becomes, strikingly, the first to preserve the Gautier "norm, " a division into two oppositional halves. With the next two strophes the syntactical running on between them recurs but is made more complex (than that of stanzas four and five, for example) because of our uncertainty as to whether it is the "ladies" who are "observing" or "Mrs. Turner." The final stanza begins with a line containing the heaviest caesura in the poem and again has no division.

Along with Eliot's sense that writing requires hard work and professional expertise comes a concomitant elitism: if, as he asserts, "The profession of poetry is fatiguing, " and if it "is in the inevitable dry times that work counts when a writer must either master a style or be mastered by a mannerism, " only a few people will have either the dedication or the talent to achieve such mastery. Furthermore, if a writer achieves such mastery, only a few people will be able to understand the work: "There will always be a few intelligent people to understand James, " he writes in "In Memory of Henry James, " "and to be understood by a few intelligent people is all the influence a man requires". These "intelligent" people are almost certain to be cosmopolitan, to be aware of and influenced by other European writings and as such they will be perceived as being dangerous by the "British reading classes" who "usually object to any writer who has actually assimilated foreign influence, grown his lion-skin, become suspect in the fold". The importance of assimilating foreign influences is asserted repeatedly by Eliot, often by arguing that this is more possible for an American. Indeed, in his obituary for Henry james he asserts that only an American can be a

European: "It is the final perfection, the consummation of an American to become, not an Englishman, but a European—something which no born European, no person of any European nationality, can become". An essay on Turgenev places a similar emphasis on the writer's cosmopolitan nature, but there Eliot argues that such cosmopolitan exile is productive because of the fusing of cultures that it necessitates:

Turgenev was, in fact, a perfect example of the benefits of transplantation; there was nothing lost by it; he understood at once how to take Paris, how to make use of it. A position which for a smaller man may be merely a compromise, or a means of disappearance, was for Turgenev... a source of authority, in addressing either Russian or European; authority but also isolation. He has a position which he literally made for himself and indeed may be said to have invented. It is not a position of popular appeal, as he neither aped French writing nor exploited the Russian backwater.

Eliot often couches the productive and vital nature of this type of transplantation in scientific, neo-Darwinist terms; he repeatedly emphasizes the "importance of cross-breeding in poetry, " for only in that way can the culture be strengthened. "The serious writer of verse, " he writes in "Verse Pleasant and Unpleasant, " must be prepared to cross himself with the best verse of other languages". Consequently, his praise or disparagement of writers is dependent on how parochial they are: he criticizes Georgian poetry for the fact that "no crossing visible" and praises the writers in Wheels, an anthology edited by the Sitwells, for being "conscious of the fact that literature exists in other languages than their own". Ignoring the advances in other countries makes a writer antiquated and redundant:

A poet like a scientist is contributing toward the organic development of culture: it is just as absurd for him not to know the work of his predecessors or of men writing in other languages as it would be for a biologist to be ignorant of Mendel or De Vries. It is exactly as wasteful for a poet to do what has been done already as for a biologist to rediscover Mendel's discoveries. The French poets in question have made discoveries in verse of which we cannot afford to be ignorant, discoveries which are not merely a concern for French syntax. To remain with Wordsworth is equivalent to ignoring the whole of science subsequent to Erasmus Darwin. This Darwinist idea of "organic development" underpins the elitist, anti-social, political edge behind much of Eliot's criticism of this time. Consequently, in "Observations" he agrees with Ford Madox Hueffer that "what we want is to disturb and alarm the public" by "point out that the intelligence of a nation must go on developing, or it will deteriorate; and that every writer who does not help to develop the language is to the extent to which he is read a positive agent of deterioration. That the forces of deterioration are a large crawling mass and the forces of development half a dozen men". These "half a dozen men" are presumably the five he mentions—Hueffer, Pound, Joyce, Lewis, who "write living English, " Jean de Bosschere, who "writes a living French"—and the one he does not: Eliot himself.

Eliot's two reviews of Lewis are especially interesting in that he praises Lewis unreservedly and there is the feeling that Eliot is also moving toward an explanation and ideal of satire and satirical intent that was the driving force behind his own "scurrilous French". The last two quatrain poems—"Sweeney Among the Nightingales" and "Sweeney Erect"—evince a sense of impending violence or violence suspended that can be seen to be formulating in his assertion that Tarr is "terrifying, [which] is the test of a new work of art. When a work of art no longer terrifies us we may know that we were mistaken, or that our senses are dulled". Tarr is terrifying because it is both a critique and a portrayal of the contemporary situation: "It is like our civilization criticized, our acrobatics animadverted upon adversely, by an orang-outang of genius, Tarzan of the Apes" (Tarr" 106). As this last phrase suggests, Eliot argues that Tarr is so powerful because it exposes the savagery behind the veneer of "modern civilization" by using the resources and knowledge of the modern mind. The review ends with one of Eliot's earliest programmatic statements of the artist:

The artist I believe is more primitive, as well as more civilized, than his contemporaries, his experience is deeper than civilization and he only uses the phenomena of civilization in expressing it. Primitive instincts and the acquired habits of ages are confounded in the ordinary man. In the work of Mr. Lewis we recognize the thought of the modern and the energy of the cave man. The end result of an "orang-outang" "animadvert" on contemporary civilization is satire. And no one needs the use of satire more than an intelligent man living among the English: No one can be so aware of the environment of Stupidity as the Englishman; no other nationality perhaps provides so dense an environment as the English. The intelligent Englishman is more aware of loneliness, has more reserves than the man of intelligence of any other nation....

Humour (I am only speaking of real humour) is the instinctive attempt of a sensitive mind to protect beauty against ugliness; and to protect itself against stupidity. The older British humour is of this sort. Mr. Lewis's humour is near to Dickens but on the right side for it is not too remote from Ben Jonson. Eliot here combines elitism, intelligence, humour, being-in-England and cosmopolitanism (savagery and civilization are cross-national) to depict a satiric tradition that has its origins in the Elizabethan period and that Eliot wanted his quatrains to revive. In the year following this Lewis review, Eliot began to publish essays on the Elizabethan and Jacobean satirists, but his attitude toward them reflects the critical filter through whom he read them, Baudelaire, specifically his essay "On the Essence of Laughter."

Baudelaire's essay is dense with Christian imagery and ideas. His argument develops out of the quotation: "The sage/ saint laughs not save in fear and trembling". The sage is a believer, someone quickened with the spirit of the lord, " and one who "trembles at the thought of having laughed". Laughter is perceived as a temptation, as satanic, as something that was a consequence of the fall. Accordingly, Baudelaire argues that the "comic vanishes altogether from the point of view of absolute knowledge and power". If this is true, he continues, laughter is therefore the preserve both of the non-sage, the "madmen, " and of the non-knowledgeable, the "ignorant". As a consequence the comic is the "clearest token of the satanic in man" since it comes from "the idea of one's own superiority"—for Baudelaire the cause of the Fall and of insanity: " idea of one's own superiority [is al Satanic idea, if there ever was one! And what pride and delusion!

For it is a notorious fact that all the madmen in the asylums have an excessively overdeveloped idea of their own superiority.... Note too, that laughter is one of the most frequent and numerous expressions of madness". Since laughter is Satanic, an effect of the fall from grace, it is necessarily contradictory in that it betokens "infinite grandeur" in "relation to the beasts" and "infinite misery" in "relation to the absolute being". It is the "collision of these two infinites" that causes laughter, a collision that happens within the person laughing: the "comic and the capacity for laughter are situated in the laugher and by no means in the object of his laughter". Baudelaire's idea of the contradictory nature of laughter helps explain why the Sweeney quatrains in particular make it difficult for the reader to secure an outside vantage point from which to observe the events in the poems. The poems manipulate the reader into taking positions of knowing superiority that are destabilized by uncertainty as to what is being portrayed as well as to whether s/he is implicated in the events, since the very vagueness of "what the hell is going on" means, to a greater or lesser extent, that the reader is creating what is going on. As a consequence any secure position from which to analyze the characters or events in the poems is precluded as soon as a reader decides that one or another is comic.

Baudelaire defines what he calls the "significative comic, " which contains "art and the moral idea". The "visibly double" "element" of this comedy insures that laughter is always "a moment late". What Baudelaire seems to be suggesting is that "significative comedy" draws the reader/watcher into the work, the "art, " thereby forcing him/her to take a position in relation to the events or characters portrayed and, by so doing, to laugh. Such laughter is deeply Satanic, since the displacing of laughter insures that when it does come it is conscious: that is, the reader's deliberate and conscious self-positioning enacts his/her own sense of superiority and thus causes him/her to laugh. When the significative comedy is "push... to its furthest limits, you reach the savage variety" of the comic and, in a sentence Eliot quoted in a 1920 review of the London literary scene, Baudelaire says that " find true comic savagery... you have to cross the channel and visit the foggy realms of spleen". What distinguishes true comic savagery" is the "violence" of the events it portrays.

Baudelaire's formulation of savage comedy clearly underwrites Eliot's 1919 and 1920 analyses of the Elizabethan and Jacobean dramatists which were collected in The Sacred Wood. In the Christopher Marlowe essay, for example, he writes:

If one takes the Jew of Malta not as a tragedy, or as a "tragedy of blood, " but as a farce, the concluding act becomes intelligible.... I say farce, but with the enfeebled humour of our times the word is a misnomer; it is a farce of the old English humour, the terribly serious, even savage humour, the humour which spent its last breath on the decadent genius of Dickens. Baudelaire's idea of the displacement of effect caused by significative comedy also seems closely related to many of Eliot's more famous and canonical poetic ideas. His repeated assertions that the work of art should only produce emotions integral to itself, that the "end... of poetry is a pure contemplation from which all the accidents of personal emotion are removed, " echo Baudelaire's notion that the double element of significative comedy causes the reader to position her/himself in relation to the work and then and only then, to affect. A similar form of displacement is acted out in

Eliot's assertion that the artist should seek an "objective correlative" in which the private emotions can inhere and, thus, become "particular, " not emotion belonging to a particular individual but a particular emotion that can belong to any individual. Eliot is aiming for the type of "frigid, " "inhuman" "intelligence" that he praises in Lewis: a distancing intelligence that enables him to utilize dark neuroses—both his own and society's—and to distance himself from such utilization; a satiric intelligence that enables him to implicate the reader through the displacement intrinsic to significative comedy; and a scientific intelligence that enables him to set up "laboratory" situations in which and to which the reader must react. In short, he seeks the sort of poetry he perceives de Bosschere as epitomizing:

M. de Bosschere is in fact almost a pure intellectual; leaving, as if disdainfully, our emotions to form as they will around the situation which his brain has selected. The important thing is not how we are to feel about it, but how it is. De Bosschere's austerity is terrifying. A poet like M. De Bosschere is an intellectual by his obstinate refusal to adulterate his poetic emotions with human emotions... He thereby limits the number of his readers and leaves the majority groping for a clue which does not exist. The effect is sometimes an intense frigidity which I find altogether admirable. The last quatrain he wrote on Sweeney, "Sweeney Erect, " exemplifies this "frigid" intelligence: it is a deeply disturbing poem which implicates any reader drawn into constructing meanings from it, meanings that are made on destabilized ground.

"Sweeney Erect" refuses to allow any representational or referential reading to settle, since how one line is read alters the reading and meaning of the rest of the poem. Eliot's idea of the mechanical, technical aspect of verse writing is relevant here since, as Hugh Kenner notes, the poem is, on one level, simply a collection of facts, arranged paratactically together, from or with which the reader creates syntactic connections. Part of the disturbing power of the poem comes from the concomitant literalization of metaphor: is Sweeney gesturing like an orang-outang or is an orang-outang gesturing? As Eliot wrote in his 1918 "Studies in Contemporary Criticism": "The healthy metaphor adds to the strength of the language; it makes available some of that physical source of energy upon which the life of language depends. 'In her strong toil of grace' is a complicated metaphor which has this effect; and, as in most good metaphor, you can hardly say where the metaphorical and the literal meet". The usual narrative of the poem told by critics concerns an "epileptic" woman who has a fit while Sweeney shaves, a narrative that, in its very specificity, creates problems as to how to read the following stanzas. Why would the women assume it was "hysteria"? A fit is like an "hysterical" attack perhaps, but why bring "sal volatile" and "brandy neat"? Furthermore, the earlier stanzas suggest that Sweeney is uncaring and unfeeling, an intimation that "epileptic" should perhaps be read figuratively—indeed as the women do: the epileptic fit is hysteria since the woman is hysterical because Sweeney is leaving her.

She could, therefore, be connected to "Nausicaa" weeping for Ulysses. Alternatively, since Polypheme was also tricked by Ulysses and proceeded to hurl abuse and rocks at the Greek hero as he sailed away, she could also be "Polypheme, " an identification that would tie in with the sense of disgust at women and with the idea that "she" is the primitive in contrast to the "erect" Sweeney. "Sweeney Erect, " in turn, might suggest that he is the missing link, homo erectus and that the reader, homo sapiens, is superior to, more civilized than, Sweeney. Yet since this seems to be some sort of description of contemporary affairs, such interpretive specifications enact the reader's involvement as well as perhaps the sense of being disgraced by an overactive imagination.

If the "epileptic" can be either Nausicaa or Polypheme, or both, or indeed neither, then strange things begin to happen to gender in the poem. If the woman is figured as Polypheme, how does Nausicaa fit in? Who is Nausicaa? Could it be Sweeney? Preposterous as such suggestions may seem, the description of the fourth stanza can be seen to merge genders:

This withered root of knots of hair
Slitted below and gashed with eyes,

This oval O cropped out with teeth: For Pinion this is a description of Sweeney's face, for Schuchard Doris's. Pinkney points out that the image can be seen as a figuring of the vagina in horrific and fearful terms. But could it not also be a figuring of Sweeney's penis, a "withered root"; "slitted below" would then be his "broadbottom, " the eyes being his orifices? Both readings of the description—as a vagina or as a penis—connect with the notion of the one-eyed Cyclops. If genders are indeed merging, could this be a description of a homosexual encounter? The close relationship between "teeth" and "root" would thus mean that the phrase "wipes the suds around his face, " is suggestive of sperm, this possible reading giving another twist to the poem's feeling of disgust and its figuring of this site as being debased and corrupt sexuality. Alternatively, since both gender, face and genitalia are all exchangeable here, perhaps Sweeney and Doris have just completed a session of mutual oral sex? The whole scene is cockeyed, creating the shifting possibilities of the Kama Sutra.

On the other hand, all such readings are dependent upon there being someone else in the room. If, on the other hand, the "epileptic" is really" not there with Sweeney, the apparent depiction of a sexual act becomes masturbatory. All the poem says, its statement of fact, is that Sweeney waits "until the shriek subsides, " the poem then moving immediately to: "The epileptic on the bed/Curves backward, clutching at her sides." If the "epileptic" is in another room, if this is another scene in "the house, " this could explain why Sweeney disappears from the poem and the women are described. There is certainly no evidence that "Doris" "enters" the same room as Sweeney, only that she enters a room where someone, perhaps the "epileptic, " probably is "bringing" refreshments. Again what this house is, whether a boarding-house or a brothel or both, is unclear.

The fourth and fifth stanzas have generally been read as a brutal depiction of sexual intercourse, perhaps even a rape (although, as noted earlier, some critics see it as depicting Sweeney and/or another waking up). William Arrowsmith pushes this further, arguing that the scene arises from Eliot's reading in anthropology and that it is a description both of defloration and of ritual. But the way in which discrete, paratactic information is placed side by side makes any interpretation dependent upon where the reader positions her/himself in relation to earlier pieces of information. For example, the sudden shift from stanza five to stanza six disorientates all of these representational interpretations: the sudden jerk from "clawing at the pillow slip" to Sweeney at the mirror suggests there might be a separation between him and the action of the previous stanza.

Rather than describing a sexual act, however, the fourth and fifth stanzas could be seen depicting either an abortion or a birth. This would fit into the idea of miscegenation, of the primitive meeting the civilized: any child produced from the union of "Nausicaa and Polypheme" would be presumably hideously deformed. Sweeney with his "razor, " his backstreet medical instrument, is cutting the umbilical cord or causing an abortion. This medical interpretation would certainly connect the "steam" "sheets, " Sweeney's washing of himself and his callous, unfeeling attitude becomes a mechanical, professional one. Either interpretation would elucidate the social concern of the household: an abortion or an illegitimate child would do "the house no sort of good."

Readings proliferate alarmingly: these past few pages only touch the problem. The whole poem is so infinitely interpretable because all these sentences, many of which are not "sentences" but fragments of sentences ("image complexes" as Veronica Forrest-Thomson calls them), can be placed into innumerable referential categories. The poem, its individual lines as well as clusters of lines, can refer to the outside world in an infinite number of ways. In effect, then, the words have meaning only in relation to one another, relationships (and referents) that are made up of arbitrary (but necessary) reader choices. In other words, to say this is an epileptic woman is to create a reference that persuades and insures that the poem is read in relation to that referent; and if "epileptic" is read figuratively, that change of reference changes the poem. An abortion seems to me more "referentially" likely than a birth, in that the poem is so mechanically violent. Yet the depiction of such a violent birth would certainly not be out of place within the poem and within the Eliot oeuvre: "Birth and copulation and death./That's all the facts when you come to brass tacks."

As far as I am aware I am the first person to suggest that either an abortion or a birth is taking place. And so, what does this say about my mind? Although he is referring to one particular interpretation of "Sweeney Among the Nightingales, " Ricks's description of this unsettling" process is apt and accurate:

Eliot wrote in his dissertation: "An idea which may appear to an outsider a pure imagination, possesses fatality for one crazed by fear or passion." The same goes for the imagination of a reader, who is both insider and outsider. Piers Gray has urged that "the connotations of animality are suggested in the name Rachel: a |rache' is a |hunting dog which pursues its prey by scent'." But the nature of this unsettling poem is not such as to assure us whether, for instance, this suggestion is a warranted deducing or a pure imagination crazed by fear or passion.

The technique of the poem—its use of "significative comedy, " its mechanized, factual language, the sense that something sexual and/or violent is going on—forces the reader to make uneasy choices in order to make sense of the poem. Each choice is conscious—and each choice can be unconscionable.

Ten years after writing the quatrains, Eliot returned to the two French writers—Baudelaire and Gautier—who had most influenced those poems. In the essay "Baudelaire" he praises the French poet for confronting his readers with the necessity of choice: "So far as we are human, what we do must be either evil or good; so far as we do evil or good, we are human; and it is better, in a paradoxical way, to do evil than to do nothing: at least we exist". The fact that the quatrains also constrain the reader to make similar conscious choices might explain why, after his conversion, he never denigrated them as he denigrated The Waste Land: "Various critics have done me the honour to interpret the poem in terms of criticism of the contemporary world, have considered it, indeed, as an important bit of social criticism. To me it was only the relief of a personal and wholly insignificant grouse against life; it is just a piece of rhythmical grumbling" (Waste Land Facsimile xxxiii). In the light of Eliot's criticism this last sentence is particularly disparaging, since it suggests that in The Waste Land the personal emotion is not distanced in the manner of "significative comedy." That is to say, emotion was not contained in the work in such a way as to effect a displacement between the "art" and the "moral element, " and, as consequence, the reader is not forced consciously to take a position. Instead the work does the positioning. The satire of "Sweeney Erect" refuses an easy vantage point: the past, the allusions, do not create a secure moral position from which to judge the present since a reader does not know what s/he is even judging until s/he has actively created the present.

Eliot moved away from this Baudelairean "savage comedy" as soon as he began to conceive of writing a long poem about contemporary London. The quatrains still exist in section three of The Waste Land—or at least the vestiges of the form—but the effect is very different. There is a definite and clear meta-narrative posited and available: "I Tiresias" perceive "all." The reader is positioned by this voice and is told how to regard, interpret the events: the "young man" is "one of the low"; the woman is "bored and tired"; and so on. It is a story arranged syntactically for the reader, not a paratactic collection of facts that the reader has to arrange syntactically for her/himself.

The same is true for The Waste Land as a whole—its title creates a narrative position from which a relatively unproblematic hermeneutical reading can be created. As Valentine Cunningham points out, it was I. A. Richards's interpretation of The Waste Land and The Sacred Wood that had become the dominant reading of Eliot by the end of the 1920s: "The poem, says Richards... expresses the post-war sense of desolation, of uncertainty, of futility, of the baselessness of aspirations, of the vanity of endeavour and a thirst for life-giving water which seems suddenly to have failed'". A reading that clearly fits in with the social position of the literary academic, alienated and tenured, looking with disdain at the squalor of modern life in comparison to the great tradition of art.

The crucial theoretical text of Eliot became "Tradition and the Individual Talent, " written immediately after the final quatrains were published. However, it must be remembered that it was a particular way of interpreting the essay which fostered its becoming "crucial." It was seen as espousing the superiority of the past over the degraded present, a reading The Waste Land clearly supports with its movement from the squalor of a contemporary assignation to the glorious past of Elizabeth and Leicester. The essay itself, however, is considerably more ambiguous, since Eliot says that "the historical sense involves a perception, not only of the pastness of the past, but its presence". This implies that the relevance of the past lies both in its difference from and in its similarity to, the present. Ulysses leaving Nausicaa could be of a different order from Sweeney's behavior, but it could also be the same. As Eliot later wrote, possibly with deliberate obfuscation:

I was not aware and am not aware now, of having drawn a contrast between a contemporary world of slums, hysterics and riverside promiscuity etc. with any visibly more romantically lovely earlier world. I mean there is no nostalgia for the trappings of the past, so far as I can see and no illusion about the world ever having been a pleasanter place to live in than it is now. Now clearly in The Waste Land this was almost certainly not the case and, whatever Eliot's intentions, it certainly was not how the poem and this essay came to be read. Accordingly, the poems of Eliot that were canonized were those which conformed to this ideology of the alienated, academic intellectual: "The Love Song of J. Alfred Prufrock, " "Portrait of a Lady, " "Gerontion." and The Waste Land.

The quatrains, on the other hand, the works that made manifest the unstable nature of hermeneutical readings and inscribed the reader into the texts in such a way that s/he was forced to make conscious choices, were ignored, disowned, down played. Perhaps as a result the quatrains are alive for me in a way that the more canonical poems are not. A poem like "Sweeney Erect" still forces readers to take positions themselves, unlike The Waste Land, whose meta-discourse does the positioning for them. Consequently, the criticism of the quatrains is a critic's dream-battlefield in that, armed with the poems—they do not even have to be read against the grain—s/he finds the prejudices of previous critics revealed with startling clarity. The poem draws people out and insures that the unwary, the unself-critical, leave hostages to fortune. Indeed, even the wary and the self-critical reveal them more than they would like. To adapt an earlier sentence: I have found myself "involved" and perhaps "disgraced" by an overactive imagination.

The voice of this Calling: the enduring legacy of T.S. Eliot

IN 1953, THE FIRST EDITION of The Conservative Mind was subtitled From Burke to Santayana; the second and every edition thereafter bore the subtitle From Burke to Eliot. Not only did this adjustment afford Kirk a bookend better consisting with Burke, but the change was also fortuitous as one element of a broader clarification of Kirk's premise and purpose. For the second edition, Kirk enlarged his discussion of Eliot and he also recast the final chapter, changing its final section from one called "The plan of action for American conservatives" to one entitled "The conservative as poet." Thus, Kirk emphasized formally an argument that runs throughout his book—that the most vital expressions of conservative thought are not to be measured so much by effective political activity as by their reflection in the tradition of humane letters, particularly in those writers who (to borrow Kirk's habitual wording) furnished anew the wardrobe of the moral imagination.

In T. S. Eliot, Kirk found just such an exemplar of thoughtful conservatism informed by an acute literary sensibility. Perhaps more importantly, in selecting Eliot as something of a latter-day counterpart to Burke—certainly as a figure more substantial than Santayana and one still living at the time of his writing—Kirk was looking ahead, beyond the tradition of thought he had surveyed, to identify possible models and resources for cultivating the "Conservatives' Promise, " as he titled his concluding chapter. The golden anniversary of the original publication of The Conservative

Mind offers an occasion to reassess that promise and to suggest what the legacy of T.S. Eliot has to offer another generation as we work the fields of a different cultural landscape, venturing to renew what Eliot called "The life of significant soil."

I

Kirk's substitution of Eliot for Santayana was not merely an afterthought but rather indicative of his sustained engagement with Eliot as he sought to honor an intellectual debt. Shortly after arriving at Saint Andrew's University in 1948 to commence his doctoral studies and to compose the manuscript that would become The Conservative Mind, Kirk discovered Eliot's Notes towards the Definition of Culture; immediately, he felt a sense of intellectual kinship. The two men met for the first time in Edinburgh in 1953 and that meeting began a friendship that lasted until Eliot's death in 1965 and which issued in the publication six years later of Kirk's long-germinating study, Eliot and His Age: T.S. Eliot's Moral Imagination in the Twentieth Century.

Kirk's book on Eliot makes explicit and endeavors to substantiate a strong claim more modestly adumbrated in his survey of conservative thought: "ours has been the Age of Eliot." In the years from the end of the First World War through the first score after the Second, Kirk argued, "Thomas Stearns Eliot, a shy colossus, bestrode the period as Virgil or Dante or Dryden or Johnson had dominated very different times." In thus characterizing Eliot's dominion, Kirk was not simply designating an era of literary history or weighing the poet's considerable influence; nor was he just paying tribute to the one who gave us in The Waste Land the preeminent metaphor for our times; rather, for Kirk, "Eliot was the principal champion of the moral imagination in the twentieth century." Eliot summed up the spiritual loss and longing of an epoch so "that, beyond the boredom and the horror, men might perceive the glory."

Kirk saw in Eliot a vital link to the past and a promising link to the future. But he was also aware at the time he finished Eliot and His Age in 1971 that the "Age of Eliot" was waning and that forces were mustering to launch a post-mortem assault on Eliot's authority, reputation and credibility: "Catholic, royalist, classicist—a writer so bold as to describe himself thus sets himself up as a mark to be shot at by folks who worship strange gods." Kirk also predicted that the figure who had been so widely lionized in his lifetime, often for all the wrong reasons, would with the inevitable sharpening of ideological knives become prey to "the rising fad of psychobiography" and grist for the mill of the hermeneutics of suspicion. Even a cursory survey of writings on Eliot over the last two decades amply confirms the worst of Kirk's fears. Yet Kirk's sympathetic study of Eliot was not, it needs emphasizing, an exercise in hagiography. Actually, the book is remarkably judicious and at points sharply critical of its subject. Kirk sought to rescue Eliot as much from misguided deification as from malicious demonization.

Accordingly, Kirk's task was (and it remains ours today) to discern the enduring value of Eliot's life and work behind the associations, misconceptions and half-truths conjured by the poet's name: the upstart American who took the European literary establishment by storm; the iconoclastic pioneer of poetic modernism; the romantic nihilist and connoisseur of the aesthetics of despair; the arch architect of obscurity; the neurasthenic neo-medievalist and fusty Anglican; the literary dictator and mandarin arbiter of elite taste (though even Kirk indulges this last one a bit, repeating a touch too solemnly the facetious sobriquet of the aging director of Faber and Faber, "the Pope of Russell Square").

Clearing the ground for a measured appreciation of Eliot requires, too, a difficult sense of perspective—he is, at once, too close to us and too remote—and an acknowledgment of those things which were peculiar to his historical moment. The Waste Land, as Kirk concedes, is already "something of a period piece, " and many of the quarrels of pith and moment that Eliot marshaled between the wars in the pages of The Criterion today scarcely command more than antiquarian interest. Even so, Kirk insists and quite aside from the insights of Eliot's definition of culture, his idea of a Christian society and his assorted critical and literary judgments, the poet continues to offer latterday "pilgrims in the waste land" a collection of perduring symbols that can help us explicate our condition and direct our way.

But those symbols, even when rightly construed, risk losing their vitality and becoming shopworn through long familiarity and our very proximity to Eliot. Much like the hallowed Kirkian invocations of the "permanent things" and the "moral imagination," holding onto their meanings requires a constant struggle of translation and assimilation. This was something Eliot keenly understood and practiced and in such understanding, such practice, resides Eliot's continuing importance. To recover and keep vital the symbols we must also reclaim a measure of the disposition that engendered those symbols.

It is a commonplace that the sequence of Eliot's major poems and the pattern of his life enact a kind of Dantean pilgrimage from the inferno of the modern soul through the purgatorial fires of self-abnegation to a foretaste of paradisal communion. Eliot's own pilgrimage, an instance of our common journey of sanctification, was hardly a holiday excursion. Rather, it entailed an unremitting movement forward, together with a concerted motion out and back—to fathom the resources of tradition that afforded the possibility of meaningful pilgrimage in the first place and to find a way clear of the apparent impasse of modernity. Eliot provides us an example and a challenge—that of combining an appetite for significance with a search for order realized through unsentimental engagement with present-day reality and a sustained and discriminating conversation with tradition, all to approach the possibility of a hope beyond tradition. As Eliot put it, tradition "cannot be inherited and if you want it you must obtain it by great labour." From him we can learn anew the habit of reclaiming tradition, not simply as an intellectual activity or program but as a kind of ongoing spiritual discipline, even a penitential regimen—yet one, for all that, not without its own sense of play. And part of the tradition we have so to reclaim from manifest distortion and misunderstanding is Eliot himself.

II

"We had the experience but missed the meaning," wrote Eliot with suggestive generality in the third of his Four Quartets. His words may have some application to understanding the extraordinary phenomenon of his own career and reputation, the "mystique" of T. S. Eliot, its making and its undoing. In a belated "obituary" for the "Age of Eliot," penned by Cynthia Ozick for The New Yorker in 1989 (a typical screed, distinguished only in the venomous puerility of its ad hominem attacks), Ozick declares that nowadays "the bookish young" can find nothing of interest, much less value, in Eliot. To demonstrate the point, she enacts her own personal exorcism of the spirit of Eliot, confessing and then repenting her youthful idolatry of the poet: "He was lyric shudder and roseburst. He was, in brief, poetry incarnate; and poetry was what one lived for.... He was, to say it quickly, absolute art: high art, when art was at its most serious and elitist." Eliot, she says, was for her generation the quasidivine oracle of rapturous despair. But now, alas!, Ozick wails and exults to the accompaniment of Nero's fiddle,

High art is dead. The passion for inheritance is dead. Tradition is equated with obscurantism. The wall that divided serious high culture from the popular arts is breached; anything can count as "text." Knowledge—saturated in historical memory—is displaced by information, or memory without history: data.... For the modernists, the center notoriously did not hold; for us, there is no recollection of a center and nothing to miss, let alone mourn.

But to pursue the implications of her words—that knowledge saturated in historical memory may point the way back to a real center beyond whirling blips of data, as Eliot understood—that would interrupt the cathartic euphoria of Ozick's revisionist iconoclasm. She gives us, instead, facile psychologizing and the summary judgment that Eliot was just another crypto-fascist. The meaning and shape of Eliot's life and writing, she informs us, are really much simpler than we had reckoned: brilliant young Tom ran off to Europe to escape his parents; he married Vivien Haigh-Wood, the poor woman went mad and the experience produced The Waste Land; thereafter Eliot's soul shriveled and he became a bitter, atavistic churchwarden, hiding in the sacristy, consumed by sin and guilt. Such is the fruit of Ozick's smug disillusionment; but some of us seek more substantial food.

That Eliot perceived through his sense of sin a larger vision of the universal human predicament, that he transmuted his personal suffering into something greater, that he approached through art the reality of a grace beyond the reach of art, that he did so through the enlarging perspective of tradition: all this Ozick refuses to consider. Instead, she chooses to dance on the grave of the slain god, wistful yet gloating: "the truth is we had the experience and were irradiated by the meaning... it is now our unsparing obligation to disclaim the reactionary Eliot." Were she not so blinded by the glow of her own self-righteousness, she could have read on in Eliot's poem just past the line her allusion willfully misconstrues and pondered, "the past experience revived in the meaning/Is not the experience of one life only/But of many generations."

Though he retains more sympathetic and tougher-minded expositors—chief among them Denis Donoghue—Ozick's depreciation of Eliot is typical of our current critical climate and part of Eliot's value today is precisely that he models an alternative to such self-aggrandizing, pop post-modernism, with its ritualistic "slaying of the father"—not only a different idiom but a different disposition of mind and heart. (A further index of these parlous times is the fact that Cynthia Ozick is often accounted something of a "conservative, " and not without reason.) To find our way back from Ozick and her ilk to Eliot himself requires opening ourselves to tradition, to a particular attitude toward tradition and to its disciplined practice.

It is not simply that Eliot understood the practical imperative of what Simone Weil called l'enracinement, the need for roots—he wrote an appreciative preface to the English translation of her book of that title—but he also had a vital sense of what we might call the metaphysics of tradition. The variety of his writings, in poetry, drama, literary criticism and cultural theory, all attests that tradition, rightly conceived, offers neither a refuge of security nor mastery of time but rather constitutes, with and through language, the very medium of our participation in the shared human enterprise, the ground of genuine self-knowledge, the pre-condition for the perception of order and for the possibility of authentic development.

Yet he knew as much without hypostasizing or deifying tradition or history as a monolithic entity; he had a keen sense of time as a dynamic field of tensions and of the fragmentary quality of our fitful resistance to both willed and unconscious uprootedness. He understood, as well, that tradition is no substitute for deeper forms of transcendence, that tradition can only point toward the discovery and the gift of the dispensation of faith handed down for our health. Though he never developed this understanding explicitly in one place, such is the persistent, unifying concern of all his work, from its first articulation as a dimension of literary experience in "Tradition and the Individual Talent" (1919) through his musings on time, memory, history and transcendence in Four Quartets (1943). The same concern is not only explored but embodied and enacted in the sequence of his major poems, in his plays, essays and lectures, branching out from specifically literary questions to encompass and characterize Eliot's approach to society, culture, politics and religion. Eliot sought to see the whole, yet he also accepted and embraced the particular limitations of his own rootedness in time and place and in the various traditions that composed his self-understanding: "Home is where one starts from, " but "History is now and England."

Far from parochial or sectarian, though nonetheless firmly situated, Eliot's work can be understood as a kind of demonstration of Alisdair MacIntyre's insight into "the rationality of traditions" and accordingly connects with an important and ongoing philosophic discussion of the meanings and implications of traditio. From Edmund Burke to John Henry Newman and on through Eric Voegelin and Hans-Georg Gadamer, a large and various body of argument concurs in suggesting that the real enemy of human understanding and development is not the dead weight of tradition—which is never quite as dead as some suppose—but rather the conditions of deracinated individualism and rootless cosmopolitanism, coupled with all the attendant species of modern ideological presumption. The result is the deprivation of relational connectedness and the impoverishment of meaningful language, inducing the modern sense of anomie that Eliot diagnosed with ruthless precision and that even Ozick ruefully concedes to be the ongoing character of our times: "Men and bits of paper, whirled by the cold wind."

However, Eliot did not use tradition only or even primarily as an instrument of critique for contrasting a shabby present with a vibrant past—though crude readings of "TheLoveSong of J. Alfred Prufrock" and The Waste Land hardly get beyond such an inference. To be precise, Eliot did not "use" tradition at all, as if it were an implement or a power to be wielded; rather Eliot's acute and cultivated consciousness of tradition constituted, as much or more than personal experience, the very nerve of his creative and critical faculties. We will come to no just estimate of Eliot and his relevance unless we also appreciate the positive function of tradition in composing his particular moral imagination. "Since our concern was speech and speech impelled us/To purify the dialect of the tribe/And urge the mind to aftersight and foresight"—since language was the stuff of Eliot's calling—it may be helpful to think about his discipline of tradition in the light of Gadamer's historical hermeneutics, with its remarkably positive vindication and development of classical aesthetics and the humanist ethics of interpretation.

III

Against the dominance of subjectivism and the rule of "method" in aesthetic and interpretive theory since the Enlightenment, Gadamer argues for the solidly historical character of human knowledge and he rehabilitates the concept of "prejudice" to help reclaim the resources of authority and tradition as means of creative insight and rational participation: "Understanding is not to be thought of so much as an action of one's subjectivity, but as the placing of oneself within a process of tradition, in which past and present are constantly fused." Gadamer's central concept of the "fusion of horizons, " the intersection of past and present, has the character of a conversation with broad ethical implications. As it was for Eliot, tradition for Gadamer is the ground of morality, the basis of education and the arena of human freedom; and in language it becomes also a mode of our participation in the ground of being.

Though language itself in Gadamer's thought sometimes threatens to usurp the place of divinity, the validity and relevance of linguistically mediated tradition in his account rests on an Augustinian notion of the function of the Logos in human understanding and on the concept of personal application (subtilitas applicandi) inherited from German Pietism. That Eliot applied the lessons of tradition to his own conversion to Christian orthodoxy does not mean that he settled into an easy chair, communing privately with the Word in religious bliss; far from it, he recognized in conversion the beginning of "a long journey afoot, " one beset with the constant struggle of wresting meaning from language and tradition. With Gadamer and with the best of our post-modern avatars of suspicion, Eliot knew that "Words strain, /Crack and sometimes break" and that "History has many cunning passages, contrived corridors."

Tradition comes to us with a variety of multifarious voices: their meaningful orchestration and application to the concerns of the current moment demands openness, tact, judgment and discrimination. Tradition is not an object that can be mastered by method or controlled by technique, Gadamer insists, but rather presents itself to us as a gift in the form of an interpersonal relationship: "For tradition is a genuine partner in communication, with which we have fellowship as does the 'I' with a 'Thou.'" It is perhaps sadly revelatory that Eliot's poetry rarely dramatizes—and even his plays only intermittently—genuine moments of human intimacy and person-to-person communion; yet his poems are rich in Gadamerian dialogues with tradition, both explicitly and more subtly personified, from the voices of Virgil and Augustine in The Waste Land through the "familiar compound ghost" of Little Gidding and indeed, his essays consist largely of such conversations. As Gadamer argues and Eliot demonstrates, the ordered apprehension, assimilation and development of tradition is the work of an ethically informed historical consciousness, situated in time and place and requires the diligent application of prudence, an awareness of human finitude together with an appreciation of the educative value of suffering and the selfsurrender of creative interaction with art as a form of "play."

To descend for a moment from the heights of hermeneutic theory, we may glean a sense of the relevance of Gadamer's approach to understanding Eliot's own habitus of tradition by pausing to hear W. H. Auden's wonderful characterization of Eliot's intermingled personae as a household with "at least three permanent residents":

First, there is the archdeacon, who believes in and practices order, discipline and good manners, social and intellectual, with a thoroughly Anglican distaste for evangelical excess.... And, no wonder, for the poor gentleman is condemned to be domiciled with a figure of a very different stamp, a violent and passionate old peasant grandmother, who has witnessed murder, rape, pogroms, famine, flood, fire, everything; who has looked into the abyss and, unless restrained, would scream the house down.... Last, as if this state of affairs were not difficult enough, there is a young boy who likes to play slightly malicious jokes. The too earnest guest, who has come to interview the Reverend, is startled and bewildered in being handed an explosive cigar.

In Auden's vignette of Eliot's multiple selves we can discern analogies for the principal dimensions of his particular stewardship of tradition.

In the figure of the archdeacon we see Eliot as an exemplar of Aristotelian phronesis as applied by Gadamer to the moral component of creative insight and critical understanding. Insofar as our conversation with tradition is ultimately ordered toward self-understanding and the application of the universal to the particular situation, argues Gadamer, the moral knowledge sought in creative and critical activity subsists in the habit of practical wisdom. Even Eliot's decision to align himself with the Anglo-Catholic wing of the Church of England rather than Roman Catholicism was not only a function of theological conviction and cultural preference but also had about it the character of a prudential judgment. More to the point, as a poet and a critic Eliot never allowed the mists of abstraction to obscure the jagged edges of concrete and particular instance. Though he is known for the arcane formulations of the "objective correlative" and the "dissociation of sensibility, " he was pre-eminently a practical critic concerned above all else to explicate and make richly meaningful demonstrable nuances of tone, voice and sensibility. He had an astonishing gift in his essays for apt and revealing quotations and in his poetry for arresting and evocative allusions. Where his poems configure the voices of tradition in vivid juxtaposition with the controlled pressure of challenging contexts, his literary criticism explicates the tensions within and across traditions through a deft counterpoint, as when he sets in contrastive play Pascal and Montaigne, Bramhall and Hobbes andrewes and Donne and Dante and the French Symbolists.

This counterpoint of tensions also inflects Eliot's cultural criticism with intricate webs of qualification, carefully delimiting the scope of his arguments and the particular force of his claims, "Restricted to What Precisely/And If and Perhaps and But./How unpleasant to meet Mr. Eliot!" Thus he painstakingly delineates the tensions between liberalism and Christianity (in The Idea of a Christian Society) and the complex symbiosis of culture and religion, class and elite, unity and diversity and education and politics (in Notes towards the Definition of Culture). However much Eliot's networks of caveat and proviso may exasperate the reader, they are central to his habit of mind and characteristic of an ethical disposition committed to honoring all of the complexity and diversity of our multiform reality.

Eliot the prudent archdeacon keeps company with "a

young boy who likes to play slightly malicious jokes, " and we recall that "Old Possum" really was a Marxist of the Groucho variety and an inveterate practical joker. But quite aside from his sense of whimsy, there is in Eliot's engagement with tradition through aesthetic experience and in the very seriousness of his art a quality of "play" that is not altogether unlike handing the importunate guest an explosive cigar. For Gadamer, the concept of "play" is both important and elusive, drawing together in a rich knot of meanings multiple senses of the word, to designate not the subjective attitude of "playfulness" but rather the nature of art itself. It is, he says—not very helpfully!—"the mode of being of the work of art itself." In Gadamer's usage, the word characterizes the gratuitous integrity and internal dynamism of the accomplished artwork, which is like a "game, " set off from ordinary reality, vitalized by its own "rules, " and to which the "player" submits in "playing" to become part of the "game." In both the making and contemplation of art, we are drawn outside and beyond ourselves into a mode of disinterested yet pleasurable participation, one in which reality is arrested and transformed in artistic representation. But the reality that "goes into" art in representation, arrested and transformed, also "comes out, " as it were, in contemplation and can issue in a new perception of reality, transformed with insight. Thus, for Gadamer, art—most especially literary art—serves uniquely as a vital carrier of tradition even as it effects the ongoing modification or enrichment of tradition: "What we encounter in the experience of the beautiful and in understanding the meaning of tradition has effectively something about it of the truth of play."

Gadamer's account of "play" helps gloss the brilliant insights of "Tradition and the Individual Talent, " especially Eliot's theory of the "impersonality of art, " while assisting our larger appreciation of Eliot's dual vocation as poet and critic. According to Gadamer, the critic, too, plays a central role in preserving and transmitting tradition: "The literary critic goes on, as it were, weaving the great tapestry of tradition which supports us." And perhaps Eliot was not altogether disingenuous when he described poetry as "a mug's game" and "a superior form of amusement." Be that as it may, in the spirit of Gadamerian "play" we can still receive the gift of Eliot's poems as so many explosive cigars, with their capacity to arrest and transform our understanding; and when they explode in our midst we may feel with the blast and the ensuing epiphany something of what Gadamer calls "the joy of knowledge."

We must not forget the place in the Eliot household of the "old peasant grandmother" with her comprehensive awareness of the reality of human suffering. Ready to "scream the house down" and speaking for herself in Eliot's verse, she requires rather less commentary than her flat-mates, restrained as she is by the prudent reverend and momentarily distracted from the abyss by an exploding cigar. Suffice it to say that Eliot perceived and recorded in his time, as Aeschylus and Dostoevsky did in theirs, both the universal pathos of human grief and the particular forms of modern pathology; and it was his special metier to reveal not the shapes of physical violence—murders, rapes, pogroms—but their subtler, less obvious psychic equivalents in the waste land of broken, desiccated, love-less souls. He saw this spectacle of suffering and he saw it steadily and whole through the blind eyes of Tiresias—through the perspective of tradition. He did so not as an act of evasion or repression, to hide from himself and the world "the inferno that was Vivien, " as Ozick would have it, but in the only way any of us can learn from suffering—through its enlargement in sympathy and solidarity, even and especially across the distance of time.

According to Gadamer, the Aeschylean dictum of "learning through suffering" (pathei mathos), perhaps the central awareness of historical consciousness, means not only passing through the vale of disillusionment, but more particularly the humbling acknowledgement of human finitude, which is the very reality of experience, not just of tradition. If the clergyman and the prankster keep the old woman in check, it is also true that the hectoring grandmother puts the other two in mind of their mortality; prudence and play are both circumscribed in and necessitated by finitude. Gadamer sums up:

What a man has to learn through suffering is not this or that particular thing, but the knowledge of the limitations of humanity, of the absoluteness of the barrier that separates him from the divine. It is ultimately a religious insight—that kind of insight which gave birth to Greek tragedy.

From this truth, says Gadamer, comes not only humility but "a new openness to new experiences" and the moral knowledge for a deeper communication with tradition. And he might have added: compassion. Recalling his first meeting with Eliot in 1953, Kirk wrote,

Nowadays I hesitate to attribute "compassion"—what with the mawkish corruption of that word—to a sensible man. Yet compassion, in its root sense, could be read in Eliot's face: not the condescending sentimentality of the humanitarian, but a consciousness of the community of souls.

Kirk goes on to quote the lines from Eliot's "Preludes" that came into his mind on the occasion of that meeting:

I am moved by fancies that are curled Around these images and cling: The notion of some infinitely gentle Infinitely suffering thing.

Unsentimental yet tender, Eliot came to see as the full measure of compassion, as the object of faith and hope beyond the insights of his beloved Greek tragedians, embracing and even constituting the community of souls throughout time, the ministrations of "The wounded surgeon, " Christ our Health, in Whom we are assured that "All shall be well and/All manner of thing shall be well."

IV

For latter-day "pilgrims in the waste land, " T. S. Eliot offers neither a program for success nor a recipe of happiness, no remedy, nostrum or elixir, but simply the counsel of hope, the example of his prudence, play and compassion, all as part of the imperative of the unremitting spiritual discipline of tradition. Tradition is a hard and rugged way—not without its consolations, but daunting nonetheless. Yet nothing else will do, arrayed as we are against the powers of darkness and the forces offorgetfulness, "But fare forward, voyagers." By his labor and in his words, Eliot modified the contours and contents of tradition with his particular fusion of horizons. He is now part of the tradition in which we find ourselves and his are the tradita handed down to us by which we must take our own bearings and respond anew to "the drawing of this Love and the voice of this Calling." The rest, Eliot enjoins us, "Is prayer, observance, discipline, thought and action."

Polyphiloprogenitive: T.S. Eliot's Notion of Culture

Tomislav Brlek

Summary: In his various writings on the subject, T.S. Eliot develops the notion of culture as a comprehensive and highly complex system of meaning production, wherein social, political and other contexts are constitutive of experience formation, while the experiences thus formed are what the cultural system consist of. The multiform dialectical interaction that is culture crucially involves the notion of community and postulates ongoing interpretation as the lifeline of all cultural activity, predicated as it is on the ceaseless semiotic feedback between the heterogeneous codes that comprise it and the communicative exchange with the "outside" through which its "inside" is actually brought about. Such considerations closely link Eliot's understanding of culture with Lotman's concept of the semiosphere.

A new civilisation is always being made: Whatever else he may be taken to be, T.S. Eliot is generally not thought of as a semiotician and his work, poetic as well as theoretical, has apparently not received much attention in the form of semiotic analysis. This is somewhat surprising as it would seem that Eliot has a lot to offer from the point of view of both pure and descriptive semiotics as defined by Morris and termed respectively the inward-turning and outward-turning tracks in the tradition of semiotics by Sebeok. Not only has Eliot studied under William James and Josiah Royce and read Peirce attentively, he has also exposed himself to and absorbed in his work a variety of other doctrines of signs, from Aristotle and St. Augustine to Indian Buddhism. Indeed, the semiotic interest seems to be dominant even when we turn to less obvious sources-one of Eliot's favorite authors, the 17th century Anglican divine Lancelot Andrewes, has of late been described to have held "a semiotic view of reality, " maintaining that "all things are also signs", while the mysterious figure of "the third who walks always beside you" in *The Waste Land* has been read as defined by a "multitude of coordinates" as a figure of the interpretative act predicated upon "this 'third' term" and proposed as one of the most important moments in the text. Moreover, if it is true, as has been argued by David Zilberman, that "the skeptical state of mind seems to be the only genuine pre-condition of semiogenesis" (quoted in D'Amato 2003: 188), Eliot's cast of mind would be exceptionally suited to such an enterprise, since for him skepticism, as "the habit of examining evidence and the capacity for delayed decision" was "a highly civilised trait, " one of the principal features of development of a culture (Eliot 1962: 29; for an extensive treatment see Pearl 1989).

In his discussion of the indicators of changes in "the metalingual structure" of what he calls the semiosphere, Lotman singles out "the studies of 'unknown' and 'forgotten' writers" as well as, on a smaller scale, the appearance of works on the subjects "such as 'the unknown Dostoevsky' and 'Goethe as he really was'" as particularly revealing. Remarking in a similar manner the dependence of a meaning of a term on its contextual positioning with respect to the dominant code, Eliot has written that as "a doctrine only needs to be defined after the appearance of some heresy, so a word does not need to receive this attention until it has come to be misused". From this point of view, it is perhaps only to be expected that semiotic readings of Eliot should eventually appear, as indeed they have, though of what is this indicative remains to be seen. In his recent survey of a host of Eliots construed by contemporary critical readings, Donald Childs includes a section on "The Semiotic Eliot", although it consists of but two members, the articles by Walter Benn Michaels (1980) and Michael Beehler (1999). The aim of this paper, however, is not to produce "the real"-semiotic, of course-Eliot by means of demonstrating his semiotic credentials, though these are by no means negligible, but to indicate a certain important affinity between culture as conceived by Eliot and Lotman in the light of the general topic of this conference, the unifying aspects of culture. The form of the argument, particularly its somewhat indulgent reliance on direct quotation, is a result of the need to exemplify this notion on a different level, taking the semblances of the theoretical insights underpinning the respective constructs to indicate unity, with the important differences in vocabulary and expository manner at the same time demonstrating variety.

In *Universe of the Mind*, the study Vladimir Alexandrov called "a book-length *summa* of his life's work", Lotman proposes the notion of semiosphere as the model for a semiotic explanation of the way culture works, the semiosphere being defined as "the semiotic space necessary for the existence and functioning of languages", the background or context always already necessary for any semiotic act to take place, including all cultural activity: "The semiosphere is the result and the condition for the development of culture". In his *Notes towards the Definition of Culture,* a study originally published in 1947, surveying many of the issues addressed elsewhere in his writings, Eliot, using a similar dialectical figure, conceives of culture "as the creation of society as a whole: being, from another aspect, that which makes it a society". The scope of his enquiry is no less impressive than Lotman's and the claim made for culture is just as enormous: "the baffling problem of 'culture' underlies the problems of the relation of every part of the world to every other". For Eliot, as for Lotman, culture is a comprehensive and highly complex system of meaning production, wherein social, political and all other contexts are constitutive of experience formation, while the experiences thus formed are what the cultural system consist of. It can therefore by no means be reduced to mere entertainment, however lofty, or relegated to the status of a marginal aspect of life-for indeed culture can tentatively be defined as "that which makes life worth living".

The specifically semiotic aspect of Eliot's theory of culture is to be found where it is perhaps least expected, namely in his emphatic insistence on the crucial relation of culture to religion, which are seen as the product of each other, depending on the point of view of the observer. As is often the case with Eliot's idiosyncratic pronouncements, this particular contention has tended to discourage even otherwise well-disposed readers (see e.g. Scott 1994 and Shusterman 2002) from further serious engagement with the text in its totality, dismissing its basic stance as reactionary and setting about salvaging what they can from it for more progressive causes. Yet it is precisely what Eliot terms the religious that informs culture with meaning, for a religion is understood to be a shared code of a society:

"A religion requires not only a body of priests who know what they are doing, but a body of worshipers who know what is being done". Eliot's attempt at a definition of religion in terms of information-circulation, as a master-code informing all aspects of human activity-and he makes it perfectly clear that he does not reduce the meaning of the term to specific rituals of worship, pointing out that "bishops are a part of English culture and horses and dogs are a part of English religion"-renders it akin to Lotman's understanding of culture as simultaneously the sum total of the messages circulated within a social structure and as the comprehensive message the society is constantly addressing to itself, which enables him to conceive of "human culture as a vast example of autocommunication". For if "we can see a religion as the *whole way of life* of a people, from birth to the grave, from morning to night and even in sleep, " then not only is it clear how "that way of life is also culture", but it is also clear that this religion-culture continuum is a semiotic space, very much like Lotman's semiosphere.

Like Lotman's, Eliot's understanding of culture takes language as its privileged model: "it must be remembered, that for the transmission of culture-a peculiar way of thinking, feeling and behaving-and for its maintenance, there is no safeguard more reliable than language". Starting from the assumption that "culture is built on natural language" and that consequently "its relation to this natural language is one of its most essential parameters", Lotman draws the conclusion that "the laws of construction of the artistic text are very largely the laws of construction of culture as a whole", which permits one to analyze it using the hermeneutic tools fashioned for semiotic readings of literature. Furthermore, the notion of culture as an all-encompassing semiotic mechanism enables both Eliot and Lotman to see everything produced by a given society as "instruments for preserving and transmitting information" and take "even the humblest material artefact" for "an emissary of culture out of which it comes". At the same time, being the basic structural matrix of our experience, it can never be completely grasped: "Culture can never be wholly conscious-there is always more to it than we are conscious of; and it cannot be planned because it is also the unconscious background of all our planning". Since by definition "the semiotic experience precedes the semiotic act, " as every communication is only made possible by there always already existing a set of codes by means of which to communicate, "the semiosphere has a prior existence" with respect to any give languages it comprises and therefore also to any individual use of them.

For Lotman, the semiotic space of the semiosphere is crucially brought about by "the unifying factor of the boundary, which divides the internal space of the semiosphere from the external, its *inside* from its *outside*". Eliot in turn opens his book on culture with the epigraph from the *Oxford English Dictionary* definition of "definition" as "1. The setting of bounds, limitation (rare)". Already in his doctoral dissertation, written in 1916, he had maintained that it is only by means of differentiating itself from something outside itself that anything can come about: "Experience is certainly more real than anything else, but any experience demands reference to something real which lies outside of *that* experience". Even though for Eliot the insight that "in any cognition there is never more than a practical separation between the object and that which apprehends it" was fundamental, perhaps due to his extensive first-hand knowledge of Eastern schools of thought (on which see Kearns 1987; on subject and object in Buddhism see D'Amato 2003: 194), while Lotman remarked only in passing that the concepts of subject and object are "the results of a particular cultural tradition at a particular moment of its development" ("Kul'tura kak sub"ekt i sama-sebe ob"ekt" 1989; quoted in Alexandrov 2000: 358), the basic similarity of attitude is of the essence in the present context, since in both cases the identity of the subject is seen as the ongoing process of self-formation against the contextual background, dependent on the dialectics of ceaseless interpretation. It is only the permanent semiotic feedback between the heterogeneous codes that comprise the collective, as well as the individual subject and the continuing communicative exchange with the "outside, " through which the "inside" of this subject is actually brought about, that provide the subject with whatever identity it has. Just like personal identity is a result of a semiotic process, as "one of the primary mechanisms of semiotic individuation is the boundary and the boundary can be defined as the outer limit of a first-person pronoun", so cultural identity is only possible through contact with other cultures: "One people in isolation is not aware of having a 'culture' at all".

For both authors the life-line of any past, present or indeed every conceivable culture is the constant exchange of information and its existence is predicated upon two conditions, the semiotic difference and the shared code, i.e. upon there simultaneously being something to communicate and the available means of doing so. While "dialogue without semiotic difference is pointless, " when "the difference is absolute and mutually exclusive dialogue becomes impossible". Likewise, in relation between any two cultures, "without the attraction they could not affect each other and without the repulsion they could not survive as distinct cultures". If culture is information, it follows that

the country which receives culture from abroad, without having anything to give in return and the country which aims to impose its culture on another, without accepting anything in return, will both suffer from this lack of reciprocity. In the light of an understanding of culture as a semiotic mechanism, it becomes clear why "a world culture which was simply a *uniform* culture would be no culture at all".

The exchange of information does not, however, occur only between two cultures or two semiospheres, it also takes place within a given semiotic space, "in a vertical direction" in the form of "complex dialogues between the levels, " as "all the elements of the semiosphere are in dynamic, not static correlations whose terms are constantly changing". Similarly, a culture, "if it is to flourish, should be a constellation of cultures, the constituents of which, benefiting each other, benefit the whole". Moreover, the various parts of the complex social mechanism should create "*friction*" between themselves, since without it there can only be ossification: "the friction, not only between individuals but between groups, seems to me quite necessary for civilisation". The multiform dialectical interaction that is culture crucially involves the notion of community and postulates ongoing interpretation as its mode of being. "Any assertion about the *world*, or any *ultimate* statement about any *object in* the world, will inevitably be an interpretation".

The exchange of information that culture consists of takes place across time as well as across space, for a culture is not only a synchronic semiotic space but a diachronic one too. "In fact, everything contained in the actual memory of culture is directly or indirectly part of that culture's synchrony". It is precisely on account of the insights about the dialectical relation of the present and the past under the rubric of tradition, of course, that Eliot is most famous (cf. e.g. Eliot 1975: 37-44). What he wrote about tradition can equally be applied to culture, as in his later writings the terms can be understood interchangeably: "Tradition cannot mean standing still". Apart from the contact with other cultures, the renewal of a culture depends on it being capable of going back to its own sources, in other words, re-interpreting itself. These considerations become especially relevant with respect to the possibility of radical change and improvement of the culture we are part of. Since the culture we live in forms the all-encompassing context for our cognition, being the total background informing all our activities, "we can imagine no other". Nor can we reach beyond it: "Outside the semiosphere there can be neither communication, nor language". Every civilization, another term Eliot uses interchangeably with culture, defines its members and a new civilization would mean a whole new mental set-up: "the people who live in that new civilisation will, by the fact of belonging to it, be different from ourselves" and we would have no way of comprehending the aspects of their culture that make it different from our own. If we can conceive of some aspects as changed, than they obviously already are part of our culture: "A new civilisation is, in fact, coming into being all the time". It is precisely this ceaseless interpretative activity that actually keeps tradition, culture or civilization alive.

For Eliot as for Lotman, both individuals and cultures are defined by the boundaries which are functions of the differences between them, which give rise to and are negotiated by semiosis. Since it is the semiotic differences that produce new meanings and interpretations and the constant production of new meanings and interpretations is what constitutes cultural change, which in turn alone makes culture possible, it is obvious that culture by definition can be neither uniform nor universal. While the semiosphere is constituted by its heterogeneity, "defined both by the diversity of elements and by their different functions", culture can only ever exist as a series of variations based on a template that can only be theoretically constructed, for "common culture is only actual in diverse local manifestations".

It should be noted, however, that for both Eliot and Lotman, in order for the interpretative system that is culture to function, too much diversity should be avoided no less than the entropy of total unification, otherwise, "the system might lose its unity and definition and disintegrate". The consequences are the same in both cases: "Excess of unity may be due to barbarism and may lead to tyranny; excess of division may be due to decadence and may also lead to tyranny: either excess will prevent further development of culture". Although Eliot and Lotman conceive of culture as a structure (cf. Lotman 1977: 213; Eliot 1962: 15), they both take great pains to emphasize its dynamic character by means of organic metaphors-although culture consists of the arts, social systems, habits and customs and religious practices of a people, "these things added together do not constitute the culture, " for "just as a man is something more than an assemblage of the various constituent parts of his body, so a culture is more than the assemblage of the arts, customs and religious beliefs".

In the Russian-language version of his essay on the semiosphere, Lotman uses a strikingly similar language: "Just as we will not wind up with a calf if we glue together separate cutlets, but will get cutlets by cutting up the calf, we will not get a semiotic totality by summing up separate semiotic acts. The semiotic totality must generate internal and external differences, or its meaning-production will come to a halt; at the same time, precisely because it is heterogeneous, the semiotic sphere must be considered as a totality, lest its diversity, plurality and multiplicity accelerate the interpretative activities to so frantic a speed as to render the system inert: "Like molecules rushing about haphazardly in a Brownian movement, a culture bustling with activity and change may nevertheless be static".

The title of this paper appropriates the word Eliot coined in his poem "Mr. Eliot's Sunday Morning Service", fusing the parts whose meanings include the notions of "plurality, " "liking/affinity" and "creation, " all of these-together with the self-reflexive manner in which the form of the word performs its compound meaning-being crucial components included in his tentative definition of culture, as we have attempted to demonstrate. Foregrounding as it does its multiple checks and balances, as well as its self-perpetuating potential for unlimited semiotic generation, the particular contribution an exploration of Eliot's notion of culture can make to the discussion of the unifying aspects of culture is that these can only come about through diversity.

The Criticism: 1917-1923

"Sound criticism is the application of a sound philosophy to works of art."—Stephen C. Pepper, The Basis of Criticism in the Arts.

IN 1929, in an essay titled "Experiment in Criticism, " T. S. Eliot declared that there is an urgent need for a criticism of a new kind that "will consist largely of a logical and dialectical study of the terms used." In the essay that follows, an attempt is made to make such an experiment. There have, of course, been many other such attempts since Eliot made his statement. If this one differs from others of its type, it does in the effort that is made to approach Eliot from a clearly defined standpoint, that of the metaphysics of his dissertation.

To do justice to Eliot's early criticism is hard work because of the number of considerations that have to be kept in mind simultaneously. We have, first, to think of that early criticism in the context of all of Eliot's work, prose and poetry. We have, second, to see it intervening between his doctoral dissertation and The Waste Land. We have, third, to read all of it, or just about all of it, for some is not easy to obtain. We receive a different impression from such essays as "Tradition and the Individual Talent, " "Hamlet, " and "The Metaphysical Poets" when we see them in sequence with a hundred or so other articles that Eliot wrote between January, 1916 and November, 1923. Moreover, in speaking about Eliot's work, as in thinking about any literary criticism, we have to spell out his critical presuppositions in advance and avoid, when exasperated, interpreting his utterances in a frame that is pseudoclassical (literature is the presentation of sound ideas in an attractive emotional context) or pseudoromantic (poetry is the overflow of emotion in a noninhibiting intellectual context).

In addition, since literary criticism is probably like theology in that the basic statements are figurative, we have to avoid taking Eliot literally. His criticism is not about literary "things, " for a poem is not a thing the way a carrot is a carrot; criticism is about acts fundamentally mysterious since they are not acts in the ordinary sense. They are not transformations of an environment by one physical body operating on other physical bodies, but transfigurations of a situation by a self's transformation of itself. Still further, in considering what Eliot says we have frequently to suspend judgment on the rightness or wrongness of his individual judgments, or their specific importance or unimportance, in order to concentrate on the concept of the literary act that his ideas are pointing at. His practical criticism is, perhaps, theoretical criticism, an instrument, mainly, for elucidating literary principles.

Finally, we have to know something of the epistemological system, the terms of which control the terms of Eliot's literary criticism; we have, in short, to be sensitive to the philosophical nuances of words like "object," "feeling," "ideas," "point of view" as Eliot uses them. It is somewhat surprising that many expositors of Eliot who would not think of interpreting what Aristotle means by "mimesis" apart from his other writings and apart from his frame of reference, or what Coleridge means by "imagination" apart from his total effort as poet and theorist, have ventured to show what Eliot means by "tradition" "objective correlative" "dissociation of sensibility" without putting those terms into a fairly complicated context. But Eliot, of course, has been a somewhat indifferent parent to his critical ideas, leaving them like infants on various doorsteps, allowing other people to raise them and acknowledging only those whose faces make up well.

In the experiment that follows so much effort goes into setting up lights and fixing focusing devices, the elements to be focused sometimes seem to be hemmed in by a forest of fixtures. There seemed no way to avoid this and this introductory statement is an attempt to say why.

- If Eliot's beginning as a poet is a metaphysical standpoint, it is tempting to see his early and most influential criticism as the application of a philosophy to literature. Because it is fragmentary although voluminous, it is exasperating; and yet because it is the response of a young poet schooled in philosophy to a problem at once personal and cultural, it is significant and emotionally charged to a degree unusual in criticism. To ask what this criticism means is to ask two questions. What did the poet write it for? and what "idea" explains and reconciles puzzling and seemingly discrepant utterances?

The answers here proposed (but proposed more as useful hypotheses than as theses literally true) are that Eliot wrote his early criticism to keep himself persuaded that poetry could be written in an unpoetic age by a poet from whom the muse had departed and to persuade others that though the poetry business was, indeed, in a bankrupt state, it was so because of the misapplication of reason and could be restored by reviving an old line of goods—"intellectual, " or philosophic poetry—which, however difficult and dry and prosaic, not only was intensely poetic but was the one right poetry for an age of unbelief.

In declining to offer these answers as literally true, I am trying to avoid the suggestion that these hypotheses reveal what Eliot consciously and literally was moved by in the years 1917-23. On different occasions, Eliot himself has testified to different motives for his criticism—that he was moved by the need to make small sums of money quickly; that be was moved by a concern that the integrity of poetry be respected, i.e. that poetry be judged as poetry and not another thing; and that he was moved by the need to make a place for the kind of poetry he wanted himself to write.

The idea that Eliot's early criticism is exciting because it has an emotional charge on it and that this charge is due to the fact that he is responding to a personal as well as a cultural predicament is a supposition on my part. But certain facts seem to support it. Eliot does seem to have been one whom (as he said of Donne and Coleridge) the muse visited early and then abandoned, leaving him a person who might have made something of his life, but for the muse. His philosophical studies do appear to have coincided with a period of poetic nonactivity and may have been undertaken to redeem the time, to assist a man who had been a poet at twenty-one to be a poet after twenty-five. His early critical activities, moreover, do coincide with a period of pump-priming; when incapable of versifying in English, he began to compose in French, with fruitful results. One might guess, therefore, that though Eliot may have written to convert others, he wrote also to cheer himself up, to preserve the conviction that it was possible to construct something poetic on which to rejoice.

Starting, however, from the supposition that there is a central motive in Eliot's early criticism and the assumption that there is a controlling idea, I must inevitably see more pattern in Eliot's random critical utterances than the poet himself perhaps saw (I doubt this) or professes to see now and certainly more than many of his critics have observed. As is well known, the critical Eliot has been charged with contradicting himself on every important issue he took up, betraying inherent incapacity for theoretical thought and playing Dr. Jekyll in the criticism and Mr. Hyde in the poetry. Anyone who has tried to read straight through the Selected Essays will sympathize with these adverse criticisms. If, as Eliot declared in his dissertation, the aim of the critic should be to avoid public formulae, he succeeded in his aim beyond expectation.

But what Eliot once remarked about Pascal Pensées is probably the truth about his criticism: "He who reads this... will observe at once its fragmentary nature, but only after some study will perceive the fragmentariness lies in the expression more than in the thought."

The problem that is a context for Eliot's criticism is, by now, an old one. A personal expression of it was Coleridge's lament for the loss of his "shaping power of imagination" in Stanza VI of "Dejection: an Ode, " which Eliot once said constituted for him "one of the saddest confessions that I have ever read, " An equally personal, semiphilosophic, semiliterary expression of the problem was Nietzsche The Birth of Tragedy, whole passages of which echo in Eliot The Waste Land. Nietzsche's formulation was: "Yet every culture that has lost myth has lost, by the same token, its natural healthy creativity.

Only a horizon ringed about with myths can unify a culture.... Man today, stripped of myth, stands famished among all his pasts and must dig frantically for roots, be it among the most remote antiquities." I. A. Richards' Science and Poetry is a contemporary analysis of the problem, one that Eliot said awakened him to the fact that there is a problem of different types of belief, one that he criticized for its naturalistic theory of value and one that he praised for anticipating the question that the next generation will be putting to themselves.

But the problem—how to be a poet in a world from which the element of depth has vanished—though easy to feel, is less easy to formulate in neutral language. Here (to keep connections with previous chapters), I shall think of it as the problem created by the decay of valid metaphysical sensibility. To follow Eliot's dealings with the question, I shall attempt to provide two formulas-one for the concept of the poetic act that seems to underlie Eliot's early criticism and one for the four dimensions of that act that we need to take account of if we are to follow Eliot's diagnostic treatment of the literary ailments of his own and earlier ages. Only after these are out of the way can we come to the real point of the essay-Eliot's prescription of a kind of poetry appropriate to an "Alexandrian" culture.

- Although Eliot in the thirties denied having a general theory of literature to offer, his early criticism implies a poetics—an idea of what poetry is and does. There are many partial observations in Eliot's early criticism of how poets work, but these usually terminate just at the point where a philosophic point of view is involved. It is as though Eliot either knew his overall position so well that he had no need to place literature in a total framework, or that he was sensitive to the difficulty of talking metaphysics in a poetry session. (Coleridge erred frequently in this regard.) But anyone who wants to think through Eliot's criticism must see it in conjunction with a philosophy. Here the difficulties arise that force me to supply two formulas seemingly out of thin air.

Eliot's practical criticism implies a poetics, but that poetics is hard to describe in complete terms because somewhere between Eliot's dissertation and Eliot's criticism, a third linking fact is missing. We could say that what is missing in an anthropology, a theory of man. Eliot's dissertation is a theory of knowing without a knower, just as his criticism is a theory of writing without a writer. I am using "anthropology" in a sense so broad that, taking it in terms of the kind of metaphysics Eliot worked out in his thesis, his statement of an anthropology would actually turn out to be a theology—a statement of man's involvement in, estrangement from and soteriological relation to an Absolute.

Much later, it will be recalled, Eliot declared that no literary criticism can be substantive except in the framework of a theology—but we have no such documentary evidence of it as we have of Eliot's epistemology. All we know is that in a seminar of Josiah Royce's in 1913 he was studying the relation between description and interpretation and reading widely in anthropology and asserting on at least one occasion that truths imply contexts of belief. It is possible to detect certain theological leanings in some of Eliot's philosophic book reviews (1916-19) for the International Journal of Ethics. But no one has ever investigated this matter and it would be hazardous to try to do so here.

We could say (and it adds up ultimately to the same thing) that the missing element is a theory of language which the dissertation points to but does not supply and the criticism takes for granted but does not provide. Throughout the dissertation significant declarations about language are thrown out by the way as it were, but the involvement of linguistic and knowing processes is never directly taken up. For example, Eliot remarks that we make a mistake to think of language as merely a development of our ideas; it is a development of reality as well. Taken in one light, this observation may seem tame: Eliot is merely saying that language develops what is felt as well as what is thought.

But taken in another light, Eliot's innocuous observation is saying that we are what we say and giving a new reality to the Biblical statement that no word shall be lost and every word uttered shall be judged. We see, on another level, why Eliot in his dissertation dwells on the peculiar anachronism of a contemporary geologist describing an earlier world in a language subsequently developed. Thus, Eliot's entire dissertation might be interpreted as a discourse on language, language regarded not as a set of things called words, but a set of acts whereby an organism which is part of the universe becomes sufficiently social to contemplate that universe of which it is an organ.

When, in The Sacred Wood Eliot says that "permanent literature" is always a "presentation, " either a "presentation of thought, " as in Aristotle, who strips thought to its essential structure, or a "presentation of feeling by a statement of events in human action or objects in the external world," as in the Agamemnon or Macbeth, revealing "the essential sickness or strength of the human soul," he is making a basic statement about the two rhythms that govern language. By one the organism fixes a world (glimpses the mysterious order of the concepts); by another it takes possession of a self—sees who the person is who has been constituted by his choices.

What is striking about Eliot's description of the second type of permanent literature is that it leaves an impression (encouraged elsewhere) that Eliot's poetics is basically Aristotelian. Poetry for him is an "imitation of an ac-tion." But Aristotle's famous formula, having been affixed to Eliot, needs to be clarified. Could we say that poetry is an imitation of an action (men feeling and doing something) in order to create an imitation Action (man recognizing and affirming his destiny by re-enactment), we would be approaching the concept of literature that lurks behind Eliot's early criticism. But to clarify the difference between action and Action (a linguistic), I must step outside Eliot's criticism and resort to a formula taken from R. G. Collingwood Principles of Art. Collingwood's concept of art-as-language (which Eliot evidently read with interest in the 1940's) seems very close to what Eliot might have come up with had he been forced to propound a theory of art on an examination in 1916.

Imagine a baby lying contentedly and silently in his crib. Suddenly an elder child steals up and drops a red silk handkerchief over the baby's eyes and blinds his vision. The baby cries aloud. The baby's cry illustrates what Collingwood calls an expression, but not language. Consider a second illustration. I walk toward a porch where my fiancée is when her Airedale leaps from his hiding place and snaps and snarls at me. I jump. Collingwood would put my jump in the same category as the baby's cry: psychic expression, but not language.

Suppose, now, that I walk toward the porch and the dog still advances with me, snapping and snarling. Being afraid of dogs, I cannot avoid flinching at every other step, ignominious behaviour that I focus from my fiancée's point of view. How can she possibly love me? At a stroke, the dog has deprived me of self and world and reduced me to a thing at the mercy of brute things.

Suppose, however, that while behaving no differently, I manage to consider the whole situation as a spectacle: dog, personal terror, humiliating responses. I should be bringing what Collingwood calls consciousness into play and transforming the original sensations and emotions into what Collingwood calls imagination, a more or less stable mosaic of raw experience frozen for contemplation.

Collingwood emphasizes that consciousness has a liberating effect on me. Sensation and emotion cease to be something imposed from without and tend to become something I have, even though having them is not one of my prized possessions. But as yet I do not have language. I have psychic expression (my cringe before the dog) and imagination (my picture of the total situation).

But, now, suppose that with an imaginative eye on my fiancée, on myself and on the dog, I recollect a dance where my fiancée broke the heel of her dancing slipper. I recall her expression of reproach as she looked at the heel, apology as she glanced at me and then I remember her shrug as she resumed the dance. Suppose now that I imitate her behaviour and do it in such a way that I see that she recognizes what I am doing. If I understand Collingwood, I am still flinching in front of the dog, but I am flinching and shrugging at the same time. My composite action becomes a kind of dance. My psychic expression has become imaginative expression or language, low-level language it is true, nevertheless language and art. The complex act, not only catches up all the pieces of the situation held by my imagination, it not only duplicates the psychic cringe, it also expresses my sense of liberation, my emotion of delight at being able to transfigure my involuntary behaviour. Thus the emotion expressed is unique. My act expresses both my involvement in the world of necessity and my freedom from it.

Collingwood's "language, " it should be clear, is not what most people think of when they think of "language." That word ordinarily calls to mind what Collingwood calls an "intellectual symbolism." He insists, however, that we shall never comprehend the real nature of language if we start to think about it at the level of intellectual symbolism, or scientific discourse. Scientific discourse is the top level of a mode of behaviour that is more analogous to dance than to discourse. And scientific discourse withers and dies unless it retains its roots in imaginative expression, which in turn is rooted in psychic expression. In an early essay, when Eliot declares that "all thought and all language is based ultimately on a few simple physical movements" he is expressing a point of view similar to Collingwood's as well as one consistent with the epistemological views expressed in the dissertation. The objects that confront us are what they are first because of the kind of physical organisms we are.

But what might be of use here is the way Collingwood's art-as-imaginative-expression combines two old positions in literary criticism and perhaps permits us to interpret Eliot's Aristotelian poetics in a post-Crocean way. In literary criticism there have been not too many basic perspectives that produce fruitful results in practical criticism. From the classic period we inherit the Aristotelian viewpoint (poetry is an imitation) 33 and the Longinian (sublimity is the echo of a great soul). Both these approaches were one-sided. Aristotle's focus showed so clearly what art comes from that what it moves toward came out blurred. To unimaginative successors Aristotle's insight became a public formula that art mirrors life for pleasure or instruction. The distinctiveness of the end of art was lost. That Aristotle meant more seems certainly possible. Mimesis, interpreted in the light of his characteristic philosophic tendencies, ought to have meant a twoway process, taking life as it appears in a flesh and blood context and putting that appearance into a context of art so that something only potential in the flesh and blood world becomes actual in the world of art. What the something is that is actualized in the mimetic context (and only in the mimetic context) Aristotle either could not clarify or did not feel the need to clarify; he called it "catharsis," a term that has puzzled his commentators.

Longinus, on the other hand, judging that writers gained an immortality of fame from sublimity a certain excellence of style that echoes a great soul and evokes transport in the reader—focused so sharply what art moves toward that what it moves from was left blurry. We are uncertain what differentiates the echo of a great soul from the roar of an African lion.

A double-barreled formula like Collingwood's has the best of both points of view. A poem is both mimetic and expressive. When I find a way voluntarily to re-enact my involuntary response to a dog, I have acted both mimetically and expressively; I have imitated my psychic expression but imitated it in such circumstances that my imitation is an expression of the emotion of transcending my initial emotion. I have thus exemplified "catharsis," Aristotelian catharsis interpreted, not as extrinsic to the art act, but inherent in it, being that liberation from brute environment that language affords. At the same time, I have illustrated "sublimity"—a way of "speaking" that fills the soul with joy and vaunting, a transport that no lion's roar can sound because it comes from one's recognition of being a self in a human community.

But the crucial feature in the development of imaginative expression, i.e. language, is something that Collingwood's formula takes for granted and does not emphasize to any great extent. We need to emphasize it because of the fundamental importance to understanding the problem, at once personal and cultural, that Eliot faced as a literary critic. This is the factor of a community of interpretation, the kind of community that, at the lowest level, exists between me and my fiancée because of common feelings and memories. This community of interpretation manifests itself in two quite different ways. It operates first to provide me with that impersonal perspective that deprives me of my assumed self. (I see myself, that is, from my girl's point of view as a shameful coward.) It operates, second, to provide me with a remembered gesture that enables me to restore my self. (I see my shameful behaviour as a reenactment of my fiancée's behaviour, so that not I but "we" respond to the dog.)

These two modes of focusing a situation correspond to Eliot's two forms of permanent literature. Both, it seems apparent, are rooted in one community of interpretation. I cannot see the facts of my behaviour except from my fiancée's point of view; I cannot re-enact those facts except to her point of view, which incidentally is not hers, but ours. Nevertheless, though rooted in one community of interpretation, the first perspective, defining what Josiah Royce called the world of description, tends to cut me off from my roots, to destroy what Royce called the world of appreciation.

What would happen if through some hypertrophy of the first organ of seeing, we all focused the world of description so compellingly that we lost the capacity to see the community between persons that every act of language implies and thus lost the capacity to believe in any real community between persons? Such a hypothetical situation is exemplified in "The Love Song of J. Alfred Prufrock" where the "eyes that fix you in a formulated phrase" have made the community between persons unsee-able.

Moreover, our hypothetical situation is one more or less equivalent to that precipitated for us by the massive successes in the seventeenth, eighteenth and nineteenth centuries of the scientific way of seeing. Here, with what I. A. Richards called the "neutralization of nature" a phrase which means the loss of a sense of community of interpretation—is the problem with which Eliot's criticism begins.

- Eliot's problem as poet-critic may now be formulated

> several ways, all of which eventually add up to the same thing. We could say that the problem was metaphysical: the loss of a community of interpretation was due to the decay of metaphysical sensibility. Or we could say that the problem was literary. The decay of metaphysical sensibility was due to the weakening of a valid poetic tradition. Or we could say that the problem was educational. The abandonment of the poetic tradition was due to the rise of science. Or we could say that the problem was cultural: the rise of an urban industrialized world created an environment that seemed to deny human community.

But if we are to talk about Eliot's literary criticism, we need to restrict attention to the language act and yet to stratify our initial general impression of that act so as to see its four-sided character. For the sake of easy remember ing, then and to keep the different dimensions of Eliot's diagnostics clear, I am going to suggest that the language act—taking it from the poet's point of view—be thought of as like Aristotle's cosmic process, involving four "causes." There is the material cause, which, in Aristotle's terms, is something to be moved and which, in my illustration would seem to be my fiancée's Airedale and the whole realm of physical necessity that he implies. There is the efficient cause, something in Aristotle's terms, to do the moving and in my illustration is the point of view of my observant fiancée.

There is the formal cause, which, in Aristotle, is the path toward the goal and which, in my illustration, is the remembered dance. There is the final cause, which, in Aristotle, is the point where the process comes to rest and which, in my illustration, would be the restored community involving me, my fiancee and the Airedale.

Let me illustrate what the poetic process looks like when viewed in terms of four "causes, " using wherever possible references drawn from Eliot's early criticism, but supplementing these with whatever others seem useful. We must begin with the final cause. In the case of my danced cringe, the final cause, what I am aiming for, is the sense of fulfillment that comes when I have fused into one significant whole the Airedale, the dread, the humiliation and the community between myself and fiancée. In "Tradition and the Individual Talent" (where Eliot warns that it is not the sublimity of the felt materials that makes art great, but the intensity of the process whereby they fuse) Eliot speaks of halting at the frontier of metaphysics. No theory of literature resembling Eliot's can really do so.

Thus in The Dry Salvages when Eliot speaks of hearing music so deeply that you are the music while the music lasts, he names this experience an "Incarnation." This, of course, is a late work. Nevertheless, in an early piece of criticism, we find Eliot acknowledging the metaphysical dimension of the final cause of the art process: "The end of the enjoyment of poetry is a pure contemplation from which all the accidents of personal emotion are removed; thus we aim to see the object as it really is and find a meaning for the words of Arnold. And without a labour which is largely a labour of the intelligence, we are unable to attain that stage of vision amor intellectualis Dei." Elsewhere when he speaks of fusion and unity of feeling, he is back in the context of the poetic act and using words that are misleading unless they are re-related to the miraculous. What is fused is not merely this superficial feeling with that, but the whole being of the poet and the reader with a situation. What makes the experience ecstatic is that it offers release from our sense of separateness.

Since there are no novelties in literary criticism or philosophy, there is nothing original in Eliot's notion of the end of the poetic process. His fusion seems another name for that reconciliation of opposites that Coleridge speaks of as the ultimate goal of poetic imagination.

But the final cause is not a term to be comprehended apart from the material cause. In The Cocktail Party, Harcourt-Reilly describes the experience of being suddenly reduced to the status of an object:

When you've dressed for a party
And are going downstairs, with everything about you

Arranged to support you in the role you have chosen,
Then sometimes, when you come to the bottom step
There is one step more than your feet expected
And you come down with a jolt. Just for a moment
You have the experience of being an object
At the mercy of a malevolent staircase.

Here we have an evocation of what I mean by the material cause of a poem. What is it? It is any situation, any organization of experience that reduces a person to a thing. When my fiancée's Airedale deprives me of my self and my world, he has introduced me to the material cause of a poem. Of course, poems do not necessarily start from the material cause. They may start with transport, or with a conventional form, or an idea, as well as with a depersonalized situation. But wherever in actual practice the poem starts, the material cause will be the Caliban who is Ariel's opposite. Eliot in his early

criticism does not phrase the matter just this way. He merely emphasizes that art starts with the physiological, an actual brain in an actual environment, our "personal animal feelings, " "our exact and practical passions." Then he goes on to speak of the poet as seeking to transmute our practical responses to our physical environment. He stresses that what makes a poet a poet is his inability to trim his feelings to fit the "quotidian." The poet is compelled to "extend" (another recurrent Eliot term) his feelings until he finds a point from which the quotidian is transformed in a new whole. The shock of surprise that Eliot finds great poetry provides comes, I infer, from our finding the world of flesh and blood completely transfigured while remaining flesh and blood. The poet regains his personality by becoming a new person. He does so by transforming the material cause into "matter" for art.

The efficient cause in the poetic process (something to do the moving) is simply good sense, or what the Augustans would have called good sense. Eliot sometimes calls it "wit." If genius is required to see the obvious, Eliot's critical genius is best illustrated by his clear view of the role of intelligence in the poetic process. Indebted as he is to Matthew Arnold's perception that the main fault in romantic art is not lack of poetic genius but lack of wit, Eliot goes beyond Arnold by virtue of his having a theory of language. Eliot sees that the role of knowledge in art is not to furnish the artist material, but to enable him to define exactly what and how much he feels in a given situation.

Harcourt-Reilly again furnishes us an elementary lesson in poetics. He shows how wit works in a poetic progression. Edward Chamberlayne has been reduced to the status of an object by virtue of the departure of his wife on the eve of a cocktail party. What does Reilly do? He calls for gin and water and gives Edward a clairvoyant description, from a devil's point of view, of the profit and loss of a wifeless situation. What is the effect? Edward sees what he really does feel in the situation and becomes dimly conscious of how much his feeling exceeds what he would feel were he merely an object in a world of malevolent objects. I call "wit" the efficient cause because it is the first step whereby the poet moves that organization of experience he is against.

Eliot's discussions of what I call the efficient cause in the poetic process do not necessarily recognize a difference between the efficient and formal dimensions of the process. It is profitable for us, nevertheless, to observe a distinction between the kind of attention that defines the material cause and the kind of attention which finds a way to the final cause. What I mean by the efficient cause is most clearly placed by Eliot in early essays when he observes that it is only by the exercise of intelligence that we avoid "rhetoric;" intelligence enables us to determine exactly what and how much we feel in a given situation. "Intelligence" as Eliot uses the term is a characteristic of educated consciousness. It is the ability to see from a social perspective what Josiah Royce calls "the world of description." In the essay on Marvell, Eliot calls this "wit, " and speaks of it as an ability to see an experience from the point of view of other experiences. It is a quality he finds lacking in artists like Blake and D. H. Lawrence.

The formal cause in the poetic process is the hardest to talk about. It is not identifiable with external forms like blank verse, sonnet form, the five act plot, or even quantity of sounds of English words, or figuration. Although without these the formal cause cannot exist, it itself, like Henry James' "figure in the carpet" escapes public formulation. When the poet is in motion, it is the pattern that Eliot speaks of in Burnt Norton whereby the poem reaches the stillness; at the moment of flight, it is not merely certain conventions, but the readiness of a public to respond to these—what Eliot in another place calls the "temper of an age."

The earlier illustration of my fiancée's Airedale may make clear three characteristics of a formal cause: it must involve a convention common to me and my fiancee; it must have the power to reproduce in some fashion my psychic response to her dog; it must "reach the stillness, " i.e. restore the sense of community destroyed by the dog's attack. The recollected dance had these characteristics.

But this illustration serves notice, again, that what is crucial in the poetic process is a community of interpretation. Without that, art seems not possible. The kind of community required, moreover, is not furnished by such naturalistic activities as a beaux art ball, or the firemen's annual Fourth of July picnic—or is not insofar as these involve the extinction of the person in a collectivity. The kind of association involved, as Josiah Royce pointed out, is one where the individual finds himself realized in the group.

The formal cause of a poem, then, is a social entity of the kind Josiah Royce has in mind when he speaks of a church, or Eliot when he speaks of a literary tradition. The essence of what Eliot has to say about the formal cause is contained in "Tradition and the Individual Talent." But Eliot's determination in that piece to avoid the metaphysical, makes his declarations somewhat cryptic.

If we take Eliot's essay, however, in conjunction with the characteristics of a formal cause already illustrated we see why Eliot stresses such points as the absolute difference between an event and an art event. My response to a dog and my mimetic dance of that response are not in the same sphere of being. We see too why Eliot insists that the most original parts of a poet's work may be those points where the dead poets, his ancestors, make their presences felt. I must be invaded, as it were, by the ghost of my fiancée's behaviour before I can join together the fragments of the situation. We understand, in addition, why Eliot judges many readers to be capable of the experience of sincere emotion in a poem (i.e. the sincerity of my response to the dog) and some readers to be capable of appreciating technical excellence (i.e. my skill in graceful mimicry), but very few to be able to see a significant emotion in a poem, an emotion having its life in the poem and not the history of the poet.

Eliot's last statement invites the interpretation that a poem does not express what a man in a situation feels, but what the man feels in that situation as a representative of a community. It is the sensibility of the community that speaks, just as in Nietzsche's interpretation of Greek, tragedy, the sensibility of the audience is given back by the protagonist through the mediating vision of the chorus.

But if, having glimpsed what in the poetic process the formal cause is, we now return to Eliot's problem as a poet-critic, we do so with the impression that his problem was insoluble. It is as though he were asking me to invent a dance to transmute my emotion in the presence of a fiancée that I know to be a fool—a fiancée, that is, who not only disapproves of dancing, but has been educated to believe that two and only two responses are appropriate to an unruly dog: scientific lectures on care and training of dogs; "poetic" falsifications of the unpleasant facts such that I am enabled to pretend no dog is there.

In "Tradition and the Individual Talent, " Eliot is discussing, it would appear, only half of the formal problem—the relation of the poet to his dead ancestors. What of the poet's relation to his contemporaries? A tradition not exemplified in what George Herbert Mead called "the generalized other" is not alive. Was Eliot's problem not merely that of living in an age that was "formless" but one where counterfeit forms had driven out good? He formulated the matter in these terms in 1920 in "The Possibility of a Poetic Drama." After stating that "no man can invent a form, create a taste for it and perfect it to, " and pointing out how fortunate Shakespeare was to have "given into one's hands, a crude form, capable of indefinite refinement, " he concluded, "But it is now very questionable whether there are more than two or three in the present generation who are capable, the least little bit, of benefiting by such advantages were they given."

- The path through Eliot's criticism is strewn with terminological mementoes of his struggle to solve the seemingly insoluble problem of how to write poetry in a formless age. His path is crooked and many of his terms do not systematize very neatly. But if we remember that Eliot was a poet with a metaphysic and a literary critic convinced that the real world is a community, then the problem seems less insoluble. Eliot's early criticism becomes an interesting three-phase therapeutic operation. In phase one, he surveys malformations occurring in the literary body when writers lose contact with a metaphysical center. "Dissociation of sensibility" is the memento of this phase of the operation. Milton, Dryden, Tennyson and Swinburne are some of the patients. In phase two, he demonstrates some of the wrong measures intelligent poets took when confronted by loss of depth, either in themselves or in their society. "Objective correlative, " "tradition" are the mementoes of this stage; Shakespeare and Blake are the subjects. In phase three, the physician prescribes a right way to write when the social atmosphere is dry. "Poetry of design" is the most memorable of his terms. Ben Jonson on the English side, Henry James on the American, are the examples.

Eliot's terminological mementoes are keys to the various phases of his literary-critical operation. None is more important than dissociation of sensibility and none harder to treat. To interpret it we need a concept and the one I start with derives from reading Eliot's criticism against his dissertation. Dissociation of sensibility is the dislocation of thought from feeling and feeling from thought that occurs when language orbits too far out from a metaphysical center (a metaphor borrowed from the beginning of Choruses from "The Rock") and spurious centers are established, the center of the restrictedly objective, or of the restrictedly subjective. The cause of the dissociation is faulty metaphysical vision that leads either to the absolutizing of some specific view or some specific point of view (some means of visualizing an order) instead of the point of view which cannot be fixed in any view or specific point of view.

Thus when the literary process sickens, declines and finally breaks down, the source of the malady is some such error of philosophic judgment as Bertrand Russell is found guilty of in Chapter IV of Eliot's dissertation. The error is that of confusing a practical point of view with an ultimate one and substituting the physically real for the metaphysically real. But the error is inherent in the nature of language and dissociation of sensibility would seem, therefore, to be an inevitable accompaniment of all maturation of language. The better a language is, the better we objectify a world; the better we objectify a world, the more easily we are taken captive by it. Perhaps one of Eliot's somewhat puzzling remarks on two early manifestations of dissociated sensibility may make plausible this concept of dissociation of sensibility. In "John Dryden" Eliot implies, I believe, that Milton and Dryden have equally "commonplace" minds. "Commonplace, " in the context, seems to mean metaphysically obtuse and supports the interpretation that dissociation of sensibility is merely a literary-critical term for loss of metaphysical sensibility.

Now the intent of Eliot's remark is clear. It is to startle us into an evaluation of Milton's vision, to force us to weigh the poet's tendency in Paradise Lost, to treat realistically matters that are not material and not susceptible of literal statement. But the point I aim to make is that such illustrations of high level, but "commonplace" minding as Milton and Dryden exemplify are symptoms of materialization of thought occurring simultaneously with a growth of scientific language and an increasing objectification of a physical world. Soon abstract universals become deified "things" as in the eighteenth-century popular philosophers' apotheosis of Newton's law of gravitation. Thereafter, the pendulum swings again and the deified world-machine is a Frankenstein monster (as Milton's God becomes a devil to Shelley) and romanticism, the heretical reaction to a heresy sets in. Aesthetic feeling divorced from reason is enthroned as an absolute in place of the discredited universal.

The end of the course appears: a Browning fabricating a world out of private ideals, a Swinburne one out of private sensations and a Tennyson, oscillating between, now anaesthetizing his feelings in order to kneel before Victorian ideas so sanctified by public opinion that he dared not question them and now anaesthetizing his ideas in order to find relief for his feelings. Eliot's sympathetic analysis of Tennyson's predicament is a fine thing. But for the diagnostician, the cause of the "dissociation of sensibility" comes down finally to a writer's compulsion to provide an illegitimate satisfaction for the metaphysical instinct of a society that has lost its metaphysical eyes. Or so it seems to me. The essay that comes closest to revealing the syndrome is Eliot's "The Possibility of a Poetic Drama" where the connection between literary formlessness and impure literary motivation is illustrated by Goethe, the "philosophic poet, " who doctors the facts of existence with ideas in order to fabricate a world his heart can rest in and by Bergson, the "poetic" philosopher, who doctors the facts of life with feelings in order to fabricate a world his head can find tolerable. Here we sense that Eliot's "dissociated sensibility" is closely akin to R. G. Collingwood's "corrupt consciousness."

No one, of course, can read Eliot's scattered remarks on dissociation of sensibility without realizing that the term points in half a dozen directions at once at phenomena occurring on different planes of experience. Eliot used it to classify pathological symptoms in the language process with no intimations given that the term had a philosophical background. His readers not having enjoyed the benefit of conversion by F. H. Bradley were unaware that the "union in all perception of thought with sense, the copresence everywhere in all appearances of fact with ideality—this is the one foundation of truth." They were unaware that unified and dissociated sensibility are matters of degree; no human mind is ever fully unified, none ever fully dissociated.

Nor were they warned that when a high degree of dissociation occurs in a culture, literary men can probably not do much about it on their own hook. A metaphysical change of climate is occurring and a metaphysician is called for to chart where we are. But in phase one of his operation, Eliot was perhaps less interested in theorizing than in classifying the classic symptoms that crop up at every level of the literary process when metaphysical awareness evaporates. He resembled a practitioner fresh from medical school filling his office with bottled specimens of the pathological. Here, illustrative of the onset of the dissociation is John Dryden: atrophy of the final cause. Here, illustrative of the end is Charles Algernon Swinburne: atrophy of the material cause. Here exemplifying symptoms at the middle of the way is William Blake: progressive deterioration of the formal cause. 63 Here nearing the end is Alfred Lord Tennyson: loss of the efficient cause.

Eliot's exercises in literary pathology hardly helped him, however, to deal with the sickness of language as it affected him. What could the poet do to be well? In the second phase of the operation we see him showing what measures not to take. William Blake, in the prophetic books and Shakespeare in Hamlet are the subjects. Two more terms, "tradition" and "objective correlative" are memorials of the moment.

William Blake's predicament was to be caught in a cultural context where the final cause of the literary act had sunk from sight and his wrong move was to attempt to remedy the situation by becoming a one-man poet, prophet and propagandist coercing a society into seeing with his metaphysical vision. He provides Eliot an instructive example of the point where a unified sensibility turns and becomes dissociated. He begins as a "naked man" whose work has the same terrifying honesty as that of Aeschylus, Dante, Villon, or Shakespeare. In his early work he presents vision, which means that, partly by virtue of his education, he is able to use ideas as idea-ings to define feeling instead of as sacred pillars of the eighteenthcentury firmament. But the later Blake reverses the order and makes feeling the servant of ideas. His prophetic books betray, according to Eliot, a tendency to be formless. It is not that they are too visionary, but not visionary enough, Eliot states. We might judge that Blake had been taken captive by his own abstractions.

When Eliot concludes that what Blake's genius needed "was a framework of accepted and traditional ideas which would have prevented him from indulging in a philosophy of his own and concentrated attention upon the problems of the poet, " he is writing a prescription, not for Blake, but for himself. When he looks at Blake, he is intent on analyzing the response of a man of genius to an and cultural situation: "The fault is perhaps not with Blake himself, but with the environment which failed to provide what such a poet needed; perhaps the circumstances compelled him to fabricate, perhaps the poet required the philosopher and mythologist; although the conscious Blake may have been quite unconscious of his motives." Eliot might well have been cautioning himself.

Shakespeare's wrong movement in Hamlet might seem to illustrate the exact opposite of Blake's. Blake had so clear a vision of the end to be attained that he tried to drive his readers toward it without regard to their habitual reaction patterns. He violated the formal cause. Shakespeare was so sensible of the need to play the literary game according to the established rules that he allowed the public formulas of his profession to dominate his vision. He betrays the final cause. But the terms of Eliot's diagnostic (in "Hamlet and his Problems, " 1919) when applied to Shakespeare's movements seemed calculated to produce a maximum of mystification. How, one wondered, if Lady Macbeth washing her hands is an "objective correlative" can Hamlet playing the buffoon before Ophelia avoid being one too? But the question shows that we are seeing the objective correlative as a material factor rather than a formal one in the artistic act. Blake's failure to be visionary enough in the prophetic books might be called a failure to find an objective correlative. For the term means the way to what has been termed the final cause. Shakespeare took a way to his vision that went in the opposite direction from his vision. His state of mind (and now I am putting together hints that Eliot drops in separate later essays) was peculiar; he was undergoing the condition of aridity that is one phase of the movement to-ward religious commitment. In Hamlet he was trying (unconsciously perhaps) to recreate the experience of religious doubt in its meaning by the instrumentality of a revenge play whose only principle of form was the drift toward realism unlimited. This principle, although defective, was not as defeating of artistic value as Eliot's strictures implied; it succeeded when the vision to be unfolded was what Nietszche called "Apollonian, " but proved faulty when the state of mind to be expressed was that of acedia, for then there could be no realistic objective correlative because the protagonist's feelings naturally exceeded the realistic facts in the situation. A symbolic objective correlative was needed, one that in painting might be called "non-representational."

Eliot does not spell all of this out in "Hamlet and his Problems, " but if we take that essay in conjunction with later ones, something such as I have described may be seen taking shape in his mind. In talking about Shakespeare, as in talking about Blake, Eliot may well have been talking to himself. If Hamlet is an artistic failure, as Eliot asserts, then so is "The Love Song of J. Alfred Prufrock." Prufrock's intensities of response to the coffeespoon circuit are in excess of the facts as they appear. In these two essays, Eliot is pointing out two directions the poet in a dry age must be wary of taking. When the depth has departed from communal life, the artist ought not to try to convert the community. And when the poet himself is in the grip of the demon of doubt, he ought not to attempt to force a formless realism to express his emotion.

If these are the remedial measures that Eliot forbad himself to take, what positive measures could he endorse? In approaching the third phase of Eliot's criticism, the prescriptive, we need to grant that at the root of the literary ailment was the malfeasance of the metaphysician manqué and that the cure had to start at the ground. A poet had first to re-establish his metaphysical standpoint. Then he had to find an appropriate form for an arid period. Finally he had to find a point of contact with the contemporary mind at a place where it met the mind of the past. The essay that lets us see how Eliot attempted to do these three things is the "Lettre d'Angleterre" in La Nouvelle Revue Française where Eliot names F.H. Bradley, Henry James and Sir James Frazer as his "masters." That essay needs to be taken in conjunction, of course, with several earlier ones, especially those on Ben Jonson, Henry James and James Joyce. "Poetry of design" is the terminological memento of this phase of Eliot's therapy.

The singularity of a young poet's naming a metaphysician as a "master" influence on his work needs to be taken account of if we are to interpret correctly the somewhat cryptic announcement of that influence that Eliot makes in the "Lettre d'Angleterre." The cryptic attitude calls attention to the fact that the poet is gratefully acknowledging, not receipt of ideas, but the development of a sensibility. The philosopher has enabled the poet to preserve what Blake had—naked vision—and then has provided what Blake had not—a tradition. If we bear in mind that Bradley's philosophizing is an instrument for cleaning the springs of consciousness, we comprehend why Eliot speaks of receiving everything and nothing from Bradley and expresses gratitude for being left in a state of "bewitched despair." Does this not seem to mean that the poet came to the metaphysician in a state of mind where he was unable to enjoy any form of spiritual life except that of thinking? What aroused the poet's interest was that he found the philosopher sitting in the same wilderness that he himself was in. What evoked the disciple's gratitude was that this master required nothing but a thoroughgoing skepticism; no water from exhausted wells, no capacity to see airborne mirages was needed. The discipline consisted of learning to pay attention to the broken images in the desert. But by that discipline the consummate metaphysician purified the poet's sense of an ultimate reality without which poetry is a game.

Thus, Bradley's dialectic freed the poet's standpoint,

recovered for him a traditional metaphysical sensibility and left him free to do the poet's work in an uncongenial age. It provided, moreover, a hint of a poetic method. If every appearance in life points to an absolute order which is the meaning of the appearance, then we can begin to take an absorbed interest in the negative forms of human activity. A poet, incapable of anything but thinking, can record observations of the moral life of the living dead, convinced that hollow men live in the Absolute too. An ultimate reality moves in their whispers and such movement is the one right subject for a dry poet in a dry season. "Preludes" (1910-11) looks like a good illustration of the way Bradley's dialectic might be applied to a poem. The quotidian urban life points perpetually to a transcendant reality that the "eyes assured of certain certainties" deny.

From seeing a poetic method in a philosopher's mode of thought to examining the procedures of the past for an unsuspected tradition is but a step. I see Eliot taking it in his essays on Marlowe, Jonson and Dryden. "Ben Jonson, " as a matter of fact, looks like a companion piece to "Hamlet and his Problems." If "Hamlet" is a statement of what not to do when caught in the dark night of the soul, "Ben Jonson" is, perhaps, a statement of what might be done. "Poetry of design, " "poetry of the surface"—a poetry that is "so very conscious and deliberate that we must look with eyes alert to the whole before we apprehend the significance of any part, " a poetry which uses surface details to create worlds "which are like systems of non-Euclidean geometry, " a poetry whose logic "illuminates the actual world" by giving us a "new point of view from which to inspect it" this is Eliot's prescription for himself. In an arid period like ours—so I see Eliot's ideas going together—poetry of the surface enables us to be tough and realistic without being victims of "realism unlimited." We can keep our wits about us; we can start with a human brain in a human environment. We can take the facts of quotidian life as they come to us—smell of cooking, noise of typewriter and by a kind of montage achieve designs that reach directly the emotions of art. We thus bypass attempts to reproduce ordinary emotional responses of actual life. 75 Ben Jonson's "two-dimensional" art is a "part of our literary inheritance craving further expression."

Although I may be wrong, Eliot's ideas on intellectual poetry do not always seem intelligible without the presence of a specific ontological outlook. When, using a shifting vocabulary, he describes the method without describing the outlook, he is apt to leave readers perplexed. What keeps the poetic designs of a "pure intellectual" (like Jean Bosschère, to whom Eliot, in the Egoist, October 1917, enthusiastically applies the phrase) from being arbitrary? What keeps Ezra Pound's historical method from dumping bric-a-brac on a reader? What is the point of Joyce's juxtaposing past and present in the exercise of a "mythical method"? (Eliot would have answered, I suppose, that his remarks were meant to apply to artists who were artists and to be interpreted by readers who were intelligent.)

I seem to see what Eliot is driving at when I find him placing Henry James next to F. H. Bradley as his second "master". What Eliot says about James's fictional characters resembles what he says about Ben Jonson's. They are real, but not realistic. They derive their peculiar reality (by contrast with other authors' fictional people who sometimes seem assembled in the same novel by accident) by the way they fit together to make a total design. But here Eliot clears up what he does not clarify elsewhere, the source of the vitality in James's designs. James's form is the result of his vision of an "ideal society, " a vision so exigent that it compelled him to achieve exact expression. The "ideal society" that Eliot speaks of must be the same as the Josiah Royce community; it is a metaphysical entity and now I know where I am, or where Eliot is. If F. H. Bradley reveals the "still point", then James shows the way to the "still point". Bradley rehabilitates the final cause of literary expression and James the formal.

If we come now to Eliot's third "master" and inquire what he contributed to the poet's rehabilitation, we may almost guess that he redeemed, for purposes of art, the efficient cause. This, at any rate, is what I shall argue. The artist's problem in an arid age is how, without falsifying the material that is his given, to move that material toward art. In an urban, scientific culture, the problem is especially difficult because the eyes that fix things in a formulated phrase have already pinned just about everything living to the wall. What Frazer does is to pin up for attention facts drawn from pre-scientific, pre-urban societies widely separated in space and time.

Frazer's facts are impressively factual so that they suit contemporary ways of seeing. But these facts embody what primitive communities did ritualistically in interim situations, in those seasons of the year when the life of the community, or the primitive sensc of the community of all life, was threatened. These facts, therefore, do something to our eyes. What they do, Eliot says, is provide a glimpse of the human soul from a new angle, a glimpse into the abyss as valuable as that provided by Freud and perhaps in the long run more useful. What Eliot means, perhaps, is that both Frazer and Freud provide insights into the real bases of psychic life, as opposed to the apparent foundations. But Freud's principles of interpretation forced him to reduce psychic phenomena to what they come from, physiological foundations, whereas Frazer, having no conceptual framework, left the way open for an interpretation of his data in terms of what psychic life moves toward, a spiritual life.

What Frazer Golden Bough offers the poet is a point where factual past and factual present meet. He provides the point where Bradley's dialectic can operate, not on abstractions, but upon concrete events. Or this is what I take to be the manner of the "mythic method" that Eliot hails in his essay on Joyce Ulysses. Frazer's facts suggest that archaic and contemporary behaviour are already juxtaposed in contemporary conscious-ness and that a poet can further refine the juxtapositions, not necessarily to disparage the latter and glorify the former as is sometimes supposed, but to disclose a ground of identity and to reveal the presence of a third entity, a metaphysical community in all men. That Frazer himself had no such vision of an ideal society as Eliot has enhances his value. His compendium of human folly, Eliot's phrase, provides a record of earlier man's misguided efforts to contain and control a life beyond life (which is my interpretation of what he means). These efforts were misguided because they were magical. But set against our own unconscious magical rites, they may sensitize us to our own folly.

The pragmatic test of Eliot's critical theories was The Waste Land, the poem which I should perhaps be interpreting but am not. (In the Appendix, I try to speak of the design of the work; but that design does not seem to me to quite reach the public domain. It is Eliot Hamlet.) I turn to Burnt Norton for illustration of Eliot's poetry of design. Although difficult, it is a public poem, the first of a series in which the discipline that the poet had won for himself in private is brought to bear on the crises of a world.

T.S. Eliot and the Revolt Against Dualism

His Dissertation on F.H. Bradley in its Intellectual Context In 1915 and 1916, T.S. Eliot wrote a Ph.D. dissertation on the epistemology of F.H. Bradley. Some critics, such as Hugh Kenner, believe that Bradley is important only for flavor. "Bradley has an attractive mind, though he has perhaps nothing to tell us. He is an experience, like the taste of nectarines or the style of Henry James." Eliot himself commented on the relationship several times and in every instance downplayed its importance. Once, however, when writing about Bradley in an unselfconscious way, focusing on Bradley's general significance for an audience that knew nothing of his own debts to the philosopher, Eliot was unambiguous in his testimony that a close study of Bradley's work is transformative. In an obituary article, he insists that Bradley had

the finest philosophic style in our language, in which acute intellect and passionate feeling preserve a classic balance.... [Upon] those who will surrender patient years to the understanding of his meaning... his writings perform that mysterious and complete operation which transmutes not one department of thought only, but the whole intellectual and emotional tone of their being. To them, in the living generation, the news of his death has brought an intimate and private grief.

By the time Eliot finished his dissertation in 1916, he had surrendered those patient years. Those who know of his own lifelong struggle to nurture both intellect and feeling and to preserve them in classic balance will find the tribute moving and convincing.

But what of the dissertation? Did the patient years surrendered to following Bradley's meaning make a difference in Eliot's poetry and his literary criticism? In several articles written between 1979 and 1986, I maintained that Bradley profoundly influenced both the shape and the content of Eliot's work; and in Reading The Waste Land: Modernism and the Limits of Interpretation, Joseph Bentley and I demonstrate through a close reading of The Waste Land that an awareness of Bradley's ideas can be enormously helpful in understanding Eliot's contribution to modernism. Several recent critics have also focused on the relevance of Eliot's early work on Bradley. Sanford Schwartz, for example, clearly demonstrates in The Matrix of Modernism that an awareness of Eliot's early philosophical studies, especially of his work on Bradley's epistemology, is immediately helpful in understanding Eliot's criticism and his position in the modernist revolution.

The context into which I would like to put Eliot's dissertation is what the Times Literary Supplement, in a leading article in September 1926, called "The Dethronement of Descartes." After describing the last three hundred years in Western philosophy as a development of Cartesianism, the writer claims that Descartes and the great physicist-philosophers of the seventeenth century had been dethroned by the physicists and philosophers of the early twentieth, ushering in a new dispensation in intellectual history. Eliot, an occasional contributor to and regular reader of the TLS, had made the same point some months earlier in his Clark Lectures at Trinity College, Cambridge. After quoting a passage from Meditations, he maintains that Descartes's crude reasoning is behind the pseudoscience of epistemology that has haunted the Western mind for the last three centuries. 4 Eliot's focus is on poetry, the TLS writer's focus is on philosophy, but both are focused on the twentiethcentury's rebellion against the seventeenth and both identify the deposed monarch as Descartes. A few years earlier in 1921, Eliot had reviewed Grierson's Metaphysical Lyrics and Poems of the Seventeenth Century, a review included in Selected Essays under the title "The Metaphysical Poets." His dispensational analysis of English poetry in that review is explicitly based on the realization that in the seventeenth century, something "happened to the mind of England." That something was the triumph of dualistic thinking and that triumph produced, to use Eliot's phrase, "a dissociation of sensibility."

The poets of the seventeenth century... possessed a mechanism of sensibility which could devour any kind of experience.... In the seventeenth century a dissociation of sensibility set in, from which we have never recovered.

Mind and matter, thought and feeling, subject and object, fell apart; poets thought and felt by starts and fits. In phrases now famous, Eliot claims that before Descartes took over the Western mind, poets could feel their thoughts and think their feelings. They could feel their thoughts as immediately as they could smell the odor of a rose.

A brilliant account of Descartes' dethronement is given in A. O. Lovejoy's Revolt Against Dualism. Lovejoy argues that Western thought has been dominated for three centuries by the assumptions of Descartes, Locke and Newton. These geniuses all believed that the subject and the object were separable, that objectivity was possible and even necessary for understanding the world. But early twentieth-century philosophers, in Lovejoy's account, joined in an attempt to escape from this epistemological dualism of subject and object as well as from the parallel psychophysical dualism of mind and matter. 5 The realization that subject and object are connected in a systematic way and that mind and body are aspects of a single world is in effect a dethronement of Descartes. Lovejoy's argument, articulated in 1929, anticipates the work of such intellectual historians as Thomas Kuhn, Gerald Holton and Jacob Bronowski. His thesis, like theirs, is helpful in approaching modern thinkers in many fields. Most of the figures who shaped the twentieth-century mind, figures as diverse as Freud, Heisenberg, Picasso, Royce and Eliot, have in common an about-face on the subject-object question and the mindmatter question; they all try to discredit the dualism that arbitrarily splits the world into pieces. Russell and the neorealists refuse to give up the subject-object distinction, but they too join in rejecting the division of the world into mind and matter.

Russell is, of course, important in Eliot's personal revolt against dualism. He was Eliot's teacher at Harvard and his benefactor in the early London years. In the fall of 1915, while Eliot was writing his dissertation on Bradley, he and his bride moved in with Russell. At this time Russell was specifically involved in trying to overcome the distinction between mind and matter, maintaining, for example, that sense-data are the ultimate constituents of matter; on the other hand, he was strenuously holding to the dualism of subject and object. Russell's general point of view at this time is preserved in Mysticism and Logic, a book that Eliot reviewed, in the process displaying an indepth knowledge of Russell's work. There can be no doubt that Eliot learned much from Russell; at the same time, there can be no doubt of Eliot's early and fundamental dissent, already clearly evident in the dissertation. In chapter IV, he analyzes Russell's realism and concludes by rejecting Russell's dualism:

The curious dualism of Mr. Russell... which has much in common with obvious, though I can hardly think correct, interpretations of Plato, will not hold good of a world which is always partially in time, but never wholly in time, with respect to any of its elements.

For a detailed and slightly different account of Eliot's indebtedness to Russell, I recommend Richard Shusterman's T.S. Eliot and the Philosophy of Criticism. Shusterman's discussion of the philosophical underpinnings of Eliot's literary criticism is valuable, despite his overstatement of Russell's importance in Eliot's development. By all accounts, of course, Eliot's situation in late 1915 was extraordinary. He was a close student of both Bradley and Russell; he had studied with Bradley's friend and disciple Harold Joachim and with Russell himself. And now, while writing a dissertation explaining and in general defending Bradley against Russell, Eliot found himself face to face with Russell across the breakfast table. Moreover, as the husband of a fragile wife to whom both were devoted, Eliot must have found life to be a kaleidoscope of brilliant and fluctuating patterns.

The subject of this paper, however, is not Russell, but Bradley, one generation older, living in seclusion at Oxford and generally considered as the greatest living philosopher. Bradley was a trailblazer in intellectual history, with insights anticipating and paralleling those of Heisenberg in physics and Picasso in painting. He was an unflinching leader in the revolt against dualism; and from the beginning of his career, he was a radical skeptic who rejected the notion that there is such a thing as objectivity or objective truth. Like all idealists, he believed that everything is connected to everything else in a systematic way and that everything is part of a single allencompassing whole. He believed, consequently, that every perspective is partial and incomplete and thus, to use his terminology, an appearance.

Bradley is labelled an idealist and often a "Neo-Hegelian, " labels that are true in a sense but very misleading to the casually informed. He began his work with one foot in German idealism but with the other firmly planted on the ground, the ground being British empiricism. His distinction is that he forged these two traditions into a synthesis, a synthesis preserving the intellectual and the experiential—in Eliot's words, intellect and feeling. Bradley believed, with Hegel, that reality is an all-encompassing unity; but he disagreed with Hegel's first principle, that is, with the notion that the real is of the nature of thought, that it is intellectual—to use a Hegelian vocabulary, that the real is the rational.

Unless thought stands for something that falls beyond mere intelligence,... a lingering scruple still forbids us to believe that reality can ever be purely rational. It may come from a failure in my metaphysics, or from a weakness of the flesh which continues to blind me, but the notion that existence could be the same as understanding strikes as cold and ghost-like as the dreariest materialism.

Bradley believed that the real includes the intellectual, but like Locke and the British empiricists, he believed that everything begins and ends in experience. As Eliot correctly stated in his 1927 review of Ethical Studies, "Bradley is thoroughly empirical, much more empirical than the philosophers he opposed". The philosophers he opposed, of course, lived in a world dominated by Newton and Descartes and to them, experience consisted of a subject, who does the experiencing and an object, which is experienced; to them, experience has two parts, mind and matter. Bradley retained their commitment to experience but dropped their dualism. Like Wordsworth, he believed that the universe is a living whole, that mind and matter, subject and object, are parts of a single whole. Bradley changed subject and object from nouns to adjectives, from things-in-themselves to the subjective and objective aspects of experience.

One must understand Bradley's empiricism to understand his work. It is best to think of him not as an idealist but as an idealistempiricist, as much a part of British empiricism as of German idealism. In keeping with his Lockean roots, Bradley claims that "Everything is experience" and also that "experience is one." "There is but one Reality, " he insists, "and its being consists in experience. In this one whole all appearances come together." Now we are compelled by language to think of experience as "my" experience, or as some other person's experience. To the extent that we think of it in this way, we are missing Bradley's point and lapsing into dualism. He is not speaking of experience as something that is experienced by an experiencer but as something that simply is, as a complex that encompasses experiencer and experienced. The Absolute is experience and it systematically includes everything that exists or can be imagined to exist. We can, with minimal distortion, think of Bradley's Absolute as a complete inventory of all experiences that have ever existed or will ever exist. This means, of course, that his Absolute itself does not yet exist in its completeness and will do so only in the moment when all experience is finished and comprehended. In that moment, it will also cease to exist.

The revolt against dualism is immediately helpful in understanding Appearance and Reality, the main Bradleyan text behind Eliot's dissertation. Bradley's field here is metaphysics, which he defines on his first page as "the attempt to know reality as against mere appearance." For unsuspecting literary critics, this definition will be congruous with a common literary theme, the opposition between appearance and reality, such as one finds in the plays of Shakespeare or the poems of Dickinson. But let us, briefly, take a closer look. Bradley's book is divided into two parts, one on appearance and one on reality.

The first is a devastating attack on traditional ways of attempting to understand truth or first principles. Thinking by its very nature divides reality into this and that, into temporal and spatial, into body and soul, into mind and matter, into subject and object. All of these divisions collapse under scrutiny into self-contradiction. The second part of Bradley's book is called "Reality, " and for the casual reader, it will promise Bradley's alternative to appearance. But instead of an alternative, the reader finds the disconcerting suggestion that appearance and reality are not opposites at all. An appearance is reality in any less than comprehensive aspect. Bradley's reality is not an abstraction lying behind the appearances in the external world. "The Absolute is its appearances, it really is all and every one of them, "—not all totalled together, but all unified.

Eliot's dissertation springs to life when it is understood in the context of the revolt against dualism. His purpose is to explain and to some extent to defend Bradley's epistemology. Now epistemology, the investigation of how we know what we know, is by definition dualistic. It involves a systematic analysis of subjects and objects and their relations. The central Bradleyan insight, however, is that the world is one, that reality is one, that dualism always leads to selfcontradiction; and in fact, Bradley argues that there can be no such thing as epistemology and Eliot agrees with him. The epistemology that Bradley and Eliot reject is the activity of that name fathered by Descartes and nurtured by Kant. Ten years later, in the Clark Lectures, long after Eliot had abandoned philosophy as a career, he speaks scornfully of epistemology as a pseudo-science. But in the dissertation, he says he is trying to elucidate and criticize Bradley's "theory of knowledge." At any rate we must insist, as Lovejoy does, that knowing is part of being human and that denying one has a theory of knowing clearly indicates that one is theorizing about knowledge. Eliot's dissertation, then, is the attempt by a man who does not believe in epistemology to explain the epistemology of a man who denies that epistemology exists.

In the opening chapter, Eliot tries to get behind the dualism implicit in his subject by grounding Bradley's theory of knowledge in something that is not dualistic. He does this, first, by making the case for Bradley's all-encompassing empiricism. "Reality,... the ultimate criterion which gives meaning to all our judgments,... is our experience". He proceeds by positing "immediate experience" as a predualistic unity, as a precognitional condition, arguing that epistemology can only begin after we have fallen away from this unity. We are forced, Eliot says, "in building up our theory of knowledge, to postulate something given upon which knowledge is founded". That something given, "immediate experience, " is a knowingand-being-in-one that precedes subjects and objects. Epistemology or the speculation on subjects and objects, experiencers and experienced, follows and builds upon "immediate experience".

The first chapter also argues that knowing is self-transcendent, that it reaches beyond itself and is taken up in a larger unity. Eliot thus situates "epistemology" in the realm of "appearance, " in the dualistic realm of relations. "Thinking" emerges from and moves toward feeling or experience and in his own analysis of subjects and objects, Eliot is always careful to indicate his awareness that his activity is sandwiched between the beginning and the end. His conclusion in the last paragraph of chapter one is:

We are led to the conception of an all-inclusive experience outside of which nothing shall fall. If anyone object that mere experience at the beginning and complete experience at the end are hypothetical limits, I can say not a word in refutation for this would be just the reverse side of what opinions I hold.

The second chapter of Eliot's dissertation takes up the question of what Lovejoy calls psychophysical dualism, or as the chapter title puts it, the "Distinction of Real and Ideal." The main point of the chapter is that such distinctions are invalid, mainly because the real and the ideal are dependent on each other for existence.

They are systematically intertwined in such a way that if one appears, the other does and if one dissolves, the other cannot survive. Eliot admits that immediate experience falls apart of itself into subjects and objects, mind and matter, but he insists that this dualism is "tentative and provisional, a moment in a process". The process, ever repeated, never ending, is the movement from the unity of immediate experience to the unity of transcendent experience. Distinctions such as real and ideal are relative and depend upon focusing on one part from one point of view, a process that automatically generates an opposite, an other-than. Epistemology, the study of subjects and objects, then, can only be carried on from some relative and shifting point of view.

The next three chapters of Eliot's dissertation are deconstructions of two approaches to knowledge, that of the psychologist, who thinks in terms of mental content and external reality and that of the epistemologist, who thinks in terms of subjects and objects. Eliot criticizes the psychologist by adopting the epistemologist's stance or point of view. Then shifting his point of view, he criticizes the epistemologist by adopting the psychologist's point of view. He evaluates idealism from the point of view of realism and vice versa. His point is that neither is right, that both are relative, that either can be reduced to its so-called opposite. Eliot's philosophical skepticism and his dialectical rhetoric make it possible to find statements that support opposite points of view, statements that contradict each other. This will not disturb those who understand his method and his position, stated at the opening of his last chapter, that every theory depends on adopting some point of view and that every point of view is no more than one point of view. The fact is that any epistemology can be undermined fatally simply by shifting one's point of view. Standing foursquare on Bradley's argument, Eliot concludes:

No [valid] definition can anywhere be found to throw the mental on one side and the physical on the other;... the difference between the mental and the real, or... the personal and the objective, is one of practical convenience and varies at every moment.

We divide the world into mental and physical, but "the mental resolves into a curious and intricate mechanism and the physical reveals itself as a mental construct". Both Bradley and Eliot are attempting to show that all thinking is relational, that any truth can be dissolved into its opposite and that since thinking takes place in a space between mere experience and complete experience, it can only proceed from one limited point of view or another. Thinking is always relative, always tentative, never final.In the last chapter of his dissertation, Eliot drops the dialectical method and summarizes his own conclusions. Although he objects to a number of points from Bradley's Principles of Logic, he accepts the validity of the major arguments in Appearance and Reality. "I believe, " he says, "that all of the conclusions that I have reached are in substantial agreement with Appearance and Reality. Eliot specifically affirms the following Bradleyan positions. 1. Reality is experience. His own words: "From first to last, Reality is experience".

- Reality is one. To quote Eliot: "We are forced to the assumption that truth is one and to the assumption that reality is one".
- Reality is all-comprehensive. The clearest one-sentence statement of this is in his first chapter: "We are led to the conception of an all-inclusive experience outside of which nothing shall fall".
- Reality is systematic. For it to include everything and still be one thing, it must be systematic. This simply

means that everything is connected to everything else and that any "new fact" that comes into being instantly becomes part of something bigger than itself, part of a system of reality. Eliot's words:

Facts are not merely found in the world and laid together like bricks, but every fact has in a sense its place prepared before it arrives and without the implication of a system in which it belongs the fact is not a fact at all.

- All relations are internal. Eliot says that he is compelled to accept the "most important" doctrine of the internality of relations. The compulsion comes from logic. If everything is a systematic part of one thing, then all relations or connections are between fragments or parts and relations are inside the all-comprehensive totality. This is important in part because it means that nothing has its meaning alone, that no action is isolated in its significance. Any change or adjustment or development in any one part changes the whole. In the opposite doctrine, the one Eliot denies, entities are complete in themselves. Thus, relations connecting them are external to each entity and moreover, changes in any one entity affect only that one entity.
- Finally, Eliot says he is also compelled to accept the idea of degrees of truth, degrees of reality. "The only real truth is the whole truth, " he says, but the fact that no one can know the whole truth does not mean no one can know truth. Partial truth is truth, to a degree. He maintains that everything, including falsehoods, errors and hallucinations, is part of reality. Eliot illustrates this by discussing the reality status of the bear that a frightened child "thinks it sees" in its bedroom. "It is... not altogether true or altogether false to say that the child sees a bear." The doctrine of degrees of truth allows him to accept both the bear in the nursery and the bear in the woods as real without requiring him to agree that they have

> the same status in truth and reality. Or, to take an example that forms part of Eliot's argument with Russell, references to the "present king of France" are and are not references to something that exists. The doctrine of degrees of reality permits him to distinguish the "present king of France" from the present king of a country like England that still has a monarch. Both are real, though not in the same way. All imaginable truth, then, is partial, although some truths are fuller than other truths.

These principles are everywhere evident in Eliot's literary and social criticism and also in his account of history. No doctrine is more important than the doctrine of wholeness, no word more ubiquitous in his prose. In talking about other writers, for example, he insists that the plays of Shakespeare are one play, the novels of James one novel, that none of these works have meaning alone, that all are systematically connected. Otherwise, of course, he could not consider many plays as one play, many novels as one novel. All six of the points just outlined are prominent features of Eliot's doctrine of tradition and the individual talent. Tradition involves the historical sense, which compels a man to write not merely with his own generation in his bones, but with a feeling that the whole of the literature of Europe from Homer and within it the whole of the literature of his own country has a simultaneous existence and composes a simultaneous order.

Eliot describes the relation between artists within the tradition as well as between the tradition and individual artists. By doing so, he provides a textbook example of the doctrines of the internality of relations and the systematic nature of the whole.

No poet, no artist of any art, has his complete meaning alone.... You... must set him, for contrast and comparison, among the dead.... The necessity that he shall conform... is not onesided; what happens when a new work of art is created is something that happens simultaneously to all the works of art which preceded it. The existing monuments form an ideal order among themselves, which is modified by the introduction of the new... work of art among them. The existing order is complete before the new work arrives; for order to persist after the supervention of novelty, the whole existing order must be... altered; and so the relations, proportions, values of each work of art toward the whole are readjusted.... Whoever has approved this idea of order... will not find it preposterous that the past should be altered by the present as much as the present is directed by the past.

What keeps this from being preposterous is the doctrine of internal relations. If every artist is related within an organic and systematic whole, then any alteration in any part changes both every other part and the whole itself; similarly, any change in any part of one's body affects not just that part but other parts and the person as a whole. Thus one can say not only that The Divine Comedy alters The Waste Land, but also that The Waste Land alters The Divine Comedy and the tradition in which both participate. Eliot's notions about organic wholes and systems of art are repeated in the opening paragraphs of "The Function of Criticism".

These ideas are also helpful in reading Eliot's poetry. "G0erontion" and the so-called quatrain poems were written on the heels of the dissertation and the principles Eliot accepted from Bradley's philosophy are everywhere apparent. To take "G0erontion" as an example: One of its major subjects is history; and Eliot brings in everything from the war between the Greeks and the Persians at Thermopylae, several centuries before Christ, to the First World War and the treaty at Versailles in 1919, the very year he was writing the poem. Not only does he bring in everything, he forces the reader to see that everything is systematically connected, that all relations are internal, fragment to fragment, both within history and within the poem; and he compels the reader to connect these whirling fragments into a unity.

His use of allusion and juxtaposition, his collapse of time and space, his comprehensiveness and complexity-all of these and more are inseparable from Bradley's ideas. Eliot incorporates other complicated influences, of course. Frazer is there and so are Théophile Gautier, Ezra Pound and others.

But Bradley is at issue here and Bradley is of the essence. The structure of the poem is based on the Bradleyan principle of the systematic nature of truth, on selftranscendence of parts always leading toward greater, more inclusive wholes. The last lines of the poem—"Tenants of the house, /Thoughts of a dry brain in a dry season"—provide the major structural clue. Eliot has composed the poem as a complex of houses within houses within houses, all decayed, all crumbling. Gerontion's dry thoughts are contained in his dry brain, which is contained in his desiccated body, which is contained in his crumbling house in his rocky yard in war-torn Europe in Western civilization over thousands of years and all of these are contained in a whirling cosmos. Both the content and the form of the form illustrate Bradleyan principles.

The epistemology, or theory of knowing, outlined and in its major points defended in Eliot's dissertation rests upon the metaphysics. All knowledge, Bradley argues, begins and ends in experience. Knowing occurs in three stages which are also three levels of experience. The first and most foundational is "immediate experience," the second is "relational experience," and the most comprehensive is "transcendent experience." Immediate experience is experience that has not been mediated through the mind; it is a knowing and feeling and being in one prior to the development of logical or temporal or spatial categories.

The first chapter of Eliot's dissertation, "On our Knowledge of Immediate Experience, " reviews an essay by Bradley of the same title. The point of both is to postulate a starting point for knowledge, a foundation upon which knowledge can be built and to which it can return. Eliot defines this doctrine by quoting Appearance and Reality. Immediate experience is: first, the general condition before distinctions and relations have been developed and where as yet neither subject nor object exists. And... second... anything which is present at any stage of mental life, in so far as that is only present and simply is.

In a later essay, Bradley defines immediate experience with even greater clarity:

We in short have experience in which there is no distinction between my awareness and that of which it is aware. There is an immediate feeling, a knowing and being in one, with which knowledge begins; and, though this in a manner is transcended, it nevertheless remains throughout as the present foundation of my known world. And if you remove this direct sense of my momentary contents and being, you bring down the whole of consciousness in one common wreck. For it is in the end ruin to divide experience into something on one side experienced as an object and on the other side, something, not experienced at all.

As an example of immediate experience, Eliot describes the viewing of a painting in which the viewer is so absorbed that he has no consciousness of self or subject, on the one side and painting or object, on the other. This directly experienced nonrelational many-inone is not the viewer's experience, for he as subject and the painting as object do not yet exist. When he becomes aware of "his" experience and of the painting as other than himself, then immediate experience has dissolved into the realm of relations, of self and not-self. Four Quartets contains several references to immediate experience, for example, the "music heard so deeply/That it is not heard at all". Immediate experience is by definition transitory. As one becomes conscious of the self, of the world in itself, of surrounding people and things as other, immediate experience dissolves into the dualistic realm of subjects and objects. The intellect, which hitherto has been an undiscriminated part of experience, assumes dominance and experience becomes relational. Reality can no longer be apprehended immediately, but is filtered through the mind. Most waking experience takes place at the level of relations, as the conscious self moves through the day and organizes experience into working categories such as present and past, knower and known, self and other. All of these categories are abstractions from experience; all are partial. This is the level of all analytical thinking, of all philosophy, including epistemology and this level is the major subject of Eliot's dissertation, which is in simplest terms an analysis of the nature of objects. This level is unavoidable, for to quote Eliot, "the only way in which we can handle reality intellectually is to turn it into objects and the justification of this operation is that the world we live in has been built in this way".

Immediate experience can be known only through reflection and intuition after it has dissolved. Time does not exist in immediate experience, but immediate experience does exist in time, for it does not last. In the following lines from "Burnt Norton, " Eliot describes relational experience, the level at which we are not fully conscious because our consciousness is primarily intellectual and reductive.

Time past and time future
Allow but a little consciousness.
To be conscious is not to be in time
But only in time can the moment in the rose-garden,
The moment in the arbour where the rain beat,
The moment in the draughty church at smokefall
Be remembered; involved with past and future.
Only through time time is conquered.

If immediate experience were all that one had, in a paradoxical way, one would not even have it, for only in time can one remember immediate experience and thereby in a sense begin to conquer time.

A third level, in Bradley's view, a transcendent experience, permits a return of sorts to the wholeness and unity of immediate experience. Immediate experience exists before relations, but transcendent experience exists after or above relations. Immediate experience dissolves of itself into relational experience, but relational experience resists resolution into the higher monistic experience. The villain is the discursive intellect and the transcendence of relations such as self and other or space and time becomes largely a matter of reforming the discursive intellect from a servant of division and fragmentation to a partner in the achievement of wholeness. Whereas immediate experience is characterized by a knowing and feeling in one that comes before intellection, transcendent experience is characterized by a thinking and feeling in one that comes after and is achieved through intellection. This idea of transcendent experience is readily illustrated from Four Quartets, which in a number of passages reads like Bradley versified. The following lines are from "The Dry Salvages" II:

We had the experience but missed the meaning,
And approach to the meaning restores the experience
In a different form, beyond any meaning
We can assign to happiness.

We had the immediate experience, say, the moment in the draughty church at smokefall, but because in immediate experience one simply exists as part of a larger unity, we were not conscious of meaning. But in relational experience, by remembering and reflecting, we can approach the meaning in such a way that it will be restored in a more complex and comprehensive form. That form will be transcendent experience and it will take us beyond the relational level where we are aware of assigning meanings to happiness.

The idea of transcendent experience runs throughout Eliot's literary and religious criticism. The famous notion of the unified sensibility in the essay on "The Metaphysical Poets" is one of his numerous uses of transcendent experience. A number of critics have said that when Eliot refers to "a direct sensuous apprehension of thought, or a recreation of thought into feeling", he is referring to immediate experience. But it is clear from his terminology that he is describing transcendent experience. One of Bradley's favorite terms for transcendent experience is "felt thought." This is precisely the language that Eliot uses to distinguish between the poets of the seventeenth and the nineteenth centuries. This is a unity that comes after thought, not before it. It is a complex of feeling and thinking in one.

There is no doubt that Eliot shared this general view of relational experience as enclosed in an envelope of undiscriminated, felt, nonrelational totality. He says so in plain words at the end of the first chapter of his dissertation. To Eliot, then, as to Bradley, immediate experience at the beginning (that is, before—yet including—intellectual consciousness) and transcendent experience at the end (that is, after—yet including—intellectual consciousness) are not mere hypothetical limits to the comprehended dualistic sphere of relational experience. Together, they constitute the reality that makes possible the construction of the relational world, the everyday world of appearances.In summary: several pervasive principles in Eliot's work directly parallel principles in Bradley's philosophy. Analytical thinking shatters the unity between knowing and feeling by breaking reality into thinking subject and object of thought.

Thinking is intrinsically limited in part because it can only proceed from one thinking subject, from one point of view, at a time. This means that the movement toward truth involves, not only development of one point of view, but also migration from one interpretation to another, occupation of as many perspectives as possible.

A main principle associated with greater degrees of truth and reality is comprehensiveness, so the more comprehensive, the more true. These matters are evident everywhere in Eliot, but nowhere more than in the multiple points of view within his poetry. In The Waste Land, for example, Eliot attempts to speak through many voices, from many points of view, from many times and places, all at once. Language is necessarily and profoundly reductive; moreover, its grammar and syntax skew propositions.

Over and over in his dissertation, Eliot says that "when we try to press an exact meaning, we find language forcing untenable theories upon us". In the first chapter, he speaks of the "embarrassment" to our theories created by the fact that we have to reduce them to words. Constantly he shows an awareness of being caught in the language trap. He says, for example, "In describing immediate experience we must use terms which offer a surreptitious suggestion of subject or object". This suspicion of language is also evident in Eliot's poetry. Prufrock is terrified by language and Sweeney moans "I gotta use words when I talk to you." Moreover, at the heart of each of the Four Quartets is an "intolerable wrestle with words and meaning." In "East Coker, " for example, Eliot refers to twenty years of

Trying to learn to use words and every attempt
Is a wholly new start and a different kind of failure
Because one has only learnt to get the better of words
For the thing one no longer has to say, or the way in which
One is no longer disposed to say it. And so each venture
Is a new beginning, a raid on the inarticulate
With shabby equipment always deteriorating
In the general mess of imprecision of feeling,
Undisciplined squads of emotion.

Eliot's rhetoric, the way he develops his discussions, is deeply indebted to Bradley's epistemology, in which feeling is transcended in thought and then both are transcended in "felt thought" or "thought feeling" or "transcendent experience." Bradley typically focuses on opposites, deconstructs both of them and then reclaims them in a new and unified form. Think briefly of Eliot's opposition of tradition and the individual talent and his inclusion of both in a greater tradition; or of his opposition of romanticism and classicism and his inclusion of both in a more comprehensive framework. The ghost of Hegel hovers here, of course, but this dialectical imagination goes beyond Hegel, especially in its emphasis on experience.

As Eliot himself said, his prose style is modelled on Bradley's. The combination of humility and irony, of feeling and intelligence, that characterizes Bradley's writings is a hallmark of Eliot's. Both the humility and the irony are genuine; both, in fact, are necessary results of the epistemology. They come from the double awareness that one has glimpsed some light and that one can only work in the dark; from the compulsion to refute error coupled with the consciousness that one's own work is bound to be in error; from an awareness that one is making a raid on the absolute with shabby equipment always deteriorating. One of the disarming aspects of Bradley's rhetoric is that he generally concludes by calling his own theories into doubt. Thus in the Ethical Studies, he shows that Kant's formalism and Mill's utilitarianism are deeply flawed ethical theories. He then presents his own ethical theory based on the idea that society is a moral organism. He concludes, however, by arguing the insufficiency of all ethical theories, including the one he has just proposed. Being ethical and formulating ethical theories, he claims, are worlds apart, not because an ethical philosopher might himself be unethical, but because being anything and analyzing it are inconsistent activities.

Each of the positions I have mentioned represents a conscious and strenuous effort to overcome dualism. I am not suggesting that Eliot was dependent upon Bradley for these insights. The revolt against dualism, as Lovejoy and others have documented, was in the air in the early part of the century; moreover, Eliot had already mounted his own revolt against dualism in his poems of 1909-11. It must be noted, however, that Eliot found in Bradley an elegant and convincing argument against every type of dualism and that he surrendered several patient years to a sympathetic reading of Bradley's work. In spite of the closest personal and intellectual involvement with a formidable neorealist, Eliot explicitly endorsed many of Bradley's ideas in his dissertation, ideas that remained to color all of his subsequent work, including Four Quartets.

Bibliography

The Flesh and the Word: Eliot, Hemingway, Faulkner, Floyd C. Watkins (Vanderbilt Univ Press, 1971).

T.S. Eliot: A Collection of Criticism, Ed. Linda Welshimer Wagner (McGraw-Hill, 1974).

T. S. Eliot, Stephen Spender (Viking Press, 1976).

Eliot's Early Years, Lyndall Gordon.

"Ulysses," "The Waste Land," and Modernism: A Jubilee Study, Stanley Sultan (Associated Faculty Press, 1977).

A Half-Century of Eliot Criticism, Mildred Martin (Associated Univ Press, 1979).

Thomas Stearns Eliot, Poet, Anthony David Moody (Cambridge University Press, 1979).

T.S. Eliot: An Introduction, Northrop Frye (University of Chicago Press, 1981).

T.S. Eliot: The Critical Heritage, Ed. Michael Grant (Routledge Kegan & Paul, 1982).

T.S. Eliot and the Poetics of Literary History, Gregory S. Jay (Louisiana State University Press, 1983).

T.S. Eliot: A Life, Peter Ackroyd (Simon & Schuster, 1984).

The Matrix of Modernism: Pound, Eliot, and Early Twentieth-Century Thought, Sanford Schwartz (Princeton Univ Press, 1985.)

The Poetics of Impersonality: T.S. Eliot and Ezra Pound, Maud Ellmann (Harvard Univ Press, 1987).

T.S. Eliot's the Waste Land, Harold Bloom (Chelsea House, 1988).

The American T.S. Eliot: A Study of the Early Writings, Eric Sigg (Cambridge University Press, 1989).

Skepticism and Modern Enmity: Before and After Eliot, Jeffrey M. Perl (Johns Hopkins Univ Press, 1989).

Reading "The Waste Land": Modernism and the Limits of Interpretation, Jewel Spears Brooker and Joseph Bentley (Univ. of Massachusetts Press, 1990).

Harmony of Dissonances: T.S. Eliot, Romanticism, and Imagination, John Paul Riquelme (Johns Hopkins Univ Press, 1991).

The Savage and the City in the Work of T.S. Elliott, Robert Crawford (Oxford University Press, 1991).

T.S. Eliot: The Modernist in History, Ronald Bush (Cambridge University Press, 1991).

A Guide to the Selected Poems of T.S. Eliot, B. C. Southam (Harvest Books, 1996).

T.S. Eliot and the Ideology of Four Quartets, John Xiros Cooper (Cambridge University Press, 1996).

T.S. Eliot Anti-Semitism and Literary Form, Anthony Julius (Cambridge University Press, 1996).

T.S. Eliot and the Use of Memory, Grover Cleveland Smith (Bucknell Univ Press, 1996).

A Reader's Guide to T.S. Eliot: A Poem-By-Poem Analysis, George Williamson (Syracuse Univ Press, 1998).

T.S. Eliot and American Poetry, Lee Oser (Univ of Missouri Press, 1998).

T.S. Eliot: Comprehensive Research and Study Guide, Harold Bloom (Chelsea House, 1998).

Eliot's Dark Angel: Intersections of Life and Art, Ronald Schuchard (Oxford University Press, 1999).

T.S. Eliot and the Philosophy of Criticism, Richard M. Shusterman (iUniverse.com, 2000).

T.S. Eliot: An Imperfect Life, Lyndall Gordon (W.W. Norton & Company, 2000).

T.S. Eliot and Our Turning World, Ed. Jewel Spears Brooker (Palgrave Macmillan, 2001).

A Critical Reading of the Selected Poems of T.S. Eliot, Manju Jain.

Discovering Modernism: T.S. Eliot and His Context, Louis, III Menand (Oxford University Press, 2003).

